MindLight

Secrets of Energy, Magick
& Manifestation

About the Author

Perhaps the most widely published Wiccan author of her time, Silver RavenWolf's books appear all over the world. She has completed nineteen books for Llewellyn Worldwide, including the bestsellers *Solitary Witch* and *Teen Witch*. Artist, photographer, and Internet entrepreneur, Silver also heads the Black Forest Clan, a growing Wiccan organization that consists of 59 covens in 29 states and 3 international groups. A wife for 25 years and mother of 4 children, Silver has been interviewed by the *New York Times*, the *Wall Street Journal*, and *US News & World Report*. Visit her website at:

WWW.SILVERRAVENWOLF.COM

Secrets of Energy,
Magick & Manifestation

Silver RavenWolf

MindLight

Llewellyn Publications
Woodbury, Minnesota

FIRST EDITION
First Printing, 2006

Cover design by Gavin Dayton Duffy

Cover images © brandXpictures and PhotoDisc

Illustrations by the Llewellyn Art Department

Disclaimer: Remember that essential oils should always be used in a carrier oil for your ultimate health safety. A general rule of thumb is for one drop of essential oil, use 10–20 drops of a carrier oil. Before using essential oils, always check with your physician first if you are being treated for a specific medical condition. Pregnant women should not work with essential oils. Body-safe fragrance oils can be substituted in any of these recipes.

Llewellyn is a registered trademark of Llewellyn Worldwide, Ltd.

LIBRARY OF CONGRESS CATALOGING–IN–PUBLICATION DATA
RavenWolf, Silver, 1956-
    MindLight: secrets of energy, magick & manifestation / Silver RavenWolf.
      p.   cm.
    Includes bibliographical references and index.
    ISBN-13: 978-0-7387-0985-7
    ISBN-10: 0-7387-0985-9
        1. Witchcraft. 2. Neopaganism. 3. Magic. I. Title. II. Title: MindLight.

  BF1571.R36 2006
  299'.9400—dc22

                                                                              2006046474

Llewellyn Publications
A Division of Llewellyn Worldwide, Ltd.
2143 Wooddale Drive, Dept. 0-7387-0985-9
Woodbury, MN 55125-2989, U.S.A.
www.llewellyn.com

Printed in the United States of America

Contents

Dedicated to Sandra and Carl

Acknowledgements to:
The members of the Black Forest Clan.
This book couldn't have been written
without you!

Introduction

Wouldn't it be nice if you could just sit down, think about what you want, and then have your desire miraculously occur? Could it be really as simple as all that?

Meditation says the magick is in the moment.

Quantum physics says this—and more—is quite possible!

If you agree, then it will be. Welcome to the world of your manifestation!

CHAPTER ONE

The World As You Make It

How many times have you opened your eyes first thing in the morning and slowly begun knitting together all the things you simply must do that day? By the time your feet hit the floor, you feel burdened, irritated, sluggish, and downright miserable—especially on workdays. No wonder they call it "daybreak"—you feel shattered even before you begin.

Where are those moments like on the television commercials where a fresh-looking person with a joyful smile laced with morning sunshine lifts themselves luxuriously from the bed with an expression of bliss?

That moment isn't in a product.

It can't be bottled, jarred, or shrink-wrapped.

It isn't stuffed in your mattress or pillow, or woven in your sheets.

That moment is actually *in* you.

If your mind is clouded upon waking with all the tasks you must complete this day, then the reality you've set before yourself will be tiresome, long, and filled with stress. If, however, you turn that first moment of magick into a thought of positive power—what then? How do you think your day will unfold?

Meditation, generally thought of as an esoteric, New Age practice for the elite few who can sit with their backs straight and legs in a perfect lotus position for hours on end, is simply an elongated thought turned into an enchantment. It is more than a tool for self-knowledge and self-improvement, though it is those things too; what we are going to focus on here is how it is a tool for daily living that can change your life and assist you in manifesting whatever you want and living the life you really want. And anyone can master the techniques to make dreams into reality.

MindLight Meditation

Right now—this minute—I want you to put this book down and prop it so that your hands are free, but you can read along with me. Are you situated? Good!

1) Position your hands as if you are holding a small ball of glowing, white light. Take your time. Just relax and build the light between your hands. This light is a part of you and a part of the Great Work: what you will accomplish for the good of others throughout your lifetime. The light is a tool that you can use to build a healthy, positive future—and the most remarkable aspect is that this tremendous power lies in you!

2) Next, move your hands apart and together as if they are held by a giant rubber band. Open, close, open, close. Keep playing with the light and, as you do so, remember what it is like to move your hands through water—nice and slow, with a gentle, flowing resistance, except here we translate that feeling through watery resistance as elasticity.

3) Add this remembered feeling of what it is like to move your hands through water to the present movement of your hands working with the MindLight—in, out, in, out. Try not to go past your shoulders when you move out, because we are working on building (we don't want to scatter).

4) Keep the rubber-band motion of your hands moving in and out shoulder-width apart, then move in for the compact ball of light, and out again. Repeat. Think of nothing but the light in your hands. If you begin to worry about other things, just gently push the thoughts away. Concentrate only on the ball of light. Stay in the moment.

5) Now we add the sacred breath. As you inhale with nice, deep breaths, draw your hands together to make the small ball. As you

move your hands out and away from each other, exhale with one smooth, even breath. Inhale (hands in)—exhale (hands out). The slower the better. Techniques learned at a nice, slow pace stay with you longer and will be more precise when you need the power.

6) Rather than dwelling on a specific problem at the moment, let's choose an energy that encourages openness of opportunity. What do you want the most right now: Peace? Harmony? Creativity? Wisdom? Happiness? Healing? Choose one of these and say the word aloud.

7) Now, look into the MindLight you hold in your hands and take a deep breath in through your nose and out through your mouth. Do this at least three times—more if you are stressed or unhappy.

8) Now, breathe fully from the diaphragm and then inhale from the chest. Practice this type of breathing with several cleansing breaths, and when you are ready, take three of these nice, deep, measured breaths.

9) On the third time, blow your desire (peace, harmony, creativity, wisdom, happiness, healing, etc.) into the MindLight. That's right, just pucker up those beautiful lips of yours and send that thought easily, fluidly into the MindLight you've created. Let the breath carrying your desire flow across your lips like fine silk through your fingers—the moisture from your body digitized by your thoughts of perfection. Once the thought is in the ball between your hands, you may feel the seemingly empty space vibrate, or your hands may tingle, or you might feel a "lightness" throughout your body.

10) Pull your hands (holding the light ball) in over your heart, allowing your body to drink in this lovely MindLight you created.

11) Breathe deeply several times, and as you breath in, think of your heart being surrounded by this harmonious, vibrant light. As you exhale, continue to relax and let go of any pent-up negativity—old hurts, pain, fear, unhappiness, etc. Every time you inhale,

THE WORLD AS YOU MAKE IT

allow the light within yourself to grow stronger and brighter. Every time you exhale, let go of more and more crusted up, gross mental garbage. Let the negativity break away, piece by piece. Keep up this visualization as long as you can; there is no time requirement.

12) When you feel you are finished for now, drop your hands to your lap, close your eyes, and take another deep, even breath. Open your eyes and pick up the book. Don't you feel great?

You've just learned two very valuable pieces of information—the benefits of deep, cleansing breathing and how to create a MindLight. Tomorrow morning, when you wake up, don't allow yourself to think of anything except that MindLight you just created. Was it for peace? Wisdom? Happiness? Say the word you associated in your mind with the MindLight several times as you rise to consciousness, eyelids slightly fluttering as you emerge to greet the day. Push *all* other thoughts aside—every single one. Just keep the word in your mind as you get up and begin the movements of meeting your day. Again, don't line up those tasks like little marching soldiers of personal duty. Instead, put that MindLight in your cup. That's right, let the MindLight of happiness, positive self-worth, peace, or creativity (whatever you called it) sink slowly into that steaming cup of coffee or chilled juice. Drink it. Say to yourself, "I will meet every task as I should. The day will progress with plenty of time to achieve all I desire, and I will feel energized, positive, and useful until I go to sleep tonight." Now, go about your day. Throughout the day, should you become stressed or overburdened, think of your MindLight like a fun bouncing ball. *Be in the moment* with that MindLight ball. Re-create the light in your hands when you are particularly stressed. Remember to breathe deeply and slowly. See your MindLight dancing on the boss's head when he's acting pushy because he's majorly stressed. Or over there at the screaming cab driver. Or under the dining room table tickling your son's feet (you know, the kid who is throwing the tantrum?). Bet you'll be surprised at what happens!

Meditation is nothing more than the *moment* you make magick.

Meditation is the wizard of the mind.

And the next night? Make a new MindLight, just like the first one. It can have the same theme or a different one. Then, when you wake up the following morning, repeat the sequence—don't think of *anything* except that bouncing, lively MindLight the first few minutes of the day. Continue to play with that MindLight all day and evening long.

Remember to *stay in the moment* with your new mind tool.

And if you make MindLights all week?

Expect your life to change and *welcome it*. You've just learned how to change your life in a positive way with very little effort—and now you know precisely what it is to meditate.

Meditation is the still point of unlimited opportunity.

Friday Night Fights!

We're standing on a big, well-lit canvas square flanked by ropes secured at the four corners by metal poles. Already we can smell the sweat and heat of human bodies mixed with the aroma of popcorn and hot dogs, stale beer and flat soda. You are surrounded by loud music and people laughing in a swirl of popping, glaring lights and you move your feet a little bit—darned shoes are too tight, they're pinching, and so you add this tidbit of irritation to your experience of "too much input"! The electric anticipation in the atmosphere flicks at your temples like a cat's whiskers before the clawed strike, so vividly that you think you can reach out and touch that energy, and for a moment, you ride a high as never before. Like the air you breathe, you can't see the charged energy, but you know that it's there. Suddenly, the crowd leaps to its collective feet, screaming and shouting, roaring into a combined beast of amazing power while a simultaneous clanging of bells heralds the beginning of the event in a cacophony of heady vibration . . . darn those shoes anyway!

And in the background, like a voice echoing in a rinsed-out soup can, you hear, "Are you ready to rrr-rumble!?"

Welcome to your life.

Every day we wrestle with the cause and effect of our own actions, which are a physical manifestation of our thoughts. Like the Friday night fights, we show up in the ring, prepared or not, to put on the gloves and duke it out with our problems, frustrations, fears, and personal foibles, now and then riding a whirlwind high that makes it all seem somehow worthwhile. On occasion we celebrate a marvelous TKO and other times we hit the mat in head-crunching pain, only to rise again in the final count. Now and then, the fight is a draw and we save it for another day, when perhaps the stars and our brains are more in our favor. We are successful when we've managed to heal ourselves to the point of acceptable re-entry into that big ring of life where we will fight courageously to obtain the world champion prize: ourselves.

The blood, violence, and gore of fight night a little too blatant for you in a book that's supposed to be about spirituality? That's the point! We are physical people in a rough and tumble, hard-core world trying to put the proverbial square peg of reality as we built it in the round hole of spirituality as we wish to perceive it. What *doesn't* help is that we create the reality we know based on a self-conditioning that often gives our power away to the roaring crowds around us and pinches us uncomfortably just to remind us that we are still living (like those shoes that are a bit too tight).

Several years ago when I was on tour for one of my books I carried a drum with me. Part of every seminar was to have the participants, five or ten at a time, scream the following into the open end of the drum: "I take back my power!" And as each group stepped up to the plate of change, I encouraged the crowd to become a cheering squad (everyone needs a little helping hand once in a while). The results were astounding. People left the seminar smiling, joyful, feeling very good about themselves. Later, I would receive letters and e-mails about how much their lives had changed in a positive way. Why did this change occur? Because for at least a second or two they had collected and solidified the courage to create their own reality at the top of its game, to send out a message to themselves and others that they had aligned their energies to create a wholesome self in control of their own destiny. Right then, right there, they stayed in the moment of power and change with the help of the cheering crowd, their very support obliterating fears and worries of the past.

Did it last, that feeling of power within themselves? Yes, for a few who went on to make positive, radical changes in their lives—for those people that seminar was the tipping point to success. Whether they knew it or not, they'd been preparing themselves for a positive change for quite some time. What about the others—those who did not go on to the success that they desired? Was there something wrong with them? Actually, no. Due to past self-conditioning, they simply weren't in agreement with themselves to let go of the negativity in their lives long enough to move forward—and, in most cases, probably because they were bored stiff with life in general.

And there's the rub. For many of us think we've seen it all, heard it all, done it all to the point where we are so unbelievably bored that we continue to seek the addictions of our old emotions to keep us feeling like we're still in the game of life—like we're still a major player, no matter what field the game is commencing on. We've created a pattern that "sort of" works for us, so in lieu of anything better, we keep dragging out the same pattern, brushing it off and twisting it in new ways in hopes that it will work better for us. The problem with this scenario is that once you've hit the critical first-time high with any pattern, every time thereafter gives us a little less adrenaline rush, and a little less, and a little less, until most crises play themselves out due to our own invariable boredom. Ever meet a person whose life is one continuing drama after another? It's because they're bored stiff and each new action packed psychological scenario loosens up the joints for a little bit so they don't remain under the Medusa's spell conjured directly by themselves in the first place. How many of you agree? Raise your hand. Mine's up first because I've done this to myself innumerable times. How about you?

Before I write any book (and I think this is number nineteen) I always go to various bookstores to see what's happening in the genre I've chosen. Then I look at other genres to see what seems to be in vogue there. Since I wanted to write a book on meditation, I found myself all over the darned place. Granted, I wrote a great deal about how to meditate in my book *To Stir a Magick Cauldron* several years ago, and this book has sold over 300,000 copies, but now I wanted to approach the subject in a different, more simplified and active way. What were other authors currently producing on this subject? My bookstore jaunt showed that some meditation books were in the religious studies section, some were in the occult section (or whatever they're calling it this season), others were in self-help, and still more could be found in the new, flashy, *huge* motivational section. In all, I found only about five titles in the whole store that dealt specifically with meditation. Why, I wondered, would such a terrific tool for self-empowerment have such minute appeal? Well, because it's boring, that's why. Meditation hit its tipping point back in the early 70s—it reached its level of saturation, and the world (most of it) moved on. Why? Because it is like everything else. We learn how to do it and then we lose interest. It no longer gives us the emotional high we first experienced. Motivational books are the same way, and frankly, this is how any fad begins. We try it, we like it . . . yawn . . . now we'll try something else because the rest of our life does not agree with what we've learned. Granted, some things were very successful while we were playing with that new high, but, in the end . . .

Aunt Jane is still a monster.

You still owe $20,000 on your credit card.

Your job still stinks.

You're still stuck in the same old cruddy house.

For some people, what they learn in motivational studies works for them. Aunt Jane goes away to Florida, they pay off their credit cards, they change jobs, and they move into a nice new house along with a plethora of other successes. They embrace the fact that since they are changing they will have to let go of the old stuff—which sometimes includes one's job, one's dysfunctional family, or the highs from bad habits—and all this can be painful. Some don't make it past letting go, and they slide into the comfortable pattern, which includes evil old Aunt Jane suddenly moving back into their lives. Others learn to deal with old problems in new ways, and so they keep advancing simply because they don't allow themselves to be bored in a positive way. What makes these successful people different from the ones who have lost interest?

Just a simple agreement.

By accepting the agreement, you are the observer who collapses energy into the form you desire.

Whether we are discussing martial arts or magick, religion or science, in the end it's all about balance and remembering to stay in the moment. A productive life is where the major player (which would be you) has attained a sense of inner satisfaction of the self, which extends a type of peace and power outside of you, touching others in a positive way. Struggling to find that grace, for some, will take an entire lifetime.

But not for you, because you have already gotten on the fast track to self-improvement in a variety of ways. Anyone who wants to take the power of quantum science (magick) and mix it with their own life has already shown that he or she has the guts, the power, the determination, and the faith that anything can be accomplished. And that, my friend, is the biggest hurdle!

Now it is a simple matter of putting it into practice.

𝒥 𝒜gree—
The Quantum Wand of Mental Magick

In his book *Gifts of Unknown Things*, biologist Lyall Watson describes his encounter with an Indonesian shaman woman who, by performing a ritual dance, was able to make an entire grove of trees instantly vanish into thin air. Watson relates that as he and another astonished onlooker continued to watch the woman, she caused the trees to reappear, then "click" off again and on again several times . . . Perhaps we agree on what is "there" or "not there" because what we call consensus reality is formulated and ratified at the level of the human unconscious at which all minds are infinitely interconnected.*

Articles like this one are all over the Internet, and some of the more cutting-edge books on human consciousness have been playing with this idea for the past few years. For about five years before writing this book I spent numerous hours searching and sifting, reading and commenting on how quantum physics affects our lives, specifically in the venue of magickal religions, which allow the idea of infinite possibilities to exist as a part of their platform of enlightenment. No matter how long or how short the Internet or magazine article, the book, the video, or the DVD, all are "agreeing" on the main theme that objective reality does *not* exist, and that what we do experience is nothing more than a consensus of the human holographic neuronet based on four agreements within ourselves—physical, mental, emotional, and spiritual—that build into the collective unconscious as a single whole *in the moment*. It is then that reality becomes such as it is.

---

* Author unknown; entire article available at http://www.earthportals.com/hologram.html.

Yes, I know. Take a deep breath—that's a lot to swallow.

Then, you say, if that were indeed true, we might throw up our hands in despair and theorize, "If reality is controlled by the whole (by everybody)— there is no hope for me because . . ." and you would list your current woes, and you would choose a structured religion that brings fate and damnation into your life, and worship the energy of that structure so that you won't get creamed again. Yet, as occultists who have worked years of ritual, tons of spells, and thousands of prayers, we know that the skilled individual in the sciences of the Spirit can, indeed, "click" an aspect of our world "on" or "off" like the dancer in the above example. Some call this natural ability magick, others call it a miracle, and then there is the "will of God" scenario. Indeed, to agree that we could simply change our lives by "agreeing" on any one issue is so profound that it is frightening.

Puts a whole new twist on the Rapture, doesn't it?

According to quantum physics, everything is energy, which changes by the direct effect of the "observer." Energy unfolds into patterns that we, the observer, create. We humans, in this instance, are the observers, and therefore we constantly affect the outcome of any situation by our participation on whether we "agree" or "disagree" that any object or situation exists. The more observers there are, the more complicated or more solid a thing or issue becomes. Now, the interesting thing about quantum physics in the realm of human existence (if we view it in this way) is that the use of this power is like breathing—we don't necessarily realize it, yet we do it all the time. In essence, we change reality every moment by our mental, physical, emotional, and spiritual agreements within ourselves and in combination with others and their inner agreements. Manipulating our environment in this way, like breathing, is second nature, and therefore we don't particularly concentrate on the skill. We just do it.

We haven't figured everything out. If we had, we wouldn't need to write books to help each other, do further study, and continue to plumb the depths of science or reach for the heights of the stars. If we had all the answers, we wouldn't even be here. Incredibly, finding the answers is the creative fun of it all.

So where does the power really lie? If a group can affect the outcome of a situation and an individual can equally affect the outcome of a situation, who wins the tug of war when the individual and the group disagree?

Ah, good question! So brave of me to ask and so bold of us to try to find the answer.

In the end, I think, it is the individual who carries "the power." We all know that magick and ritual (as the Pagan world understands it) done in secret will statistically work well and with some semblance of speed:

a)   if we do not discuss what we are doing with anyone, thereby limiting the number of observers, *or*

b)   when our inner agreements coincide with the inner agreements of others, such as in group prayer work. This works because we all agree to be in the moment.

In essence, quantum physics tells us that we have the freedom to choose our own world, but this choice is predicated on those four agreements. The four agreements I'm talking about could be categorized in this manner: If you think about it, we have four ways of responding to any event—physically, mentally, emotionally, and spiritually. Our biological systems being what they are, any one of these agreements can outweigh the other, making things rather lopsided— which puts the desire out-of-kilter. Result? No manifestation—or, worse, a misfire.

When we are desperately in trouble and we pray to a higher power, the totality of our being is giving that issue to a higher power (as we personally visualize it) to agree for us, because we obviously haven't been able to flip that switch by ourselves. We can't flip the switch because one of those four "elements" within ourselves is holding us back. A higher power, as I define it here, is absolute and total perfection. Perfection must inherently agree. When we agree that perfection agrees, miracles have been known to happen. This doesn't mean that you *must* believe in a higher power—this is just an example of how today's human usually operates predicated on religious bias/belief when they are deeply in trouble.

Then there are times when miracles don't happen, even though we've invoked that higher power. Why not? Because we didn't *really* agree that

Perfection actually has a handle on the situation. If we see God as something vengeful, cold, and retaliatory, then we have made Perfection imperfect. If we are angry with the cloak of Perfection—the religious clothes we dressed God in—then failure is most likely an absolute. If we don't trust the intermediary we've created—the "face" of God we've chosen, the archetype, you name it—the issue is a wash. We're done for.

If we do, indeed, create our own reality, then how can something we inherently and naturally do *every day* be so complicated when we try to tear it apart and reconstruct it in a focused way to make our lives better?

Because we really *don't* agree, that's why. Our individual agreements (physical, mental, emotional, and spiritual) simply aren't in sync. We're out of balance (and how many times have you heard that one?).

Perhaps we should look at balance in a new way.

Perhaps balance is agreement within the moment.

Psychoneuroimmunology

Psychoneuroimmunology is a modern science that studies how what the mind manufactures (attitude, emotion, belief) affects our physical health. *Psycho* means "mind," *neuro* means "nervous system," *immuno* means "system of health defenses," and *ology* translates to "the study of." This new study has discovered that our minds constantly communicate to every single cell in our body. Emotional chemicals, called neuropeptides, are the information highway of the body, transmitting to every cell with a steady flow of emotional data, which at any given moment greatly affects the physical stability of "you." What I find interesting (and amusing) is that for years people outside of the occult world (and those within it who are convinced they know it all, which means they know nothing) have laughed at us when we say "Fill your body with white light. Fill the room with mental white light." Yet recent studies have found that by mentally staying in the moment, breathing deeply, and filling your body with mental white light affects the neuropeptides,[†] encouraging them to carry healing energy to all points necessary.

Rather than read about it, let's try it. Right now! Here we go!

---

† Bill Douglas, *Anthology of T'ai Chi & QiGong: The Prescription for the Future* (www.smartaichi. com, 2002).

The White Knight

Read through this little exercise, and then try it for yourself. Won't take long. Promise. It has no religious bias, so it's cool for you to do. Ready?

Close your eyes. Take three deep, even breaths. Nice and easy, nice and slow. As you breathe in, visualize the air coming into your body filled with pure white light. Still a little tense? No problem. Take three more deep, even, relaxing breaths. As you breathe in, see the white light rushing into your lungs, then traveling up to the crown of your head and down to the tips of your toes. Take your time. With each breath, let the light advance further and further into your body. If you are currently sick, you may find this a slightly difficult visualization. That's because you are filled with icky energy that doesn't want to budge. It's partying in there and doesn't want to get out. However, the light says, "The bar is now closed." The white light is the ultimate bouncer—if you let it. Which means, of course, that you have to *agree* to allow the white light to haul the trash out of the establishment. Now that you have expanded the white light in your body, make it glow! Feel yourself pulsating with pure white light. With every breath, the white light grows stronger and stronger. In your mind, see the area around you also glowing with white light. When you are totally relaxed, open your eyes and stretch. Doesn't that feel cool?

Now I want you to think of a problem. Ugh. Do you feel tense, unhappy, constricted? Especially around the shoulders and neck—like you are carrying a horrible weight there? This time, I want you to close your eyes and see your body filled with chattering neuropeptides that have their knickers in a twist over your problem. The beating of your heart is the thundering of hoofbeats on cobblestone. It comes nearer. And nearer. Suddenly your mind is filled with a huge, glowing, white horse (a Lippizan is a good choice). Feel the power of this magnificent animal fill your being! Straddled high upon the horse is a man (or woman—your choice) cloaked completely in light. The left hand holds the reins of the horse, the right hand is in a fist over his/her heart. The horse rears and the rider screams "Ye-Sah!" in a thundering voice while snapping the right arm out with a powerful thrust. Blazing white light streams from the fist and into all the upset neuropeptides, which change from a dull, grumpy blob to glowing, pure white light. Feel the warmth of emotional peace fill your entire body, and say the word "perfection." Take several deep breaths and open your eyes.

There is much more you can do with this healing visualization. For example, maybe a white light feels too inanimate to you. Then pick a positive form of deity. In Pow-Wow German healing techniques, the focus is on the Holy Spirit. And what is the Holy Spirit but the agreement of perfection often visualized and shown in books as pure white light that has power in the moment! Children respond well to hero-type characters—a White Knight that battles the sickness, or a white dragon (I used that one often for my kids), or an empowered female in battle garb, or a favorite martial arts individual, etc. There is nothing wrong with an adult using character visualizations such as these. Many adults will call on Holy Mary to fill them with the healing energy of God. In the end, it doesn't matter the religion or the archetype—what matters is your agreement that perfection exists *and* can touch you.

If you use this little visualization for small ills, you'll find they pass quickly; but what about the big stuff? Just keep doing it in combination with your regular medical treatment. As the Pow-Wows always say, "You didn't get sick in a day, you won't get healed in a day"—meaning that you allowed negative thoughts to pile up, now you have to systematically clean them out, and it may not happen overnight because negative thoughts include patterned behavior. Pow-Wows always recommend that when you are very ill you should work at least three times a day with the mental visualizations and the agreement to touch perfection (which in their realm is the Holy Spirit, as I mentioned before).

What if, however, you want to meditate for Sally, or Joe, or Harold? Can you do this visualization on them? Certainly! I do it for my children all the time. Oop—I heard that! Someone just said, "But what about their free will?"

I'm so glad you asked. Let's put that monster down right here and right now. You have the free will to work on anyone you want. If they don't agree within themselves—guess what? You can visualize until the cows come home and it ain't gonna work. I tell my students to go ahead and work for anyone they desire; however, I also tell them to include a prayer or statement (depends on your belief system) that if the healing energy is not accepted, to ask that the energy be given to the person in the universe who needs it most at that moment.

When someone says, "May I pray for you?" take it! Accepting good thoughts is never a bad thing. And the reason why magickal people often ask if they can "work" for you is to set up the energy-shot (just like in volleyball) for the serve to go through to success. By asking you are receiving a verbal agreement, which helps to push the healing energy forward. If you are nervous about accepting what the inquirer might fling out at you energy-wise, then an appropriate response is: "I will accept all good (or positive) thoughts. Thank you."

Deep breathing helps to fill those little neuropeptides with whatever you want to put in them. Breathing in fills, exhaling expels. Breathing in gathers and balances, breathing out repels and sends out information. While studying this concept I went back to the Pow-Wow healing information Preston Zerbe taught me. I discovered that all the chants he gave me worked on breath in a way I had not previously considered. Yes, the words are important because what was being done had to match the faith base (although most Pow-Wows simply whispered to make the healing more effective). However, every chant works on the premise of breath. You breathe in the power of "God," you expel the chants, which carry the healing—except it isn't the chant, per se, it is the breath. That's why they called it the Breath of God or Ghost Breath (Holy Ghost)—the energy of perfection carried on the expulsion of air. To really factor it down for you: if disease can be airborne, so can God; ergo so can perfection; ergo so can healing.

This is why we must stay in the moment—because in a single moment, we can reach perfection. And it only takes one moment to build.

You can do it!

Healing—Oh, How Tricky It Can Be

Let's run through an example so that I can bring my thoughts into agreement with yours about the difficulties in healing anyone, and let's make it rather complicated—just to keep us all from being bored. Let's say that

Doris comes to you with a healing issue. You don't know Doris very well, so you have no presupposed ideas about her that would necessarily imbalance your four agreements. You've done lots of healings, had lots of successes, so Doris should be healed in no time, right?

But maybe Doris, consciously or subconsciously, is *not* in agreement with the healing at all. Maybe she thinks she deserves this horrible disease because of something she's done in the past. Maybe she's been told by some goofball that God is punishing her. Maybe she's experienced some sort of physical or mental abuse in the past and this is how it is manifesting because she's never really dealt with it. Maybe Doris has been thinking that living really is pretty hard, and maybe checking out in a way society accepts would be okay—like getting sick. Could be that Doris is being hounded by bill collectors, family members, or whatever, and she is just so tired of it all that she secretly feels she can't go on. Maybe Doris is so bored with her own life that it has manifested in sickness. Yet, a little part of Doris has come to you asking for help.

Now what?

As our healers have been saying all along, you can't treat just one part of the body. You have to treat the whole. If for one second you can get Doris into "agreement" with herself that she really wants to be well, then you can get her to add another second, and another, and build a new neuronet for herself. Then a miracle through your healing is not only possible, but probable. If you cannot get Doris to reach a point of integration—a point of successful agreement—you may fail. Remember, Doris is feeding information to her neuropeptides *all* the time.

What may really twist the problem are the people Doris interacts with on a daily or weekly basis when she doesn't come to you for a prayer session, a hypnotherapy appointment, a Reiki experience, even a typical office visit with an upbeat physician, etc. For example, let's say she visits her specialist who tells her there is no hope. His staff agrees, and because they are supposed to be experts in these things, Doris believes them. They are in agreement that she is a dead woman walking and that's what Doris becomes if she buys into their diagnosis. Sort of kills that word "hope." Or, maybe there is a family member who is secretly looking forward to clutching Doris' bank account in their greedy little hands, and therefore makes fun of Doris on a continual basis when she talks about alternative healing. Conscious behavior or subconscious, it doesn't matter, the result is the same. That person, by moral standards, is a murderer. Or, how about the religious person in Doris' life who tells her that she is sick because she is paying for her sins? By playing on Doris' fears and poor self-image, they are enticing Doris not to agree with the healing on an emotional level, which affects the physical one, which affects the mental one, which affects the spiritual one. And those neuropeptides are running rampant with negative junk.

In this scenario, who really has the power? Doris does! She just has to accept that she has it and to agree within a single moment that she has personal power that isn't predicated on past fears and negativity. If she can come into agreement with herself in the moment, the rest will fall into place if she acknowledges the moment and then chooses to make another, and another, and another.

Perhaps what makes orchestrating reality difficult is the idea we hold that the process must be complicated because our world appears to be such an incredibly intricate place. If constructing our reality is so simple, then we'd be eagerly doing it every day, right? We'd never make any mistakes and our lives would be perfect.

The joke, the illusion if you will, is that we inherently weave our reality without "thinking" about it based on a lot of shoddy emotional input, and when we do concentrate on something, it is often clothed in the negative feelings we are experiencing. Where is the money going to come from to pay my bills? Why can't I get better? Why am I always sick? Why won't my husband or partner listen to me? Why does my boss treat me so terribly? Why is my friend ignoring me? I hate my house. I hate my aunt. I hate rush hour traffic. I hate people who don't think the way I do because they make me uncomfortable. And on, and on, and on. We collectively fill our days with so much negative frustration it is amazing that the world has kept revolving!

And yet, the planet has continued to spin on its axis because somewhere within us all, we want to be in that ring with the lights, the action, and the emotional high (even if it is an old one), slugging away at our foes and, at the end of the day, we desire to march home victorious as the world-class champions of owning ourselves. Past self-conditioning fibs to us, telling us that Fight Night is the only way we will win.

Well, I have another way. It's a lot less violent, but it can be a real head trip the first time you try it and succeed. If you're game, move on to chapter 2—but *not* until tomorrow.

Because tonight you are going to do a cleansing exercise in the shower and tomorrow morning you are going to remember to do your MindLight. We agree, right?

And honey, this is only the beginning!

Shower Cleansing Exercise

This exercise is so easy you'll want to do it every time you take a shower once you've experienced how great it makes you feel! And, assuming no one watches you in the shower, you have all the privacy you need. For young parents or a busy household, normally the one place you have all to yourself for a few minutes each day for total privacy is the bathroom.

In the shower with the hot water running and all that luscious steam surrounding you, cross your hands over your chest. Take a deep breath. And another. Allow yourself to be in the moment. Note the feeling of the water on your skin, the sound of the falling water as it strikes the walls, curtain, shower floor, the gentle steam that opens breathing passages. As you stand there enjoying the sounds and feelings of the water, bless the water in your own way. Thank the water for providing cleansing energy. When you are ready, take a deep breath. Then, as you exhale, fling your hands down over the front of your body and out, visualizing all negativity being cast off from your body. Do a quarter turn. Repeat. Another quarter turn. Repeat. One last quarter turn. Repeat. Now, raise your arms over your head and allow the water to rush over you. As you breathe in, think of white light filling your entire body from the tips of your fingers to the soles of your feet. When you are feeling very good (stay in the moment—no thinking about anything but being right here in this shower right now), keep your left hand up in the air, palm facing the heavens, and move your right palm down to your side, palm toward the ground. Heaven is above you. Earth is below you. You are in the center. *This* is balance. The ability to walk between two worlds. Take three deep breaths, staying in the moment. Move the right hand up into the air, right palm facing the heavens, and move your left arm down, palm facing the earth. Again—this is balance. Stay in the moment. Totally secure. Totally at peace. Finish by crossing your arms over your chest. Say to yourself, "I am!" while you close your eyes and fill your entire body with white light. When you are finished, turn off the water and flick water drops from your fingers three times in quick succession. This portion of the meditation is done.

As you dry off, dress, and attend to any other bodily needs, think of nothing but what you are doing. Stay in the moment. No worries, no feelings of fear, no to-do lists. Stay in the moment until you open that bathroom door. If you practice this every day you will be amazed at the concentration and ease with which you go about your daily tasks. Even if you don't do another single meditation in this book, if you just manage to keep up this simple, relaxing daily practice, you will see amazing results within yourself.

I know I did.

CHAPTER TWO

You in the Driver's Seat of Your Life

In Brian Greene's book *The Fabric of the Cosmos: Space, Time, and the Texture of Reality*, he says:

> I remain as convinced now as I did decades ago . . . that life's value is the ultimate question . . . but the insights of modern physics have persuaded me that accessing life through the lens of everyday experience is like gazing at a van Gogh through an empty Coke bottle . . . By deepening our understanding of the true nature of physical reality, we profoundly reconfigure our sense of ourselves and our experiences of the universe.

Acknowledging that the universe is built on vast amounts of energy that is individually available to us at any given moment to mold and shape as we please is an incredible step toward personal fulfillment. In order to harness this energy, we first have to agree that it exists.

Do you agree?

Throughout history, this potential for excellence has gone by many names. Pythagoras called this energy *pneuma*. Other explanations over the years have included words and titles like animal magnetism, vital force, ether, and bioplasma. Post-relativity physicists like David Bohm have postulated its existence and called it the superquantum field. Author Michael Talbot discussed this energy as the holographic field and more recently Lynn McTaggert, an investigative journalist, speaks of this amazing power simply as "the field." From ancient Chinese medicine to Hindu prophets, from martial arts to New Age philosophies, from Voodoo rites to Catholic mass, for centuries the world has tried to explain in the language of various cultures, histories, secret societies, esoteric practices, and religions just exactly what this incredible potential entails and how it can be used in a positive way. And for as many people who tried to harness such power for good or ill, there were exponential numbers of people who tried to run from it, hide it, debunk it, belittle it, and turn it into superstitious fluff for the general masses, preferring the noose of disease, death, and taxes to an ultimate harmony of spiritual creation. From Christ to Einstein the descriptions, explanations, and teachings of this infinite potential have worn cloaks of many colors, and, if their followers didn't tell you how to use it, instead they told you how to worship it.

Got shivers running up and down your arms yet?

Recent studies of the new physics involving quantum dynamics infer that, like our example of the priestess dancing in chapter 1, we have the capability of "clicking" matter on and off, thereby creating our own reality, and that everyone has this natural ability. From the zero point, you affect how energy collapses in and out of the matter state. The zero point is in the moment, a place where there are no cares, no worries, no recriminations— some people call this phenomena "the zone." It is a place of "just being," and we are all quite capable of going there. In essence, you are the rod of the caduceus, and the snakes therein depicted are the energies that you are capable of manipulating. What these scientists are saying is that "stuff is here because we say that it is here." When we tend to forget about things, they disappear or break (ever noticed that)? We simply have to "agree" and at the same time stay in the moment, and when we do, energy collapses into matter by following the path of least resistance. The more resistance we've built into our lives, the slower this matter will manifest. The more codicils we add to the action, the longer it takes. The more people who are privy to our business, the more convoluted that business becomes, especially if the core observer (that would be you) is in any way unsure of your personal power (filled with doubts, negativity, anger, etc.). The more we worry about a situation, the worse it becomes, because worry sets the stage for failure, building visualizations toward defeat rather than accomplishment. How do we overcome these self-imposed limitations? By simply agreeing that we don't need miles of mental, emotional, physical, or spiritual red tape to get the job done while staying in the moment!

Can it really be that easy?

The Concept of One

I am sitting in a United States Army award ceremony. My daughter has gone before the board and received her sergeant's status. She has also earned Sergeant of the Quarter. As I wait for the ceremony to begin, I look at the flags decorating the room. My daughter is in a medical unit, and the caduceus catches my eye. I study the design. We are all familiar with the rod and the intertwined serpents, yet, for the first time, although I've talked about how the snakes make the shape of the infinity sign, I see it plainly on this flag. I think about the concept of the sign, and how it demonstrates that there is no time nor space, just an unfolding of energy predicated on our own choices—in the moment. And I think about the motto of the United States Army (at least the people I've known in it): "Never leave a man behind." My mind jumps to a biblical passage—"If you harm your brother, you are harming yourself," and an old Christian song, "We are one in the Spirit." Then I think about the Buddhist teaching "We are one." My brain skips to a wonderful Pagan song by the Faerie people—"One." I think of history and the fuss in the Egyptian world when the pharaoh tried to move from multiple deities to one deity, and all the flack that caused. I think of how the Cathars were slaughtered because in the early Christian world, deity was considered both male and female, and how their ceremonies and lifestyle tried to reflect the balance of one. And how they died horribly for it. And how people today just can't get over the argument of who gets to keep and play with the One True God. What a waste.

Because One is "in the moment."

And I realize that perhaps, just perhaps, we are perceiving the idea of "one" not as it was first meant to be. One doesn't mean "your one" or "my one," it means that in the still point of the void, that place that is not a place, in a time that is not a time, the zero point of the totality of the dynamics of meditation, there are none—which is one—united in nothing, yet bonded in everything; wholeness in the moment where there is no past nor present.

No opinions.

No individual perceptions.

No tawdry emotions.

No unmitigated anger.

Only perfect agreement.

Only potential.

Only one.

In the moment.

And in that one—anything can be done.

The One is not ego-centered. The One is not "a person" or "an energy"—it is a unification of everything. It isn't "some thing"—it's just . . . "no thing."

It is . . . now.

Many times what we choose to signify deity represents the neediness in our lives. Deity in its worst personification symbolizes what we deeply lack, and what we desire most that we believe cannot be found within ourselves or within others. Deity, then, is not always seen as ultimate perfection, but a personification of what we do not have. Indeed, this is true in most cases in most religions.

And when we feel we have no personal power—no control—that's when things get very nasty on a physical level, because what we are really doing is allowing the ego to run rampant, rather than using the ego for its intended purpose: a check and balance vehicle within ourselves. When we can resist ego gratification then we are at our most powerful. In many religions, this resistance idea has gotten skewed into the word "abstention." The problem with this is although the person can abstain from sex, violence, money, and all those things that tickle ego gratification, it doesn't take the desire for those things out of the person. That is a whole different ball game, and, for the most part, it is totally ignored. Reminds me of the old adage, "You can lead a horse to water, but you can't make him drink." If you desire something you can't supposedly have, then (many times subconsciously) you make poor, ego-centered decisions based on that desire. You will either bow to the temptation, or the temptation will play out in another way. Therefore, we are left with what we started with—the insatiable needs of an ego-centered lifestyle.

"To resist," however, implies that work must be done. Work is effort. Therefore, many people have no desire to resist, and if they can't play out their fantasies one way, they will look for a different venue. Take, for example, that totalitarian boss at work. Cruel, heartless, bossy, mouthy, etc. Every time you see a person like this, invariably they feel they have no power. Therefore, their behavior, which exerts negative energy, is a way to gratify the ego. This person does not believe in harmony because there is no personal attention in a harmonious atmosphere (as they see it). Harmony starves an ego-centered lifestyle.

They believe that harmony is boring.

Yet, harmony is a very, very busy energy in itself. It carries pure potential where anything can be accomplished. Ever listen to a really good choir? When they build that incredible vibration of total unison? And they suddenly stop?

That hush?

That edge?

That silence?

That no-thing?

That moment?

That is the power of the One.

You can click it on—or you can click it off. It's your choice.

Using the Power of One

Many years ago when discussing the power of magick one of my teachers said: "You never use up what's in here," pointing to himself, "you use what's out there," motioning to the world around him. If he had added, "because what's in here IS out there," I would have understood what he meant a lot sooner (or maybe not). Our ego draws a line so it can be top dog and run the show. If you break down that invisible barrier, the ego loses ultimate control and must be integrated into the totality of our lives. But, as all good teachers are incredibly mysterious because they force you to think for yourself rather than telling you everything, he said nothing more, just . . . "think about it."

You've always had the power of One at your disposal, most of us just don't realize we can use it. Once we agree with the four parts of ourselves "in here" (mental, physical, emotional and spiritual) then there is no barrier to "out there." We move smoothly into the power of the One, without any visible effort, without resistance, without emotional attachments, without negativity.

Once we agree, we create harmony.

And once we have harmony, we have potential.

And once we have potential, we are unlimited in what we can achieve.

All you have to do is agree to flip that switch.

In the Moment— Learning How to Get There

Once we agree that the four internal agreements exist and begin to work with them, we need to expand our personal power by learning to live in the moment. If we teach ourselves to do this, then reaching the still point when we need it is so much easier to obtain!

Learning to live in the moment can be difficult due to the patterns we create for ourselves in life. When I was little my mother and grandmother had a saying that used to irritate me to no end. They would expound with great gusto, "What's the matter with you! Life isn't a bowl full of cherries!" Now, fifty years later, I understand that they were trying to teach me responsibility. Yet this statement set me up for a ton of negative junk. No, it isn't their fault—it was mine. Because I bought into the idea that worry was a good thing. Everyone's parents or guardians had their favorite sayings (I'm sure you've got one from your past on the tip of your tongue) that were meant to help you take control of your own life. The problem with many of the concepts is that they are fear based. Fear creates worry, and worry creates sickness, heartbreak, and so much more.

Right now I'd like you to write down all the negative things you heard as a kid, and burn them. And once we've gone down memory lane, we're not going to go back. It's not that we will refuse to accept responsibility for our own actions—not at all. We are going to take responsibility for everything we do, and we are going to go forward armed with that personal power. Because in owning our actions, we own our strength. And if we are strong, the world around us also becomes empowered in a positive way.

Next, we are going to write down all the things we are worried about. The job, the house, the kids, the partner . . . whatever! Burn that list. From this point on—we aren't going to worry—we are going to "do." If one of these worries comes up, we are going to tell ourselves to stay in the moment. We are not going to fantasize and make things worse. Every time we worry about something we are going to take several deep breaths, we are going to agree that the right thing will occur, that we will embrace it when it does, and we are going to fill our minds and bodies with white light. We are going to do this every time we are worried, afraid, nervous, etc. Every time. And as we do this, we are going to tell ourselves to stay in the moment—because in this still point is the power to solve any problem.

Practice this for at least a week. Once the week is over you'll want to keep doing it because staying in the moment is a very cool place to be.

The Missing and the Found

Even conventional quantum physicists believe that the vacuum is an incredibly seething flux of energy. According to one estimate there is enough virtual energy in the vacuum of a light-bulb to boil the world's oceans. Another estimate says that you could construct another universe out of a cubic centimeter of it if you converted it to matter. All this energy exists beyond our space/time and the sum of its vectors (direction of the movement of energy) cancels out. Think of football linemen pushing each other to a standstill at the line of scrimmage. No detectable movement within what scientists used to call the ether may take place but no one would argue that energy isn't being employed. Scientist Thomas Bearden has pointed out that in physics equations if two vectors crash into each other the force mysteriously disappears according to conventional physics and the value of the force is "0." In other words, it disappears! This is not only illogical (where'd it go?) it seems to defy such hallowed precepts as the conservation of energy in which energy cannot disappear but only be converted to another form.[*]

---

* Gerry Wolke, "Tachyon Healing and the Physics of Love" (www.naturalhealthconsult.com, 1995).

When what we agree (vector A) crashes into "out there" (Vector B), the potential of the universe (zero point)—"the moment"—gives way to the manifestation we desire. The zero point morphs into birthing your creation.

The only way to determine if a method works is to try repeated experiments for yourself, and that's precisely what our family did as we began studying the quantum idea of manifestation; not through reams of mathematical data, but by actually putting various theorems to work in everyday life. We moved from the postulations of the printed word to physical analysis. For us, the question is not whether magick exists, but how to make it work faster and better in day-to-day living. Since magick is truly a science as much as it is a philosophy, we delved into the territory of the current new physics for the answers. I have learned one thing: I don't know what reality is, but I know what it isn't—and it definitely isn't what we think it is!

I started with situations as they presented themselves rather than trying to force the issue, thinking that since operating in reality is a natural process, I should go with the flow. I wanted to see if, in everyday life, this clicking on and off business could really work. I was astounded when the first time I actually tried it, it worked!

My journey into quantum manifestation started with a copper wand. A customer ordered one and I thought, okay, this is my last one, now I'll take the listing off my website. I couldn't order additional wands because the supplier had previously announced that these items were out of stock. I went into my website to delete the offering, and to my dismay, someone else had ordered another wand within a matter of minutes of the previous order. Now, I had one wand—and two customers. On the surface, my choice was to contact the second customer and indicate that the item was sold out. I don't like to disappoint people, and as a customer myself, I hate it when I order something and then the business comes back and says too bad, so sad, we don't have what you wanted. *Okay,* I thought. *Let's see if this quantum manifestation thing actually works!*

Up the stairs I marched, visualizing the wand as an oscillating picture in my mind and saying out loud, "It isn't here, it's here. It isn't here, it's here! Somewhere! I know that it is here! I agree that there is an extra wand up there—somewhere. I just have to find it!"

I found it.

Within five minutes.

Okay, so one success does not a convincing argument make, and we could always say that I'd ordered more than I originally thought, except for the fact that I found the wand in a box that had been empty the previous day. I waited for another opportunity. This time it was a missing DVD, and there were helpful parameters here. First of all, the DVD had been rented by my son the night before. He hadn't taken the DVD out of his room after he watched it, and no one in the house had been interested in seeing the movie, so we knew that it had to be in his room still. He and his girlfriend tore the room apart looking for this movie. Lucky for me this son is relatively neat, therefore, the number of places that movie could have been were exponentially smaller—a helpful plus when something is missing. Both my son and his girlfriend had heard me talk about quantum manifestation previously, so I said, "According to quantum physics, all we have to do is agree that the movie is here, and it will appear. Therefore, let's, for expediency's sake, all say aloud that we agree the movie is here and we agree that you will find it in the next five minutes." They agreed. I walked out of the room.

Ten minutes later no one had said anything, so I went to investigate. "Did you find the movie?" I asked.

"Oh, sure!" was the reply. "We found it about five minutes ago."

Thanks for sharing, I thought, but I said, "Where did you find it?"

"Oh, right here. We must have overlooked it," and he pointed to a shelf.

"Huh!" I said. "Quantum mechanics—it's here, it's not here, it's here. And there you go."

They both laughed. They both laughed because things like that only exist in the movie *The Matrix,* not in a teenager's room in broad daylight on a spring day. And that's what most of us do when the quantum field actually works for us—we rationalize it away without understanding its intrinsic value.

All right. Two experiments do not an alchemical genius make. I waited for a third opportunity. This time it was a simple can of gravy. My daughter was coming to visit and I wanted to make a nice turkey dinner. I went to the grocery store and bought everything I needed. When I returned home, I cleaned out the cupboards (it being spring and all that), so I knew what was on each shelf, and basically where everything was. About four in the afternoon I pulled the luscious turkey out of the oven and continued to prepare the other items for the dinner. That's when I realized that I'd forgotten to purchase the gravy. Yes, I do make homemade gravy, but some members of my family love gravy and there's never enough, so I always add a few cans to the meal just to ensure there's plenty (it's a Pennsylvania Dutch thang). Anyway, so there I am, dinner almost done—and no gravy. No one to send for the gravy either. No way I could leave everything cooking and zoom down to the grocery store. Besides, with my dogs, there would have been no turkey left by the time I returned.

Time for quantum manifestation! I stood at the cupboard and said to myself, "It's here. It's not here. The gravy is here. I know that the gravy is here. I agree that there is one can of gravy on one of these shelves." I started with the lower shelves, getting frustrated, knowing full well that I hadn't subconsciously hidden a can of gravy in there. Next shelf, still repeating that the gravy was here. Then I flicked my eyes up to the top shelf. Lo and behold, sitting among old, dusty glasses and other sundry unused items was a clean can of gravy.

Three for three! Hot dog! I was on a roll. Yet each and every one of these situations could be fully rationalized in a different manner. I decided to keep on experimenting. So far I'd chosen living scenarios—meaning I picked situations that were presented to me as I lived my daily life. I wanted to understand how quantum mechanics can work naturally in one's day-to-day affairs. Again, I waited for another interesting situation to come along, and again applied what I was learning. This time it was the successful completion of a test that a friend was taking. Up to this point, my friend had failed his test three times in a row. Yes, he'd studied. Yes, he'd put in the required amount of hours. What was the problem? Many people freeze during tests, allowing the anxiety to overcome their thinking process and I believe that this was what continued to happen here. Finally, out of the blue, he announced he was going to go take this test—again! This time, instead of saying "good luck," I said, "You remember our discussions on quantum physics? This time, let's agree that you will pass this test without any difficulties today. Do we agree?" The answer was a strong affirmative. A few hours later, I received an excited phone call: my friend had passed the test, getting every single answer right.

Now, let's review what I was doing before we move on so that you can replicate my experiments in your own way.

1) I chose natural life circumstances to begin.

2) I chose small situations and issues to create positive feedback for myself.

3) I know that energy moves in waves, and that it is both particles and waves. I used that knowledge to imagine my visualizations shimmering into form like a heat wave.

4) I know that there is this massive amount of energy that anyone can use (in the occult they call it "the void"), and in the confidence of knowing this I told myself I'd be using this energy to create what I wanted; understanding that the birth of manifestation comes from coalescing energy at the "still point" (zero point, the moment) and compacting this energy into my visualization of solid form. I knew that it could be done, I just didn't know how we do it naturally.

5) I always began with deep breathing. At least three breaths, more if I was upset, nervous, or anxious.

6) With missing items, I began with the statement "It's not there." I started with emptiness because that is what I was experiencing. The items did not appear to be there when I wanted them, so I was affirming what my mental, emotional, physical, and spiritual selves had agreed upon. They had agreed that the item wasn't there. Now, we were going to change that to agree that the item was there. So, we started with what we knew—absence—and then created fullness with products and items and situations that my emotional, physical, mental, and spiritual history was familiar with.

7) I agree that reality isn't what I thought it was. I know I don't have all the answers, but I also know I'm darned determined to keep looking for them.

8) I began by setting "the field" of manifestation by touching my finger on the ground and rolling (in my mind) the field of manifestation out and around me in a large circle, thinking of this

field as a vibrating mist. This, then, is like the magickal circle occult students have been taught for years.

9) I stayed in the moment.

Trying to explain how humans naturally do this feat of manifestation on a daily basis is very difficult. We've been trying to explain it to each other for centuries. Do you remember the television series *Bewitched?* The main rule for Samantha's character was that she could not invent something new. She had to take it from somewhere, she couldn't just coalesce energy (like we can) and flatten it into form. Instead, Samantha's main gift was actually the ability to teleport known objects and people. I remember an episode about a designer car that someone wanted. She produced the car, but since it was the only one on the planet, her magick had removed it from the show room and brought it into form someplace else. Of course, as there was only the one car, she was in for a stint for grand theft auto. Unlike Samantha's designer car, we can create anything, but it appears that *we can create only what we know*—at first. This isn't as stupid as it sounds; it took Edison over 2,000 tries to get the filament right in the light bulb. He started with what he knew, and he kept working to learn more. Eventually his experimentation proved successful because he now knew what he'd first envisioned—a light that works. That's the gift of being human: our ability to take thought and make it into form; our expertise in using creative energy. Edison didn't just create with his hands, he created with his mind, and anyone who has ever drawn, painted, built, etc., knows that you invest your entire self (mental, physical, emotional, and spiritual) when you work on creating a project of any magnitude.

In my first experiments, I worked with items I knew. I'd held over twenty of those wands, so I knew the weight, the feel, and had even worked with one of them in ritual. I knew what the gravy can looked like (I've been making turkeys for, let's see . . . at least twenty-four years), and I've been renting DVDs for a long time, opening and shutting the cases, etc. I know what it is like to successfully pass a test—that great rush-y feeling that you have succeeded. The other similarities in these experiments? They all revolved around something I (or someone else) needed.

Over the next several months I took my experiments further. Every year for fifteen years my Black Forest Clan met for their annual Clan Camping Event. At the last event I gave an impromptu lecture on my experiments in the world of quantum physics and magick. I gave them the agreements theory. As a group we brought errant food into form and dispelled a gathering thunderstorm or two. For the rest of the weekend I heard people all over the camp site "agreeing" for a variety of items: lost car keys, a missing hair brush, and someone's notes that had gone missing. All were successful.

I also discussed my experiments with my father over the successive months. He is in his late seventies, and like many older people he would often find himself forgetful—or so he thought. "What if," I said to him one day, "you are not really being forgetful at all? What if you have so many things on your mind that you simply aren't bothering to manifest the item you are now looking for?" He thought about this for a moment and smiled. "Out of sight, out of mind," he muttered, and then he brightened. "So they are temporarily out of my universe!"

"You got it!" I said.

"It's not there because I'm getting older, and there's no reason, really, to hold it there."

"There's a thought," I said.

"I like that concept!" he exclaimed.

Before you go on to the next section, why not be a bit adventurous? Start employing the agreement technique on little things. Begin by going outside and looking at the world, saying to yourself, "Wow! What I thought was real all these years *isn't!* I wonder just what it is?" Then endeavor to experiment with what it might be!

I'm not asking that you believe what I've just written. No, indeed! These are my perceptions. The purpose of bringing this information to you is that you try it for yourself!

Don't believe in me.

Believe in you!

Enter the Wild Cards—Those Pesky (Or Not) Observers

The study of quantum physics tells us that the wild card in any scientific scenario is called "the observer." The observer affects the outcome of the experiment, supposedly, just by being there. This is why quantifying experiments is so darned difficult and why I can't stand up on a stage and make a wand appear out of thin air. Changing the observers themselves, changing the number of observers, etc., changes the experiment and therefore will change the overall outcome of the experiment. Frustrating. Physicists are still playing with this one.

In the examples given so far, the number of observers was limited (except at Clan Camping, but by then I had done enough experiments to ensure we were all on the "same magickal page"). For the wand and the gravy can—it was just me. With the DVD and the test, it was one or two other people who had already been prepped on the nature of quantum physics. Now, let's move on to an experiment where at least one of the players wasn't in the loop of the nature of the new physics and see what occurred.

Sally had listened intently as I told her about what I was trying to accomplish with quantum thought and she wanted to run her own test. By now I'd managed to manifest a missing broom, a new treasure chest of mahogany, and an Aladdin's lamp. (Not the real one, a replica—minus the djinn. He must have fallen out in transit.) Seriously, these things didn't suddenly appear out of thin air as I watched. The chest and the lamp came via U.S. Postal system (meaning they came into my life as I understood their possibility for travel) after I had considered their existence for several weeks. What was so odd about the chest and the lamp was that I didn't "wish" for them; in reality, I was contemplating writing an article for my website on how our world is like a treasure chest of energies lit by a magick lamp (the energy of Spirit). Imagine my surprise when the chest and the lamp appeared at my doorstep! And, in case you are wondering, no, I didn't talk to anyone about the article idea.

Back to Sally. We decided that she would pick something important in her life, a pressing need, but she would not tell me what it was. Sally is also a magickal person, working with many flavors of magico-religions over the past twenty years. Here's what happened!

The problem: A few years back Sally and her husband, George, went through some pretty rough financial times. Although they managed to dig themselves out, there were still a few loose ends. One of these loose threads entailed penalties for state taxes not paid. Sally had paid the taxes, but she didn't have enough to pay the exorbitant penalties. Just like anyone else in this hectic world, Sally's life was a busy one with a job, children, a husband, relatives, etc., that all vie for her attention. She knew she owed the penalties, but she'd been so tied up with other things that she forgot about them. Along came a letter that said the state wanted to garnish her husband's wages for the penalties. Her husband flew into a panic (naturally). Sally raised an eyebrow. She did not relay this information to me at the outset. She simply said that she was going to run her own experiment and let me know the result along with the details. We chose this method so that I, now an additional observer, could not tinker in any way with what she planned to do.

Later, she sat and thought about all the ways she could handle this problem, but, right away she had a wild card: George. He was in a tizzy and insisted that he was going to take care of this problem, himself, once and for all. This immediately took a few options away from Sally. Okay, she thought, I'll let him come up with a solution because he needs to feel he's handled the problem, and I'll wait to hear what it is, and then I'll give it a little quantum boost.

Two days later her husband announced that he was going to a particular bank for a personal loan to take care of the penalties. They'd worked their credit back into some semblance of good standing, so it was worth a shot. Sally had a bad feeling about this, given their past jousts with banks, but this was what he wanted to do, so she said, "Okay, when are you going for the loan?"

Because Sally felt a little foolish about mentioning it, she didn't say a word to George about the "agreement" part of quantum thought that she and I had discussed. Later she said that he would probably have listened and even done it after a long, exhausting emotional discussion (which was his habit when handling problems). "Quite frankly," she said, "I just wasn't emotionally up to another charged conversation while he worked his thoughts out on my feelings."

As her husband was already so upset over the matter, she decided that she'd just keep her mouth shut and try this her own way. You see, Sally's husband is one of those people who will state out loud how something can't be done repeatedly before he stops and thinks it through—it's a bad habit that's been driving her nuts for years and they've had many arguments over it. To Sally, he'd already done enough damage to the situation with the vocal negative repetition over the issue. Silence, she determined, was the best course of action.

The day of the loan appointment came. While George drove down to the bank and met with the loan officer, Sally sat at her dining room table with the penalty statement from the state in her hands. Her visualization was counting the penalty value down from $3,000 (a little over the stated amount) to zero. The only things she visualized were the numbers 3,000 and zero. She went through the four agreements: "I emotionally agree. I physically agree. I mentally agree. I spiritually agree." If she got stuck on one (which she did) she repeated it firmly aloud. The one you get stuck on, we've come to find out, is where the negativity lies. In Sally's case it was the emotional agreement. When she was satisfied, she put the paper aside and found something else to do that didn't include thinking about the loan.

An hour later her husband came back. "We'll know in a few minutes," he said. "The loan officer is going to call me."

Once more Sally agreed in her mind that they would be offered the $3,000 they needed from the bank to pay off the debt. Just as she made her mental affirmations, the phone rang. George handled the conversation. Sally could tell by his statements that they had not gotten the loan. He hung up disappointed and left the house. Sally sat at the dining room table feeling a total loss. What went wrong? Maybe this quantum thought thing didn't work after all, or maybe George was just too much of a wild card with his feelings that he destroyed the energy form she was trying to manifest. She shook her head in dismay. Still determined, however, she said out loud, "I want to know why it didn't work!"

Over the next three days, Sally tried other quantum thought experiments that worked quite well. She was still stumped by what had happened with that loan. In this scenario, there were three relevant people: Sally, George, and the loan officer. Maybe it was the loan officer? Maybe that person was the wild card observer? But, that just didn't feel quite right. Maybe it didn't work because both Sally and George felt that the penalties were unfair in the first place, and they didn't really want to pay them. If this is how it is, thought Sally, with all these blasted wild cards, then quantum mechanics isn't much help even if you know it can work!

On Friday night of that same week, George took Sally out for dinner to a restaurant that was a good forty minutes away from their home. It was a beautiful evening and Sally watched with appreciation as the sun sank toward the horizon in a fabulous display of beautiful colors. She thought about what she'd recently been studying about the nature of light and how the hues are scientifically created by the lengths of oscillating waves. Her mind was far from the derailed loan as she reveled in the sunset.

"I didn't tell you everything about that loan," said George, breaking the pleasant silence.

Sally could feel a frown collapsing the skin on her forehead as her eyes slid nastily to George. Her shoulders tensed liked she'd been hit by a bucket of ice water. And, like any spouse married for a long time, Sally said, "What do you mean you didn't tell me everything?"

George shifted uncomfortably behind the steering wheel. "I asked for $15,000."

Sally exhaled a short puff of air as everything collapsed into form like an extended slinky snapping together in her brain. "Why would you do that? We didn't need $15,000," she said softly.

George explained his thought process with a litany of what they could do with that money, ending with, "Well, they did offer me three grand, but I refused to take it."

Sally could not help herself. She burst out laughing and buried her forehead in her hands for a moment, then said, "You know, George, next time you do something like that, would you mind telling me exactly what you're doing?"

"I don't see what's so funny," said George, rather miffed at the idea that he should report his every decision to his wife. Sally, wisely, changed the conversation until she could think this new development through. At dinner, in the middle of a conversation about something else, George paused and pointedly looked at Sally over his coffee cup, then said, "What did you mean earlier when you said I should have told you exactly what I was doing with that loan?" George has been married to a magickal wife for over twenty years—it just takes a while for the light bulb to go on sometimes. You know, a little like good old Edison and his filaments.

In this scenario, the loan officer was not the wild card observer. Sally did achieve success with her quantum thought. The bank did indeed offer George the amount of money that Sally concentrated on. The problem here was George—his miscommunication to Sally, his ultimate decision, and Sally's fear of telling George what she was trying to do. First, George changed the dollar amount so the two were not working together on this point. Secondly, he stubbornly refused the $3,000 loan because he didn't get his own way. For George, his denial was an emotional one that was not thought out—just a knee-jerk reaction as a result of not receiving what he wanted. His emotional tantrum shot her manifestation right in the proverbial foot. Sally, on the other hand, constrained her options, also by emotional choice. She didn't want to go through hours of explaining to George exactly what she was about to do, and then she didn't account for George changing the game plan. This wasn't in her mental equation on the issue; therefore, she hadn't considered adding the words "or better" to her quantum thought. Had she either told George what she'd planned or at least added the words "or better," perhaps they would have received the loan. Then again, maybe not.

It makes you wonder, doesn't it, just how many times circumstances are manipulated in negative ways due to our choices (George narrowed the field of possibilities by choosing to go for a loan, and Sally chose to let him do it, and she chose not to tell George what she was doing in the realm of quantum thought), our lack of control over our emotions, or to our personal fears of facing emotional energy? And, if that is so, is there a fail-safe way of affecting events once they are in motion? Or is the universe just a chaotic bunch of silly humans running around and mucking things up with their emotional drama with no hope for a positive future?

Sally Gets Her Money

A week has gone by and even though Sally has celebrated success, she also encountered failure. She learned that quantum thought is all well and good, but there are ways in which it can be used better. She also learned that what can make simple situations very difficult at a speed faster than light is the power of the emotion that's fed into the issue and the human reactions that ensue. Now, we could have told Sally all this in the beginning; however, she needed to learn these things for herself. Quantum thought is a tool, and just like any tool, it will work differently in the hands of the artist. You can use a brush to paint the town red, or you can use it as a headdress.

Sally still has a number of choices on how to handle this debt even though, on the surface, the reality of the situation appears limited. Here are some logical, surface choices of a moralistic couple (we're not going to go into the shady ones because Sally and George may feel desperate, but they are not stupid):

They could pay off the debt in installments by calling the state and asking how to do this. They could ignore the debt and pay the consequences. Sally could go to a bank or credit company for her own personal loan. They could ask their parents, a relative, or a good friend to lend them the money. She or George could find a part-time job to pay off the debt. Unfortunately, all these choices still make Sally and George cough up the money from their current budget, which just covers their expenses and allows them at least one night out at a restaurant a week for a little relaxation. Sally doesn't want the additional burden—she's sick of that. There has got to be another way!

So first, Sally says to herself, "I agree that there is another way to pay off this debt." Then she said to George, "Do you agree that we will find a positive solution to pay off this debt?" George hemmed and hawed, spitting a few emotional nuggets here and there, but Sally stood strong and George finally relented. "Yes, I agree, but I don't see how that's going to help us one little bit!"

"You don't have to see it," snapped Sally. "Just agree!"

"Fine! I agree."

Sally smiled.

Now, this is what she said, but are you seeing other parameters here? Is your mind now working for a possible solution for Sally and George? Maybe you came up with a different one. Maybe Sally could say, "I agree these penalties are unfair. I agree that I don't have to pay this! I agree that I will find another way that doesn't include paying this stupid bill. I agree that they made a mistake!" Indeed, Sally could have done that—but, this is a true scenario, so we're confined in this example to what Sally actually did. However, if you started flipping possible scenarios in your brain you are absolutely on the right track! There are, the sages say, 101 ways to make hamburger.

If Sally was into the multiverse quantum study, she could acknowledge that there are infinite possibilities all unfolding concurrently. Which one she brings into form is her choice—and she could choose one that doesn't include any observers to muck up the scenario. Sound too much like science fiction? A group at Oxford University doesn't think so. If you've got the time, pick up *Schrodinger's Rabbits: The Many Worlds of Quantum* by Colin Bruce and you'll discover a very different view of the new physics. And, just so ya know, many hard-core physicists hate Schrodinger's cats, his rabbits, and anything else on that issue because telling people they can click stuff on and off does not go over well with the penny-pinching bean counters of funding—the possibility of proving that everyone can do what they wish in an environment they design does not fit into their expectations of controlling the world banking system to their benefit.

When you realize you truly do have a choice that isn't necessarily logical given the current parameters of the situation, but possible—the world will change for you. You betcha!

It did for Sally.

It is postulated that nothing can "happen" to us unless we accept it—that our lives are truly based on our personal agreements within ourselves. What makes this difficult to believe is that we are certain that many of the unfortunate events we've experienced in the past were beyond our personal control. We've set ourselves into a false "knowing," a reality that accepts problems. Yet, if we sat back and thought about the mental chatter going on in our heads right before the event (sickness, accident, marital discord, success, gaining a raise, or moving to the next level of spirituality), we might be shocked to realize that we truly did set ourselves up for that particular scenario, by agreeing physically, mentally, emotionally, and spiritually on that reality. We reached into the multiverse and chose which scenario best fit our worries. We feared that if we did not "accept" the current societal view of reality we would be killed, incarcerated, thought the fool, or ostracized— the list goes on.

In Sally's situation, she and George set themselves up for this debt problem by not paying the state taxes on time. Hindsight is 20/20, and, to not repeat the problem, Sally could endeavor not to bring this debt option to herself again. However, none of this particularly helps Sally now as she stands there holding the bag of responsibility. The idea is to handle the "now," not moan about the past.

Sally sat quietly in her dining room, took a deep breath, and thought about the "field of perfection." (To magickal people this is akin to casting a magickal circle of white light.) She relaxed and let her mind drift into calmness. Then she said aloud, "I agree that there is a positive solution to this $3,000 debt that does not affect my current budget. And, I choose the most positive solution possible. Even George agrees!" During the day, whenever she worried about the debt, she would repeat the four agreements—that she mentally agreed, that she physically agreed, that she emotionally agreed, and that she spiritually agreed.

Once Sally agreed within herself that she would accept a new solution that would not affect her current budget, and that the solution would be positive in nature, a very strange thing happened. The next day she received a check in the mail for the precise amount that she owed the state. Flabbergasted, she quickly signed and deposited the check. That night, George came barreling through the door in a panic. Did Sally know that there was a hold on their bank account? What were they going to do? Sally shook her head and smiled, explaining to George that she had deposited that wonderful check, and that she was waiting for it to clear.

And, much like the fictional Samantha and Darren, George slid his eyes from left to right, saying, "Did you . . . ?" and then he wiggled his fingers in the air.

"Of course!" said Sally. "And you helped me do it!"

Not only is this story perfect for explaining the four agreements to success, it also shows you that the wild card observer can be handled with a little finesse.

No Room at the Inn—Wild Card Strikes Again! (Or . . . Does It?)

It's Mother's Day and George and Sally are once again going out for dinner. They've chosen a restaurant that is in another state, planning to meet some of their grown children there. This restaurant is not normally busy, and even on holidays they have always gotten in with a minimal wait time. They picked this particular establishment because it was halfway between where everyone lives. Sadly, Millie, one of their children, cannot attend because of a previous commitment. George is highly miffed at this, but Sally says, "George, these things happen, you know, when there are a plethora of mothers and grandmothers in the extended family unit. She's just trying to find a happy medium in her new life. She's going to the Hunter's Inn in an attempt to fit in. Forget it."

Now, everyone in George and Sally's family knew that Millie was going to Hunter's Inn, but it wasn't a restaurant the family frequented, so they didn't know the precise location—all except George, that is.

Yes, it's George again.

When Sally and George hit the halfway mark on the highway between their home and the intended destination, Sally's cell phone burrs to life. One of the children has already arrived at the restaurant only to discover that the place is packed. She's in a panic as she rapidly relays the circumstances over the phone. "No big deal," says Sally, "just put your name on the list. We'll be there shortly." Everyone in the car (there are four people) hears Sally's conversation with her daughter and now knows (repeat the word "knows") there may be a problem in the seating.

Sally decides she will experiment with quantum thought as she stares out the window watching the farm land fly by. She whispers the four agreements based on the idea that there are plenty of tables for the family in which they could be seated quickly. The phone vibrates again. And again, it is the daughter, now in a complete emotional surge because she's having trouble getting her name on the list. Someone has stepped in front of her while she originally called, and they took the last available table. Sally reiterates not to panic. Again, everyone in the vehicle has heard Sally's side of the conversation. They now "know" there is a problem. They are all visualizing the full restaurant with no tables—only Sally is thinking of empty tables. They can't help it because that's what they've heard. Sally's phone rings again. This time it is her son in a different vehicle and she tells him there is a possible seating problem. As they motor along Sally thinks about the number of possible observers in this situation, and realizes that she has stupidly opened the field to at least four people (her son in another car, and the three listening in on the conversation in her own vehicle), one of whom is the dynamic George—George who loves food, hates to wait, and isn't happy that Millie isn't going to be there.

And, Sally thinks to herself, "Oh. Shit."

Sally realizes that she now has two emotionally charged observers—the daughter who is being ignored at their destination and . . .

George.

Not to mention the other passengers.

Sally continues to try her quantum thinking through the rest of the ride, but she emotionally feels that she's fighting a losing battle. Upon arrival at the restaurant the now angry daughter is relaying how the hostess is ignoring her and that if they want a table, they will have to wait three hours or more. With a sinking heart, Sally says, "Let me see what I can do," and marches up to the door. The field has widened because now there is a hostess in there who doesn't want to cough up a table, most likely because of the altercation with the daughter.

Right outside the door sits an old woman, who says, "If you don't have a reservation, they won't let you in." The lady isn't being mean, she's just stating a fact as she knows it and Sally realizes that this stupid field is getting wider by the moment. Something gold drops to the ground and rolls to Sally's booted feet. Sally picks it up. It is a pill case with "Millie" inscribed on the back. Sally stares at the golden container with a bit of surprise, then turns to the old woman and says, "Does this belong to you?" "Oh yes!" is the answer. "How did that get there?" the lady goes on to twitter as she pockets the case. She thanks Sally, who accepts the kind words with a smile, then with determination walks into the darkened restaurant. Sally patiently waits for the hostess, who tells her there is no room for her family. Sally replies, "But there are plenty of empty tables!" to which she is told they are "reserved." Sally says, "But you never took reservations before. Please, we just drove in from another state. We've visited your establishment often in the past; perhaps you could make an exception." The hostess is cold and unyielding. Wait three hours or go home. Your choice, babe.

Outside the family reconnoiters. Sally is thinking that if she had enough leverage, she could still probably make this go her own way, but George is stomping around the parking lot, loudly stating that he will never come here again! (And he won't, either.) Sally is also mentally kicking herself. Once again, to a degree, her quantum thought worked. There were definitely several empty tables in there at which her family could be seated.

With George in such a tizzy, Sally says that it is obvious they cannot stay here. Waiting three hours for a table is unacceptable. Several possibilities as to where they could go are thrown about; unfortunately all of them are miles away because the family is unfamiliar with the area, and every option mentioned is historically packed on a holiday. "We need a place," said Sally, "that has plenty of room for us today. A place where we won't have to wait. A place where the food is good. A place that isn't hours away. Does everyone agree with this?" Everyone agreed with those statements.

The field now compacts to the family members who are in a calmer state (George has already headed for the car the moment the agreement was struck) and who are now all in agreement that a place needs to be found that has plenty of room for them today, where the food is good, and that is somewhere between the current restaurant and where George and Sally live—the hostess is no longer a player. There are also unspoken agreements in any family unit because you all know each other—what you like to eat, what type of place you normally choose, etc. Everyone gets back in their cars, and heads for Sally and George's home, knowing they will stop somewhere along the way, but not knowing necessarily where they will end up. Sally is concerned about how far they will drive because she knows that some of their party has been awake since four in the morning, and by now they are tired and hungry.

Halfway back Sally is thinking about the gold case with "Millie" inscribed on it. Wasn't that just the oddest thing? She does not, however, say anything to George about it. Suddenly, George slows down and takes a back road. "Where are you going?" asks Sally.

"This is a shortcut," said George. Over hill and dale they drove with the caravan of family members chugging along behind. After about eight miles, Sally said, "Hey! We're right outside of Mt. Charles. Isn't that where Millie was going?" And just as she said it, the restaurant that Millie had mentioned was on the horizon—and better yet—the parking lot was virtually empty. "Let's stop here!" said Sally.

"I don't know," said George. "It's probably full like everything else, but if you want to stop, no problem." George, if you haven't gathered by now, is the proverbial pessimist.

Sally hopped out of the car and went in to ask if there was room. There was plenty, and they were immediately seated.

And no, Millie wasn't there. Her party had visited the restaurant hours before and had already left.

What is the point of this story? First, it is a real-life situation, one that we all find ourselves in from time to time. On one level it demonstrates how a situation is affected by increasing the number of people you have on the "field" of any desire. The more people Sally either directly or indirectly told about the problem of seating at their intended destination, the more their success at eating there narrowed because everyone was focused on the problem and its level of emotion—not the solution. Yet, even as Sally was moving toward defeat, the universe provided a "clue" for her to follow. Simply follow Millie! What if we look at this story on a deeper level? A family is a group mind, especially if it is a loving one. Everyone was subconsciously thinking about how Millie would not be present, and each person in their own way had emotional feelings attached to the absence of Millie and where she was. Is it so strange, that once a verbal agreement on surface issues was met, that the family found itself consolidated at the place where it knew the missing member had been? Finally, there is an old adage: You are always in the right place at the right time—work with it.

All Observers Are Not Major Players

You would think that if quantum dynamics are true, that every observer on the field is an equal player. After much experimentation, I don't think that is correct. It's not their mere presence that will change things, it is their vested interests attached to ego-driven needs of what they know (meaning how they use the sum total of their personal experience) that can kick the bucket and spill the wash water or, conversely, help you along, should they choose to act out their desires on your playing field. If you are flying under their radar on a particular issue that they couldn't care less about, then they cease to be an active player on your field of desire. Hit the button where they become emotionally involved (for good or ill) by accident or design, then you're stuck with a wild card. Silence, then, about your quantum thoughts is not only desirable for your success, but inherently necessary unless you can get the observers to agree on the same goal-oriented outcome. If we consider the multiverse scenario, then, perhaps, we should direct our choices to involve the fewest observers possible in a positive way both physically and astrally.

Perhaps any business meeting should be less about "success" and more about agreement. There'd probably be a lot less meetings with double the normal goal attainment!

The Field of Success— Is There a Way to Load the Dice?

Where do people go to seek enlightenment? Normally we gravitate toward a place that is free of emotional activity, whether it is a mountain top, a retreat in the desert, a trip to the sea, or even the silence of our own backyard on a summer afternoon. What's there? Hopefully not a circus (actually that happened to me once as a kid—I woke up one morning to find a real elephant in my backyard stomping through my dad's tomatoes—no lie). Inherently, when seeking enlightenment we look for . . . silence . . . a representation of the "zero point" as best we can create it in this physical world without those cumbersome elephantine emotions. When attempting to obtain personal enlightenment we hunt for places that are uninhabited by life-forms with negative agendas. From this pure field creativity is born, solutions are obtained, and peace fills the body. Indeed, the perfect field for quantum thought is the practice of meditation because no one is in your head but you. No major players. No minor irritations. Just you. This is a place where you can exercise the four agreements without George, the wicked hostess, or the emotional sleep-deprived daughter screaming on the cell phone that there's no room at the inn.

By experimenting with the quantum field in meditation, can we load those winning dice to roll the way we want them to?

Only you can decide.

Getting Things Unstuck

Okay, so we've all been there—where something is stuck in something else, and it just won't budge. You've tried everything—now try this:

Create a MindLight circle of white light around the stuck object.

In your mind, while looking at the object, see it move the way you want it to. Apply the pressure as you would normally to remove one item from another.

Now, here's what happens the first time. You see it move or feel it move a teeny tiny bit. So you stop. You look at it again and it doesn't seem to have moved, so you think, this is my imagination. This doesn't work. This is stupid. (You won't after you try this technique the next time—but, for the first time, this is probably what is running through your brain.)

Stop.

It did move. But your mind allowed the previous state to snap back because you didn't believe you could do it.

Try again. It helps to say, "I know it moved." Create the circle again (because you just busted it with your disbelief). If you keep trying and visualizing at the same time, it will definitely move.

If, of course, you believe.

I have managed to get an enormous amount of things unstuck this way—from a determined candle stuck in a mold to a piece of furniture wedged in a doorway. You try!

Unlocking Doors

This is a fun one. You've locked the door, you are messing with the mechanism, and you just can't seem to get it open. Try your MindLight. Since you may not understand the concept of the lock, your visualization will be auditory, hearing the lock click open in your head.

Create a white light around the lock. In your mind, see the tool or key turning and releasing the lock mechanism. Add the sound.

Here's what commonly happens. Someone there with you is grumbling and adding negativity, so you must ignore them. You KNOW you can do this. And you will. Keep that in your mind. Don't stop concentrating until the job is done.

Searching Through Tons of Stuff for Something You Want

You have fifty bottles in the cabinet and you want one particular bottle. Create your MindLight. Visualize the bottle label. Hold out your hands, palms facing the cabinet. Spiral the energy in your hands as you think they are a homing device. Reach in the cabinet and randomly pull out a bottle. The more you practice this one, the better you get.

Hey, if you practice, you'll save valuable time.

Click On, Click Off

At night I'd like you to go into a dark room in your house or apartment and stand by the light switch. Do not turn on the light yet. Stand and quietly study the dark. Our universe began in a darkness called the great void. The velvet blackness contains all possibilities—a field of "what might be." It is up to you to switch on the light and flood your life with accomplishment. When you agree within yourself that you are ready to go forward, to fulfill your desires with dynamic, powerful energy . . .

Flick on the light.

CHAPTER THREE

Your Creative Mind

Keeping the thinking mind quiet long enough to move forward in an uplifting, spiritual way can be extraordinarily difficult. There are bills to pay, tasks to complete, errands to run, projects to finish, miscommunications to smooth out—our mind whirs and blends thousands of thoughts a day. It is no wonder that our reality sometimes feels like a rigged game show where we definitely are not the preselected winning contestant. If we follow the premise that if there is chaos within, so there is chaos without, then it is readily apparent why the world as a whole is in such a mixed-up mess.

Have you ever noticed the link between your errant thoughts and supposedly unrelated repercussions? One night a student of mine, Daphne, was making tacos for dinner, frying up the hamburger and basically going about the task in a mindless way. "For some reason," she said later in our discussions on quantum thoughts and their power, "I started mentally kicking myself for procrastinating on a particular project, and saying to myself, 'How could I have been so stupid? It's all my fault.' Just as I finished the thought, I tried to stir the hamburger and the darned mess exploded all over my stove. I finished dinner contemplating the unstable taco mixture in relation to my thoughts at the time. It suddenly dawned on me that every time I felt emotionally overburdened, objects in my reality had a habit of blowing up. I decided to sit down and write out a list of what household items in the last year required replacing and what the focus of my emotions in life had been at the time. The list was fascinating. During the past year I'd allowed rambling, fear-based negative thoughts to take out most of my major appliances and a website business like Annie Oakley in a shooting gallery!"

To consistently attain peace of mind and clarity of vision, we must be willing to create thoughts that move in harmony rather than chaos. We must master our own inner dialogue and tune in to our spiritual selves, overriding the cultural, religious, and societal conditioning that eats at us through inner, negative, fear/anger-based dialogue that inhibits our power over quantum thought. Once we stop the defeatist chatter we can use the vast and powerful energies of our minds to create a dynamic and harmony-filled lifestyle with ease.

How do we stop those wicked little thoughts? By employing at least two of our senses to interrupt the negative mental dialogue and creating sensory input that draws the focus of our minds from the inner world immediately to the outer one. When the mind is busy with the world around us negative thoughts are instantly cancelled. How can we do this? Very simple. The next time you start worrying or ruminating over something to the point of anger, breathe deeply three times and snap your fingers. Or breathe deeply three times and immediately focus on outside sounds—birds singing, the traffic going by in the street, the chatter in the next cubicle, etc. Stay in the moment! It doesn't matter which two sensory points you choose. What is important is cutting the flow of negativity. Sometimes your mind may try to trick you because it likes dwelling on junk. You may use two senses and have great success for a day or two, and then your mind tries to negate what you are trying to do. Simply switch techniques to two different senses (or even three). Like an errant child, your mind is trying to push the envelope. Don't let it get the best of you! To best use the meditations offered in this book, I recommend that you spend at least two weeks learning to switch from the inner, negative world to the outer, open, functioning one. You won't regret the practice.

The Inner and Outer Worlds of You

While I was preparing for my spiritual coronation a few years ago, author Ray Malbrough taught me a new way to empower the water used in the various rites of celebration and magick in spiritualism. The technique was very simple, yet took a bit of practice to master. Using a four- or six-ounce bottle of spring water, draw an equal-armed cross with the bottle in the air, tapping the bottle in the air at the compass points as if you were knocking on a glass window.

Unlike the north/south, east/west scenario, this technique began in the west, moved to the east, then up to the north, drawing down to the south. I always thought this was odd given the compendium of present discussions and teachings on the movement around the altar in the magickal sciences. All answers make their way to you if you are patient enough to receive them, and recently I happened upon a historical text that mentioned that the ancient Egyptians often started their rituals moving from west to east because they felt that the west was the gateway to the unseen. This bit of trivia stuck in my mind because in many ceremonial magickal enchantments the authors explain that one always moves from east to west because the east is the point of rising from our planet into the heavens. Maybe the ancient Egyptians were on to something!

The drawing of the equal-armed cross in the air with the bottle is only the set-up of the empowerment process. It is as if one is knocking on a universal gateway, asking respectful permission to enter. Once you have made the appropriate motions the bottle is thrown through the center of the invisible cross and quickly caught by your own hand (rather than disappearing like that errant Tiddly Wink). This is just as difficult as it sounds and takes a bit of practice (and if you try it, be sure there are no animals, good china or windows in the near vicinity). If you think about it, the technique requires that you take the power from "in here" and punch it "out there," then draw the combined force back "in here" to be used in your magickal endeavor. Playing on the alchemical idea of "as above, so below," this particular exercise teaches you to bridge the gateway between "here" and "there" both mentally and physically. Esoterically speaking, the little exercise says: It isn't just in here. It isn't just out there. It is at the point of integration that success is achieved.

It resides in the moment of balance.

Scientists of the mind have recently discovered that switching from the left brain (analytical) to the right brain (creativity) actually fires the area in between the hemispheres of our brain with incredible electrical power. It is from this function, by integrating the two halves of the brain, that the

magick and the might of quantum thought takes place. The more you practice the earlier exercise, switching from the inner self to the outer world, the
more success you will have at creating your desires. The point in between
the "two worlds" takes the energy of the inner, creative process and fires it
into quantum manifestation—an expression in the outer world. This is why
several of the latest meditation and mind programming techniques have
you visualize scenarios outside of yourself on some type of picture board of
the mind and then instruct you to switch from "viewing" what you want
into an active fantasy where you imagine that you step into the picture
you have created, making it so. Every technique, if you will notice, also has
its own form of "agreement" from positive affirmations to repetitive statements of intent, grabbing the power from the gateway between the two
hemispheres of the brain and sealing this power with a pact more binding
than any contract on earth. Ritual and spells do the same thing—in every
magickal working there is an inner period (of reflection, meditation, visualization, prayer, etc.) and an outer working—lighting candles, grinding herbs,
chanting, drumming, dancing, hand motions, etc., accompanied by a repetitive statement of intent. When you work magick, you move from the inner
to the outer. The difficulty in manifestation is not that we cannot move
from the inner to the outer, but that we forget to combine the energies and
internalize them in the moment. The gateway swings both ways and can be
stopped from either direction by the ego, which translates into thoughts of
self-doubt or feelings of failure.

If we drop our ego at the crossroads of the two hemispheres of the brain,
from the inner world to the outer, sensory domain, the quantum zero point
of "in the moment" unfolds for limitless possibilities! Indeed, it is our own
ego that guides the realm of our reality for good or ill. Our ego, then, is
the gatekeeper to success or failure. I find it interesting that in Voodoo the
guardian of the gateway is Papa Legba, a distinct cultural personality known
for his wisdom and communicative abilities. In this belief system, it is he
who has the power to open and close the gate of information and inspiration at will. Voodoo is not alone in designating energy with a human
mask—we find a plethora of deities throughout history attributed to gateway manifestations. Here, we are not giving our power away to an archetype. Instead, we are reclaiming our own ability to "open the way."

The idea, then, that we are already creating our external reality with our internal, unbridled thoughts can suddenly become a truly frightening one, simply because we know the mess we've got brewing in our brains at any given time of the day. The possibility that this bubbling cauldron of garbled (and sometimes wicked) little electrical impulses is capable of leaking out into the world around us is a frightening concept. If quantum thought really exists, if we can truly click material items on and off (not to mention the non-material events), then who needs dynamite? Or nuclear bombs? Or assault rifles? What's the point of having Democrats or Republicans? If we're so powerful, how come we don't know we're powerful? Why doesn't what we think manifest as reality instantaneously? Either we can't really change thought into form or there is a control mechanism somewhere that keeps us from blowing up the world by accident. Maybe that's what God is all about. Some guy sitting up there in the heavens zapping our bad thoughts into nothing with a hand-held controller. When bad things actually happen, is it because he missed a few? Oh, well. Game over. Lock 'em, load 'em, and try again!

However, maybe . . . just maybe . . . we are our own control mechanisms. Maybe we accept only what we condition ourselves to accept, which would make us appear to be a victim of circumstances when turmoil hits us wave upon wave or; conversely, when we obtain the success that we desire. Could the key to failure be that we simply don't know what we truly want in the first place, because we don't bother to quiet those nasty little thoughts? A major step, then, in determining the direction of our own inner work would be to learn to achieve that state of total calm—the still point that leads to manifestation.

Clearing the Gateway— Creating Your Own Zero Point

The following exercise is a great way to begin working with quantum thought. Practice it for at least two weeks every day, and if you have been sick or very unhappy, practice this exercise at least twice a day.

+ Agree that you have the ability to create your own world.

+ Sit quietly. Straight back. Feet flat on the floor.

+ Take several deep breaths in through the nose and out through the mouth. Expand your diaphragm as you breathe in, collapse it as you breathe out.

+ In your mind, surround yourself with white or golden light. Stay in the moment.

+ Acknowledge that everything is "One." Close your eyes. Stay in the moment.

+ Shut down all negative thought. Switch from inward to outward focus using two senses if necessary. Stay in the moment.

+ Find the still point where all is calm. This still point is where the inner you and the world of outer manifestation is in agreement. Stay in the moment.

+ Hold your hands out in front of you, palms up, as if you are holding an invisible object.

+ Visualize a MindLight in your right hand. Stay in the moment.

+ In your mind, color that light red. This is fire. Positive charge. Male. Stay in the moment.

+ Make it move clockwise. Stay in the moment.

+ Make a MindLight in your left hand. Stay in the moment.

+ In your mind, make the light blue. This is water. Negative charge. Female. Stay in the moment.

+ Make it move counter-clockwise. Stay in the moment.

+ Slowly move your hands together, MindLights still spinning. If you have trouble making them spin, the next best thing is to make them glow in your mind. Stay in the moment.

+ Between your hands, focus on the intent—peace. Stay in the moment.

+ Bring your hands together until they are almost side by side. Stay in the moment.

- Merge the colors so that they are moving in a figure-eight pattern —the sign of infinity. Stay in the moment.

- Turn the pattern to gold. Stay in the moment.

- Turn the pattern to white. Stay in the moment.

- Know: As above, so below—what is within, is without. Stay in the moment.

- Together, move your hands up slightly and out slightly as if you were letting a bird go.

- Do not separate your hands. Let the energy move out from you in waves. Stay in the moment.

- Keeping your hands together, let the energy return to you in waves, and then pull it into your heart chakra. Take a deep breath. Repeat sending out your intent twice more, bringing hands back to heart chakra. After the third time, open your eyes. Thank deity. Stay in the moment.

- You have created the future. Stay in the moment!

Within every cycle of events there is a gateway where we can move to the next level of positive experience and thus find harmony in our journey. Although we have a multitude of choices before us, many will not lead to the portal of smooth transition—they will either keep us running viciously on the same track, or take us into a whirlpool of negativity flinging us far from the light of positive unfolding. There is always, however, at least one solution of right action that is the best possible movement for the present cycle that will allow us to transform to the next stage of harmonious development. After you have practiced the above exercise to the point where you are comfortable with the technique, announce that you are looking for a positive solution for a particular problem at the beginning of the exercise and use the four agreements (I agree mentally, I agree physically, I agree emotionally, and I agree spiritually) to confirm that you wish to find a positive solution. Then continue the exercise. Rather than manifesting on the keyword "peace" in this meditation, concentrate (without negative chatter) on the gateway opening to the solution. Do not try to force thoughts of inspiration. They will come when they are ready. Sometimes it occurs during the meditation, but many times the solution appears later, during the waking hours, in a flash of insight. For others, the answer may come through a dream. If dreams often speak to you in this way, be sure to keep a pencil and pad on your nightstand to jot down your first thoughts as you awake the next morning.

Learning to Focus the MindLight

Earlier in this book I discussed the priestess who danced her world in and out of focus. Yes, you read that right—focus. Everything is "there." You just have to "light it up"—bring it into your line of observation and participation. To teach myself to focus better I decided to create an exercise for myself using a flashlight and a darkened room. I simply sat in a comfortable chair, worked on deep breathing and relaxation, and when I felt ready, I clicked the flashlight on and played the light on different points of the room. I spoke to myself like a teacher:

"Click on the flashlight. See how the light hits a particular point? Let your eyes follow the beam to the target. This is what you want to do with your MindLight. We know that light travels in waves, just as your thoughts do. The trick is to stay focused on a particular point, and then fill that point with your MindLight. With the flashlight on, follow the light and then, at the target point, also fill it with MindLight—just a round ball of light will do for the moment. Try it."

And I did.

"Now breathe deeply and stay completely in the moment as you hit the mark with a beam of mental light."

Argh!

"Try again. You can do it."

Muuuffff!

"Do not tense up. That's not how it works. Stop screwing your forehead up, you look like a cross-eyed chicken. Natural. Be natural. Relaxed. Better! Nice, deep breaths. You lost it. Try again."

Sigh.

"Why are you rubbing your forehead? Think about it!"

"Because this takes effort." Yawn.

"Did you know that yawning is an excellent way to relieve stress?"

"No! What does that have to do with it?"

"Everything! Try again."

"Got it!"

"Excellent! Now, turn the flashlight on and off several times. Each time you turn it on, put a pleasant thought out there in the light."

"Like what?"

"I don't know . . . peace? Harmony?"

"How about winning the Powerball?"

Frown. "Let's stick to spiritual pursuits, shall we?"

"Killjoy."

"Could we please stay in a harmonious moment? Click the light on and off. Each time the light goes on, put the thought in the light. More than twice, please. How many? Fine, you want a number—do it twenty one times."

"Aw, come on . . . "

"You wanna learn this or not?"

"Fine!" Click. Click.

"Slower! Send the thought like you are swimming in water and the last time I checked, you don't swim too darned fast."

"Do not pick on my age."

"Stay in the moment!"

Click. Click. "Fourteen. Harmony! Nineteen. Twenty-one! Hey! That was pretty cool!"

"Indeed. Now, practice this every day for a week."

"You've got to be kidding me."

Raised eyebrow. "With practice comes excellence."

Click. "Harmony." Click. "Harmony." Click. "Harmony." Click . . .

"Stop!"

"What?"

"Now you need to add the four agreements."

"You've *got* to be kidding. Okay. Right."

Click on. "I emotionally agree that I bring positive harmony into my life. I physically agree that I bring positive harmony into my life. I mentally agree that I bring positive harmony into my life. I spiritually agree that I bring positive harmony into my life." Click off. Click on. "I agree!" Click off. Click on. "Harmony I agree!" Click off. Click on. "Harmony I agree!" Click off. Click on. "Harmony I agree!"

"Now you've got it!"

And that's how I taught myself to focus.

The Group Mind— Our Quantum Physics Healing Circles

During the summer of 2005 a varied group of us met for biweekly healing circles at my home in our outdoor ritual area. We've been doing such circles here for over ten years, but this year we decided to completely revamp our techniques and incorporate the various aspects of magick and quantum physics experiments. The results were astounding! From healing dying people to lowering crime, we worked on love, prosperity, healing, protection, justice, and more, and here is how we did it.

First, each request was written on a piece of paper and folded (just as we've been doing for years). Then, on the outside of the paper, we wrote the category. As we were dealing with many "observers," we kept the papers folded throughout the working to keep the number of observers to the issue as limited as possible. Once this was completed, we separated the requests into categories: Love, Money, Health, Career, Healing, Protection, Justice, and "Other."

Next, we empowered a large bowl of water and placed a good-sized crystal in it and put this bowl in the ritual area. As water is both a collector and dispenser of information and crystals are great generators, we used the water to boost our working. Later, each individual would take some of this water home. From making plants grow like a jungle to being washed over injured areas that healed incredibly quickly, that water was definitely put to work after it left the ritual circle!

One of the difficulties we experienced at first was that at each healing circle, different people attended. This in itself was defeating as we had to explain what we were doing for the new people at least six weeks in a row.

By the fourth circle, however, just about everyone had been there at least once, so that circle worked far better than the first three. Also, by the fourth circle we'd written down a specific pattern of quantum ritual that we could all follow. Because we had several people (our numbers varied from thirteen to twenty-one), we included drumming and rattles to facilitate flowing energy.

To keep everyone active, the categories are handed out to various participants. We ask, "Who is feeling successful this week?" or "Who is feeling healthy?"—matching categories with individuals who felt they were stable in those topics to lead the workings. This also worked extremely well.

Before the actual cycle of work began we practiced different types of cleansing. Some would sprinkle themselves with Florida Water, others used sage. We often burned Nag Champa incense. I would sprinkle the area with empowered holy water to dispel negativity that was likely brought into the circle, etc. Sometimes we would join hands and sing, other times we would begin with a chakra cleansing exercise, etc. Someone was also chosen to begin the circle with a blessing (incorporating Spirit) and when we were finished, close the working with thanks to deity and blessings to all participants. We did not, as time passed, petition the gods with each working. Only in the beginning and the end—alpha and omega—was all that was necessary.

Each working for a specific category actually starts as a group meditation with deep breathing as we settled into our still point. From there, the real work begins. I've found that the easiest way for people to do this on a short basis is to sit quietly and allow your ears to first listen to sounds close to you while your eyes are closed, and then to allow your hearing to expand outward. As this occurs, your breathing becomes slowed and you will experience a "quiet" inside. The trick is to allow the appropriate amount of time to settle in and do it. If you rush it, you've blown it.

The person who is running the category then says, "There is one power, within and without."

The group repeats this line.

"The mist of becoming unfolds."

Again, the group repeats the last line.

The leader for the category then says, "I physically agree for positive healing for those individuals who have requested this energy either for themselves or for others. I emotionally agree for positive healing for those individuals. I mentally agree for positive healing for those people and animals. I spiritually agree for positive healing for those individuals who have requested this energy either for themselves or for others." Sometimes the participants will simply say "I agree" after each of the agreements.

Then the leader says: "I agree that healing shaped by the power of infinity and molded into being by agreement is brought into being with the light! I agree!"

As the person is reciting the agreements, the participants are visualizing an infinity sign over the working area. This infinity sign represents both the concept of deity and the concept of the work that is coalescing.

As the petitions are burned in a ritual fire, energy is raised using the drums and the rattles, with everyone shouting, "I agree!" at the crescendo of energy.

Each category is treated the same, and very carefully worded. As you become used to working with this technique you will see that as you move through the chakras of agreement, you choose to tweak your desire to the most positive spiritual conclusion. Very interesting indeed!

I think the most unusual of all the issues we worked for that summer was the request to lower crime in one participant's area. To do this we found a map in someone's glove compartment, spread it out on the ground near the ritual fire, and circled the target area. In our agreements we decided to ask for angelic healing and protection of the area, choosing angel energy because it is widely used by various religious adherents in that part of the country. Whether our participants believed in them or not was not the point. We took an archetype of the collective group mind of that area and simply put it to work. By the next healing circle the crime had dropped significantly in that area—so much so the local newspapers were hooting on about it.

A few months later one of the participants e-mailed me. She was concerned because crime had again risen in the area. "I thought we took care of this. Why do we have to do it again? Shouldn't once be enough?" she wondered.

My response to her was, "As long as people are living, breathing, and thinking, they will continue to manifest energy. The need for us to continue to work toward harmony and balance will never cease. This is the Great Work."

Meditation Altar

Many of us running experiments in meditation and energy movement in the summer and fall of 2005 found that setting up some type of altar/sacred space helped to enhance our individual workings. Rather than dedicating a flat surface to deity/spirits/angels/archetypes, etc., we kept the area free and uncluttered of specific energy patterns. Items on this virtually empty altar would change per meditation and were based on simplicity as the need presented itself. The stock items of the altar included only water and incense (or perfumed mist), although the third favorite standard vehicle included a clear quartz crystal point. Other items such as candles, gems, herbs, statues, symbols, altar cloths, etc., were added on a per-meditation basis and removed after the meditation was completed. There were times when we didn't use an altar at all, choosing to place an empowered crystal in a bowl of fresh water set on top of a mirror at an outdoor location, or employing a portable fire pit, a clay plate, or even a small cauldron. We even hung tapestries on a bright September day to catch the winds of positive change in meditative form. For one meditation in particular we used only a map of a specific area. To banish negativity, we used a white altar cloth to represent the light of protection and the fire of movement. To create or manifest items and situations, we used black to represent the void, the place from where all things (scientifically) began.

For indoor work you may wish to set up a small, uncluttered space that is used specifically for meditation—a place where you can control the vast number of distractions that can haunt you while attempting to focus. The primary requirement is that the area be kept clean and uncluttered. You may wish to add something comfortable to sit on (large pillow or chair), as well as the ability to include music should you wish to add harmonious sounds to your meditative activities. I would also suggest enough space to move comfortably as many of the meditations in this book incorporate the movement of body, mind, and soul.

Quantum Conversation

If you think about it, there are three types of conversation—sharing of information, planning, and the voicing of one's opinion. All involve a mixture of thought and emotion and the direction of energy. Naturally, certain fields of conversation would be quantified as constructive and others as destructive. By the fall of 2005, several of us involved in quantum magick meditations discovered an astounding revelation in our work—that what we talked about in the realm of conversational planning began to manifest without magick, without ritual, without spells, and without meditation.

It started with Nancy and the pizza delivery guy. Nancy always tipped the fellow well because she knew he had a wife and two children at home. He was repeatedly very gracious and never forgot to sincerely thank her. One time he also added, "I see your husband bought himself a new truck!"

She smiled. "Yes, he really needed it for his business."

"That's very cool," he said, and then brightened with an odd smile on his face. "So, when do you get new wheels?"

Nancy laughed. "I'm afraid such a thing just wouldn't fit in our budget, but I agree that it is a nice thought."

"I agree," he said, "that you deserve it!"

Nancy laughed at his exuberance and shut the door. Nice young man, she mused, and let the conversation go, but not before she envisioned a flashy little burnt orange car. "Just like a pumpkin—that's the focus!" she said softly and giggled to herself. She never mentioned the conversation to anyone. Why should she? It was a trivial, albeit pleasant, exchange. It was a moment of harmony and joy.

Or so she thought.

Eight days later her husband took her out for dinner and instead of arriving at a restaurant, they pulled into a Ford dealership. They pulled up right beside a burnt orange Ford Focus that was prepped and ready to go. Her husband turned to her and said, "Over the years you've worked very hard and made a lot of sacrifices for our kids and our friends. You've done so many wonderful things for people and I know sometimes you don't feel appreciated. Let me be the first to say that I am thankful for all you have done for me. All I have to do is sign the papers and it's yours. Do you like it?"

Needless to say, Nancy is extremely happy with her pumpkin-mobile! And that's not all.

Next we move on to Dorothy, another member of the summer healing circle and a participant in our quantum magick experiments. Dorothy's story is a bit different and serves as a wake-up call on the power of the verbal exchange between individuals, especially magickal ones. Words aren't just words and they don't have to be in an unintelligible language to carry amazing consequences. It is a story that you should certainly stop and think about, no matter your religion or whether or not you believe in magick. And then think about it in the context of your own life.

Dorothy had raised several children by the fall of 2005. The last girl, although out of high school, couldn't seem to find a direction. As a result, she was hanging out with the wrong sort of peers. Rather lost and adrift, the girl was extremely talented but had no idea where to put her numerous skills. She hated school and really had no desire to go to college, even though she could be a straight-A student when she applied herself. Yet the confines of academia truly did not suit her personality. With the girl over eighteen but still living at home, Dorothy was becoming increasingly concerned at her daughter's outrageous nocturnal behavior. One evening, Dorothy spoke to a close friend, also a part of our circle, and they agreed that something should be done to bring her daughter to her senses. During the following week the daughter's attitude grew more irresponsible. Time and again Dorothy reiterated to her daughter that if this type of behavior continued, the universe would undoubtedly balance the girl's life in a way that she hadn't anticipated, and in a manner that would most likely be unpleasant. But, like most teens/almost adults, "Mother! I will be fine! Stop worrying!" became her mantra-like response. Her daughter had also invited a negative friend who had been thrown out of her own house to stay with them, which had made matters worse. This did not suit Dorothy at all, and she said as much, which resulted in the friend sneaking in the house to take showers when Dorothy was asleep or out running errands. Now Dorothy wasn't just concerned, she was extremely angry. The youngest daughter was definitely pushing the envelope.

The following weekend yet another circle member came to visit. The conversation turned to Dorothy's problems with her daughter, the negative young lady who kept mysteriously surfacing like the Loch Ness monster, and Dorothy's anger and concern over the entire situation.

"What my daughter needs," said Dorothy, "is a wake-up call. She's not a bad kid. Not evil. Not unkind. Just gullible and stupid. Something must happen that will open her eyes. Make her think."

"I agree," said the friend. "Something where she won't be physically hurt, but something so influential that she won't ever forget it."

Dorothy sighed. "I agree."

And they began planning a spell.

"Eyebright for clarity," said Dorothy.

"Amethyst for cleansing and transformation," said the friend.

"I have that."

"What about juniper berries for protection?"

"That I don't have, but I do have juniper berry essential oil."

"Might work. We'll need two candles. One for her and one for the negative friends. We'll want to work a separation spell."

"Without harm," said Dorothy.

"I agree. Do you have lemongrass incense?"

"I have sage and lemongrass—a good combination for getting rid of negative energies."

Dorothy shook her head. "She has no concept of being responsible for her actions. It's like she lives in a dream world."

"Then," said her friend, "as we have all had to learn, she must understand that she must be responsible for her own actions. That Mommy and Daddy or friends or siblings can't cover for her. She creates it—she must ultimately pay the price."

"I agree," said Dorothy.

"We need a focus piece," said the friend, tapping at his third eye.

Dorothy considered. "You mean a taglock? Like a piece of her hair?"

"That will work, but I was also thinking about something you could carry with you. Something to banish the negativity, yet something that pulls your common sense into the situation. We're going to that festival thing tomorrow. Let's see if we can't find an unusual focus piece. There should be tons of magickal vendors there."

Dorothy nodded. "Okay, then. Sunday is the dark of the moon and switches into the new. We'll work then. We'll work for protection, clarity, and removal of negative influences. We'll work that she finds common sense and clarity."

"I agree," said the friend, and the topic of conversation led elsewhere.

The next day, at the festival event, Dorothy found a smoked glass scrying pendant surrounded by a sterling silver dragon. She showed it to her friend, who agreed that the piece would be perfect for both protective and banishing magicks. Dorothy immediately cleansed the pendant (hey, there is a lot of spring water at a festival on a hot day) and proceeded to put it on. Dorothy held the pendant up to the sunlight and declared in a loud voice that the unwanted guest her daughter kept dragging in the house was immediately and summarily banished!

When Dorothy arrived home, the Loch Ness monster brushed past her, jumped in the car, and blew down the road. She never did return. This story, however, is far from over. One holiday weekend, the entire family was gathering to go out to dinner. Everyone present tried to convince the youngest daughter to join them on the family outing. Although the girl almost acquiesced, she finally turned them down and went to a party instead.

The following morning Dorothy and her husband awoke to a ringing phone at 7:00 a.m. They discovered that their eighteen-year-old daughter had been held hostage since 3:00 a.m., with the people in control demanding $2,000 for damages they claimed had occurred to their property during the party. When Dorothy immediately indicated that the police would be called, they slammed the phone down. Dorothy had no idea where her daughter was, but she did have the phone number on her caller ID, along with the name of the person who had disturbed her sleep. She rushed to her computer, paid fifty bucks on the spot for a public records search, and found out the exact address by matching the name and phone number to the public search records. Then she used the Internet to figure out where the heck her daughter was. Dorothy's husband and other family members drove out to the property, which was an hour and a half away, and when threatened and extorted for money upon their arrival, promptly called the police on their cell phone. When the police arrived, the owners of the property immediately backed off and refused to press charges. Why? Because they had provided alcohol to minors—several of them—many only fifteen years old.

Needless to say, a very meek young lady was brought home that afternoon, many years wiser than when she'd left at dusk the previous day. She was lucky.

Now, you could say (for argument's sake) that this girl was destined for trouble—I would agree and so would Dorothy. But what we found most interesting is that everything Dorothy had discussed with her two friends happened precisely. Protection—they never touched the girl although they threatened her repeatedly. Not only that, but that evening the girl had been in a vehicle that careened down a steep embankment—not a scratch on her person, and yes, she was wearing a seatbelt. Clarity—the young lady had no concept of how cruel strangers could be (now she knows) or how her so-called friends could turn on her (she now understands that, too). Or how people will lie rather than admit to the truth of their involvement (she's seen that first hand). And how one must be responsible for one's own actions (a very hard lesson to learn). Removal of negativity—all of her "buddies" scattered like the wind after the fiasco, leaving her holding the proverbial bag. It was indeed a wake-up call, one that taught her real life is not a picnic and there are people in the world who will extort anything they think they can out of you if you give them the opportunity.

Yet not one finger was magickally lifted—it all started and ended with two quantum conversations.

Think about it.

What have you been talking about lately?

Perhaps next time you might wish to choose your words more carefully. The field of opportunity is a very busy place—it hears and sees all. The field of possibility is omnipotent and omnipresent. And that field can be accessed any time, any where, any place—through simple meditation.

Click on. Click off.

CHAPTER FOUR

Basic Meditations for Your Life Enhancement

In the first three chapters I gave you many things to think about, opportunities to expand your infinite world of possibilities, and basic techniques to assist in bringing relaxation and balance into your life. We talked about a few real-life scenarios in conjunction with the art of meditation and quantum physics and how we can make the energy work for you. Chapters 4, 5, 6, and 7 are packed with various meditations and mind exercises based on the foundation of deep, cleansing breathing, your MindLight, your four agreements, reaching your still point, and remembering to "stay in the moment." With quantum physics of the mind built into these fundamental ideas, we are ready to add different types of meditations to meet your various needs.

The meditations in this chapter are general, uplifting sequences that can be used for any type of energy manipulation training, problem solving, or goal programming techniques. They are all short and can be done in fifteen minutes, many times less. If you like a particular meditation and feel it works well for you, continue the same meditation (although your focus can be different) for a seven-day period to familiarize yourself with the technique. They also work well as basic, beginning practices that can be coupled with ritual work, spellcasting, focused prayer, or other meditations. Under some of the meditations I have listed suggested candle colors, herbs, or oils that can be used to expand the meditation into an actual working that requires physical movement. It is my suggestion that you do the meditation first (the inner you) and then move to the working (the outer you) where appropriate. Finish by internalizing the working (back to the inner you) with deep breathing and relishing a moment of absolute stillness.

Many of the meditations provided in this book can be linked together for a longer working or meditation practice, especially when you find yourself under duress or need that extra mental oomph. For example, while writing this book I had to make a television appearance after being out of the limelight for a few years. Although I love doing public seminars, the media is a different venue, with its own set of pitfalls, especially when you write about the magickal world—I've had both wonderful and upsetting experiences. On the day of the interview I used several of the meditations at different intervals, including Take Five; The Field; Up, Up, and Away; and Crossing the Rainbow Bridge.

Remember the following:

+ Always use deep breathing before you begin

+ Stay in the moment

+ Don't forget to click on your MindLight

+ Be patient to reach the still point

A world of success awaits. Let's move onward!

Take Five

One of the easiest and most relaxing meditations takes five or less minutes to do and is excellent to employ anytime during the busy day. You simply stop what you are doing, take a deep breath, look out on the horizon (or close your eyes) and take five deep, even breaths, concentrating on the air flowing in through the nose, and out through gently parted lips. After the fifth breath, close your mouth, and continue breathing deep, even breaths, through your nose, allowing the muscles in your shoulders and upper back to relax (if they haven't already). Continue to concentrate on the in/out flow of air. When you feel calm and stabilized, count from one to five and simply open your eyes. If you have difficulty calming your busy thoughts, you can say to yourself, "I am at peace with the world and everything in it." And, right at that moment, you are.

Suggested Variations

If you are at work or have been in a stationary position for some time, get up and walk to another area, then employ the Take Five sequence. If you are at home, you can always light a scented tea candle to enhance this short period of relaxation. Take Five also works very well when you are studying. Read a page, then Take Five. Read the page again. If you thoroughly understand the material, move on. If you are having trouble assimilating the data, get up, walk around, come back, Take Five, then read the paragraph or page again. For some reason people think that a page need only be read once, which truly isn't the case if you are trying to internalize new information (no one ever said you are a bad person if you read a passage repeatedly). Sometimes we need to think about what we've just read and how it fits (or doesn't) with the totality of our experience. Once you feel comfortable with the information, move on. You can always go back and read a particularly sticky area again if you like.

Another helpful technique is to read the passage, Take Five, and then practice free association on a notepad as you go over the page again. As you read, write down any word that pops into your mind. Take your time and follow the thought (if you like) with your own notes. Sometimes doodles help, too! Later, when you review what you've written you may find some interesting correlations, or perhaps realize why a particular area appears difficult to understand.

This meditation is good for:

+ Stressful, daily situations
+ Coffee breaks and lunch times
+ Stopping negative mental chatter
+ When you feel overburdened with a particular problem
+ Creating a more relaxing day or evening

The Field

This meditation is in direct relation to quantum physics in that you are setting aside a specific space with your mind that is pure white light that turns to translucent "nothingness." It is a designated area that contains no mental clutter of any kind, and I recommend beginning any meditation, ritual, prayer, or working with this short sequence. "The Field" in this meditation is like the blank white page of a book. If you are having trouble visualizing "just white," use an empty journal page as a key. Then, concentrate on two things: your gentle breathing and the sounds you hear around you (don't strain). This is a "no pictures" sequence once you have visualized the white light. Soon, the white will melt to translucent nothingness where you aren't visualizing anything at all. Instead, you will feel a wash of peace and tranquility—a sense of "just being."

Suggested Variations

If you have a particular problem and wish a solution, name the problem first and create a "field" just for the solution. Then work through the short sequence. If you are feeling lonely or abandoned, unhappy, sick, or hurt, reach out in your mind and "touch God" (as you believe God/dess to be) at the end of the sequence. This is a nice bedtime meditation to help you release all the negativity of the day before you go to sleep. Light two white candles and spend several minutes at your personal altar, then reach out and "touch Spirit" before you complete the meditation. Extinguish the candles before retiring.

This meditation is good for:

- Preparing for the day
- Preparing for bed
- As a beginning sequence to any prayer, ceremony, spellworking or other meditation
- When you are tired, sick, fearful, or upset

$\mathcal{U}$p, $\mathcal{U}$p, and $\mathcal{A}$way

Like balloons? This meditation is designed to help you release your fears. Our fears often grow, making us miserable because we hold on to them so tightly. Rather than grounding your fears in your everyday life, use this great meditation to release them!

Take three deep, relaxing breaths, concentrating on the air moving in and out of your body. Let your shoulders relax. Envision yourself holding the strings of several helium-filled balloons. The balloons represent your fears. Some of them may have names, others may not. Entitle at least one balloon "fear of the unknown." Take another deep breath, and as you exhale, in your mind let one of those balloons go. Watch it drift up into the heavens until it becomes a pinpoint and disappears. Keep breathing slowly and easily. Release any named balloons first, such as "fear of failure," "fear of flying," "fear of verbal attack," "fear of looking (or sounding) stupid," "fear of being late," "fear of sickness," etc. Then release the "fear of the unknown" balloon. Finally, you may find you are still holding a bunch of balloons. These are the fears that are subconscious, circling just under the surface of our conscious thoughts. But they are there just the same. Let these balloons go all at once rather than trying to define them. Once you have released all the balloons, take one last deep breath, enjoy the peace you are feeling, count from one to five, and open your eyes.

$\mathcal{S}$uggested $\mathcal{V}$ariations

There are several physical variations of this meditation that you could try. In the fall, write your fears on dried leaves and release them on a windy day. In the summer, collect a small batch of creek pebbles, hold them in your hands, and then throw them back into the stream, releasing your fears with each one. Be sure to ask the flowing water for blessings and harmony in your life. I knew one woman who, during spring cleaning, named all her fears with pairs of old shoes, then pitched them in the trash, visualizing her problems walking out of her life. Another sweeps her dining room floor every day with a broom, putting the powdered debris in a dustpan. Rain or shine, summer or winter, she carries the dustpan outside every day and clearly states that she is removing all problems, fears, and sickness from her home.

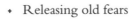

* Releasing old fears

* Combating and negating new fears

* Releasing problems

Crossing the Rainbow Bridge

Okay, so you've got to do something and you're not that thrilled about it. Maybe you are worried that you will fail, or that circumstances are going to be unpleasant and you really don't want to deal. Although we always have the choice not to do something, there are situations where we feel the heavy weight of responsibility to go forward. Conversely, there are times when we are so excited about something that the anticipation itself can be stressful in a different way. For occasions like these, you might like to try this meditation.

Close your eyes. Take three to five deep, even breaths. Visualize a pleasant woodland scene complete with a footbridge up ahead. As you move toward the bridge in your mind, count down from twenty-five to one. If you can, add singing birds, the sunlight upon your face, etc. When you reach the bridge acknowledge that on the other side there is a sphere of golden light heralding the successful completion of the event. All along the bridge there are colorful flapping flags. You can hear them snapping gaily in the wind. Begin walking across the bridge, passing the red flags. Then past the orange flags . . . the yellow . . . the green. You are now halfway across the bridge. From the green you walk by the blue, the violet, and finally, at the edge of the other side, are the white flags. Move past the white flags into the golden light of success. Count from one to five and open your eyes.

Suggested Variations

If this meditation is too hard to visualize, try taping the instructions on a small recorder and then listening to your tape as you do the meditation. You can also visit a real bridge and actually walk through the meditation. If it is a big event that has you nervous and you have the time, paint a thirteen-inch dowel rod gold, then tie ribbons of the corresponding colors, beginning at red on the bottom and moving to a gold ribbon at the top. You can visually touch the ribbons as you repeat the meditation sequence. When the event is concluded successfully, burn the stick and ribbons outdoors, thanking Spirit for the assistance you received.

This meditation is good for:

+ Quieting feelings of negative anticipation
+ Releasing worries about an upcoming event
+ Right before an important appointment or meeting: envision golden light around you as you cross the threshold to the room, office, or establishment

Chakra Breathing Meditation

Chakra breathing exercises are excellent for clearing out the energy vortexes of the body and revitalizing the mind/body/soul connection. Read through this section first before actually practicing the meditation, as the traditional colors, names, and body points of each vortex are given after the meditation sequence.

1) Close your eyes.
2) Take three deep, even breaths to stabilize.
3) Surround yourself with white light.
4) Imagine a ball of red light entering your root chakra with the next intake of breath. Allow the red light to energize the body as you breathe in and to leave the body as you breathe out. Do this three times.

5) Imagine a ball of orange light entering your sacral chakra with the next intake of breath. Allow the orange light to energize the body as you breathe the light in and to leave the body as you breathe out. Do this three times.

6) Imagine a ball of golden-yellow light entering your solar plexus chakra with the next intake of breath. Allow the golden-yellow light to energize the body as you breathe the light in and to leave the body as you breathe the light out. Do this three times.

7) Imagine a ball of green or pink (your preference) light entering your heart chakra with the next intake of breath. Allow that light to energize the body as you breathe the light in and to leave the body as you breathe the light out. Do this three times.

8) Imagine a ball of blue light entering your throat chakra with the next intake of breath. Allow the blue light to energize the body as you breathe the light in and leave the body as you breathe the light out. Do this three times.

9) Imagine a ball of violet light entering your third eye chakra with the next intake of breath. Allow the violet light to energize the body as you breathe the light in and to leave the body as you breathe the light out. Do this three times.

10) Imagine a ball of white light entering your crown chakra with the next intake of breath. Allow the white light to energize the body as you breathe the light in and to leave the body as you breathe the light out. Do this three times.

11) Take three deep, even breaths to stabilize. Open your eyes.

Suggested Variations

You can turn this into a more active meditation by lighting a candle of the corresponding color as you breathe the light in and out of your body. If movements are steady and slow, you can remain in the alpha state and still complete the meditation.

This sequence also works well for an active gemstone meditation. Choose gemstones that correspond to the chakra colors. Hold the chosen stone in your hand or place on the chakra point as you follow the breathing sequence. This is a nice morning meditation to help you prepare for the day. Suggested colors for a gris–gris bag might be rainbow or white.

This meditation is good for:

- Healing (emotional and physical)
- Stress
- Learning to breathe
- Learning the chakra vortexes
- Negating negative thoughts
- Raising self-esteem
- Stopping fears

TRADITIONAL CHAKRA MEANINGS

Root Chakra: The support

Sacral Chakra: Sweetness

Solar Plexus Chakra: City of jewels

Heart Chakra: Unstuck

Throat Chakra: Purity

Third Eye Chakra: To know

Crown Chakra: Thousandfold

GEMSTONE CORRESPONDENCES

Hematite: Grounding (root chakra)

Red Jasper: Power (root chakra)

Carnelian: Happiness and generosity (sacral chakra)

Yellow Jasper: Protects energy work (solar plexus chakra)

Citrine: Protection, success (solar plexus chakra)

Moss Agate: Eliminates depression (heart chakra)

Rose Quartz: Unconditional love (heart chakra)

Labradorite: Protect aura from leaks (throat chakra)

Sodalite: Wisdom (throat chakra)

Amethyst: Transformation (third eye chakra)

Flourite: Enhance mental state (third eye chakra)

Crystal Quartz: Energy booster (crown chakra)

TRADITIONAL CHAKRA COLORS FOR RITUAL WORK

Root Chakra: Red

Sacral Chakra: Orange

Solar Plexus Chakra: Yellow

Heart Chakra: Green

Throat Chakra: Blue

Third Eye Chakra: Purple

Crown Chakra: White

The chakras. From bottom to top: root, sacral, solar plexus, heart, throat, third eye, and crown.

Simple Daily Gemstone Attunement

1) Begin by holding the hematite in both hands. Close your eyes and take a deep breath. Continue taking deep, relaxing breaths until any tension leaves your body.

2) Following the gemstone correspondences list (see page 76), pick up each stone and breathe deeply. Consider energy moving in and around your body, concentrating on the chakra that stone represents. Take your time. Allow your energy to attune itself to the universal energies. Associate positive thoughts with the meaning of each stone.

3) When you are finished, allow yourself a few moments to "come back up" from your meditation. Hold the hematite stone again for grounding. Rinse your hands and the stones in clear water as closure.

Advanced Meditation

Begin in the same manner as the Simple Meditation on page 77.

1) Once you have activated each chakra point, envision the Cho Ku Rei Reiki symbol (pictured below) on your body. This may take some concentration if you are unfamiliar with visualization and might need several sessions to perfect. Don't get frustrated. Just note in your mind where you got stuck. That chakra probably needs more work!

2) When you have the Cho Ku Rei (meaning "put the power here") symbol in place, imagine that your right hand holds fire energy, that your left hand contains air energy, that your right foot is connected to earth energy, and that your left foot is connected to water energy. Imagine that the top of your head is connected to Spirit energy. Hold this as long as you can, then fold this energy into a mental ball over your heart (you can use your hands over your heart to help). You can also "light the balls" in your mind using a pentacle diagram (below). Finish the meditation in the same manner as in the Simple Meditation sequence.

The Cho Ku Rei symbol, left, and the pentacle, right. The Cho Ku Rei symbol is often used at the beginning of a Reiki session to bring the power of Spirit into the working.

Gateway Solution Meditation

For every situation there is a "best possible solution"—sometimes we simply have trouble finding it! I designed this meditation to help myself find harmonious answers to difficult problems and have found it to work extremely well. It takes only a few minutes to do and can be squeezed into any active lifestyle. The focus is a gate, ornate or as simple; before you begin, agree with yourself that the gateway is always open to you and that the best and most harmonious solution for all involved lies on the other side. When I look through the gateway, there is a beautiful, fruitful garden that holds exactly what I need. All I have to do is walk through the gate to receive my answer.

1) Close your eyes.

2) Surround yourself with white light.

3) Say to yourself, "I am creating the pure field I need to find the answers I seek."

4) Take three deep, even breaths to stabilize.

5) State clearly to yourself that you wish to find the best possible most harmonious solution to (fill in the rest of the sentence).

6) Envision the gate. See the garden beyond it. Take a deep breath, smile, and transport yourself with a flowing, undulating motion through the gate. Take another deep breath and smile—the solution is yours. Open your eyes.

Within the amount of time needed, your solution will manifest.

Suggested Variations

Go to a real archway or gateway and perform the meditation. Slowly rise and physically walk through the gateway. Keep the movements slow so that you can remain in the alpha stage and open your eyes, returning to the beta state on the other side of the gateway. Place dirt and a smooth stone from this physical gateway in a gris-gris or conjuring bag after you have done your meditation. This is a nice student exercise that works well on a camping trip, day outing, or festival.

Add an archetype on the other side of the gate with arms open and beckoning, ready to give you the answers. I recommend creating this archetype only if you have complete control over your meditation sequences and know how to keep negativity out of your field of visualization.

Couple with an "attraction" spell that includes herbs, powders, talismans, and gemstones that correspond to this purpose.

SUGGESTED HERBS OR OTHER ITEMS FOR RITUAL

Tonka Beans (do not eat, they are poisonous): Attraction

Lodestones: Attraction

Magnets: Attraction

Fava Beans: Attraction

Sunflower Seeds: Attraction

Rose: Navigation and transformation

Eyebright: Clarity and transformation

Fenugreek: Cleansing and clarity

Mint: Cleansing and clarity

Herbs can be ground together to make a magickal power that you can sprinkle around candles or place in conjuring bags. Herbs can also be mixed and used whole. Suggested conjuring bag and candle colors: blue, silver, or white.

This meditation is good for:

+ Problem solving
+ Finding lost objects and missing information
+ Enhancing your creativity
+ Eliminating disagreements between yourself and others
+ Finding a "happy medium" in any given situation
+ Drawing career opportunities toward you

Rocking Chair Meditation

The rocking chair meditation combines the left and right hemispheres of the brain and is based on the old Southern lifestyle of patience. Therefore, it is an excellent training tool that also provides the added benefit of relaxation. The only thing you need is, of course, a rocking chair. You can begin with either of the two previous meditations, or you can simply relax in the chair and pleasantly work through the suggested technique.

Begin by rocking the chair as long as you like, preferably until you feel relaxed and at peace. Close your eyes and surround yourself with white light. Agree within yourself that you are creating a pure field of positive manifestation. Take three deep, even breaths. Think about what you would like to manifest, then, gently rocking the chair, allow your thoughts to be transformed into waves of manifestation (bright bits of sparkling light works well). On a forward motion, stop the chair, open your eyes, and exhale, agreeing that what you would like to manifest is leaving you in waves. Now close your eyes, and allow that energy to flow back into your thoughts. Repeat this flowing out/flowing in visualization two additional times. Then, once more, let the visualization flow out into the universe. Take three deep, even breaths to stabilize, and you are finished.

I actually had a friend manifest a brand-spanking-new pickup truck using this visualization (and her credit wasn't the greatest). This meditation is extremely useful when you don't have any tools at your disposal.

Suggested Variations

You can use a porch swing, tire swing, even a kids' playground swing for this one. A friend of mine added a hand fan on a hot summer day to her rocking chair work, definitely snapping it shut to seal the spell. The next day she received an unexpected check for $3,000 in the mail. In a group format you can hold hands and rock back and forth, everyone stopping at once and exhaling, then beginning again. Now, if done this way, it can produce a lot of laughter; however, joy is the best magick and the giggles don't hurt the manifestation. Another friend focused on a complete altar setup, burning candles and concentrating on the pieces of his altar as he rocked. He obtained a coveted entrance position at the college he desired. This is also a wonderful way to empower gris-gris bags and candles for friends and loved ones; simply hold the item as you rock.

This meditation is good for:

+ Manifesting physical items
+ Stress reduction (add lavender essential oil or lavender candles)
+ Prayer work (hold prayer beads or picture of individual you wish to assist)

Gifts of Spirit Meditation

Write down seven qualities that you would like to enhance within yourself, or qualities that you would like to handle better when you have the opportunity. In this meditation the word is associated with the "feeling" you receive when you think of the word. What does that word mean to you? How does it make you feel? Once you have the list as you wish, take three deep, even breaths, then as you breathe in say the quality you wish to instill in yourself in your mind (as if you were actually breathing in that energy). When you exhale, release any random thoughts. Do each quality three times, then take another deep, even breath, count from one to five and open your eyes. If you work on this particular meditation every day for thirty days you will most likely experience a markedly improved lifestyle.

Love

Patience

Compassion

Grace

Helpfulness

Loyalty

Responsibility

This meditation is good for:

+ Strengthening current strong points in your personality

+ Developing new, powerful character traits

+ Finding solutions to current problems in a creative way

+ Relieving stress by concentrating on positive qualities

Energy Movement Meditation

As with the Gifts of Spirit technique, this mini meditation focuses first on the word, and then on the feeling. The idea is to learn how the energy feels to you so that you can access it at any time by breathing in, saying the word in your mind, and exhaling. Work with each word five times through the sequence, exhaling any random thoughts (this will help you focus). You can work with all the words given, or add some of your own. This is a great exercise for centering in group work.

Peace

Strength

Joy

Love

Speed

Power

Repair

Build

Banish

Protect

Balance

Suggested Variations

Throughout the day, when you think of it, breathe in the type of energy you feel you need at least three times. Seven or nine times is also a helpful variation. Some students enjoy taking pictures of events or objects that they feel represent the energies and tacking them on a bulletin board as a focus when needed.

This meditation is good for:

+ Learning what energy feels like

+ Learning how to expand your energy control

+ Calming after a busy day or during an upsetting time

+ Tightening your focus

+ Enhancing your self-esteem

Divine Wisdom Meditation

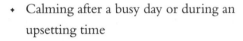

The focus of this meditation is the all-seeing eye of Spirit.

1) Sit in a comfortable chair and take a deep breath. Then another, and another. Close your eyes. Place fingertips of both hands on your solar plexus chakra and envision a golden light surrounding that area. As you move your fingers gracefully up to your crown chakra, say: "Spirit to Spirit."

2) Slowly bring your fingertips down to your heart chakra and envision white light around that area. As you bring your fingers up to your third eye chakra, say: "Mind to Mind."

3) Repeat this sequence at least three times, more if you are particularly worried about something. Each time you touch your third eye chakra, envision a light blue light that deepens into violet light.

4) When you feel calm, empowered, and comfortable, end by flipping your palms outward from your third eye and push outward with your hands, saying: "Peace and wisdom of the universe

The eye of Horus

abide in me." Envision the "Eye of Spirit" entering your third eye chakra.

5) Physically seal the chakra by drawing an equal-armed cross on your own forehead. If you don't remember to seal, you may find yourself with a headache.

Note: The ancient Egyptians believed that the heart and the brain were made of the same auric matter (and I've since read that the brain and the heart are virtually made of the same organic material, with only a few percentage points of difference), and therefore this meditation means Loving Mind (the heart) to the Creative Empowered Mind (the third eye chakra). This meditation can also be done standing if necessary.

Suggested Variations

Draw a stylized "eye" (the Egyptian Udjet or eye of Horus[1] is an option). Write what you need around the eye. Place your eye drawing at the chakra points as listed above in the same sequence. Jewelry can also be used, although I recommend silver or gold (not pewter). You can also empower a white candle and rub it with eyebright herb, repeat the sequence as given, then burn the candle until it has completely finished.

In Egyptian mythology, Horus had two eyes—the white and the black. The white represented the sun, while the black represented the moon. Another variation of this meditation is to use two stones—one white and

---

1 The eye of Horus mathematically represents a healing formula. Each portion of the glyph stands for a different fraction. One of the most popular ancient Egyptian amulets, it was used to protect the wearer and bestow desirable qualities such as health and vitality. See my book *Solitary Witch* for a complete explanation or, if you like Eyptian magick, check out *Egyptian Magick* by Gerald and Betty Scheuler (Llewellyn, 1997).

one black—in the sequence asking for wisdom, balance, and personal power. After empowerment, carry the stones with you in a black or violet conjuring bag. The idea is to gain control and possession of your own mind and your own emotions to create a level of balance within the self. If you do not wish to use a black stone, an opal works well because in the ancient texts, the opal contains water (as did the stones sometimes used for the eye of Horus).

This meditation is good for:

+ Connecting with Spirit in a positive way
+ Strengthening your connection with the divine
+ Learning how to quiety reach out for assistance
+ Clearing your upper chakras, especially when you have been ill
+ General emotional healing

Ankh Meditation for Universal Love and Long Life

Although associated with "free love" in the 1960s, the ancient Egyptian symbol of the ankh (a stylized version of the glyph for the planet Venus) stands for the life force, universal love, and compassion, and it is considered the key to immortality. Meditating on the ankh symbol brings warm, loving energies to the aura.

Where the loop on top is considered passive, the staff is thought to be active; together they create the required balance for all levels of the individual. Some use the ankh as a magick knot in spellwork applications. If you are feeling lost and alone, or are working on a health issue, meditate on the ankh symbol for at least five minutes three times a day. Carry a representation of the ankh with you on a piece of paper or empower jewelry of the same design. Silver or gold is best; avoid pewter unless you want to "set" long life.

This meditation is good for:

+ All matters of healing work
+ Stress relief
+ Learning to combine energies
+ Long-distance healing for one in need

Basic Water Magick Meditation

This is a very nice outdoor meditation. You will need a clear glass bowl of water and a colored symbol on a piece of paper that represents what you desire. For example, if you are looking for healing energy, try the caduceus. If you need money, try using a dollar sign with the amount you need written around the sign or eight one-dollar bills arranged in a fan shape. If you are trying to get into a particular university or business, use (if you can) a photograph of the establishment with you standing in front of it, etc.

Take the bowl outside (or if inside, in a darkened room surrounded by candlelight) and place on top of the focus item (picture, money, drawing) so that you can see the item through the clear glass of the bowl. Sit in a relaxed position and take several deep breaths until you find your still point. The water should also be perfectly still (unless there is a breeze outside that affects the water). Very slowly, conjure the image of what you desire up and to the left of the bowl, so that you are looking out into space. When you have a handle on the image and a handle on the feelings you will have when you are successful, slowly drop it into the water. Some people find it helpful to be holding the glass bowl with their hands as they mentally drop the image into the water. At the same time, say: "I empower this water to bring my desire in a positive way or better! I empower this water for . . ." (and fill in what it is that you need). Take three deep breaths and say, "It is done!"

Suggested Variations

There are variations on what you can do with the empowered water. If you put drinkable water in a clean bowl and the work was for healing yourself, you can drink the water. If it is healing for another, place the water in a vial or bottle and put on top of the sick person's photograph, or, if they are magickal, you can give them the water. If the water is for money, a new career, a car, a new apartment, etc., pour the water on your doorstep, making sure a bit splashes inside the house. You can also sprinkle your loose change, your purse, or your wallet with the water. My daughter puts all the loose change from pockets when doing the laundry into a toad bank, and then sprinkles the bank with the water on a weekly basis. The first week she tried this she'd collected over eighty dollars! This meditation can be repeated every day until your desire is obtained. In our healing circles, we add a large quartz crystal in the center of the bowl, and on holiday mornings, you can place a bowl of water outside where it will collect the first rays of the sun. Use this water to promote healing and well-being throughout the season by sprinkling it on all doors of the house with a sacred broom. Bless all doors and windows with clove oil and Nag Champa incense.

This meditation is good for:

+ Learning the subtle power of energized water
+ Manifestation of any physical object
+ Healing yourself or others
+ Stress relief

Cauldron Meditation for Self-Purification

An excellent meditation for spring, summer, or autumn outdoor work, the focus of this meditation is to bring the cleansing energy of the ritual fire into your body and remove all negativity. For this meditation you will need a fire-safe metal cauldron, sacred wood of your choice, and a bit of crushed incense (I recommend sandalwood; you can simply use sandalwood chips). Add a little dried yarrow herb (excellent for cleansing), if you like. You should also have a staff or stick and a lighter.

Outside, in the sand or dirt, draw a circle around the cauldron in a clockwise direction and say, "I set the field of purification and healing."

Sit inside the circle with the cauldron. Take three deep breaths and relax. Enjoy your surroundings. There is no rush or hurry. Light the fire, and say "I bring the purification of Spirit into my mind, body, and spirit in a positive way." Meditate on the fire as it burns and envision a fire dragon or phoenix (whichever fits your life circumstance) emerging from the fire and entering your heart chakra. Hold your hands over your heart to seal in the positive light energy. Close your eyes and let this positive energy move up and down your body—all the way down to your toes and all the way up to your crown chakra. Breathe deeply as you fill your entire body with the light. Imagine that all negativity is pushed out of your body and out of your aura (light body). Let it dissolve into the air or into the ground (as you desire) or back into the cauldron to be transformed. Then, release the dragon or phoenix as you open your eyes and gracefully open your hands with arms extended. Take another deep breath and say, "It is done! I am cleansed and purified!" You can add "In the name of deity!" if you so desire. Allow the fire to burn out and the cauldron to cool. Scatter the ashes to the wind, giving thanks for your positive transformation.

This meditation is good for:

+ Removing negativity
+ Overall cleansing

Flag Meditation for Self-Empowerment

Oriental cultures have long used flags or banners to capture and then release specific energies for empowerment and success. For this meditation you will need to fashion your own flag or banner. If you are not a sewing diva, you can always use a handkerchief and any of the many interesting products to decorate cloth that can be found at a craft store. Choose symbols that are important to you in your quest for personal empowerment when designing your enchantment. Working in a sacred circle and blessing all tools with holy water and incense will help to keep the object free of negativity and stress.

When you are ready to work with the flag, go outdoors on a day that has at least a bit of a breeze to it. Secure the flag on a tree or pole in an area that will ensure it can catch the air. Choose what type of empowerment you require this day, and position the flag at the quarter (north, south, east, or west) that best corresponds to your desire. For example, if you desire self-empowerment with stability and strength—choose the north quarter. If you are looking more for mental aspects of self, then the east would be a good choice. For creativity, the ability to love physically, passion—these energies are equated with the south. The west corresponds to closure, transformation, and the power of flow in one's life.

Sit quietly facing the flag and relax. Breathe deeply. Close your eyes. Let all the tensions flow out of your body as you physically feel the breeze. Let your fears, worries, and cares be ferried away by the air. Open your eyes and concentrate on your flag or banner. As the air lifts the fabric, visualize the cloth capturing the type of empowerment you desire. Allow the flag to build as much energy as you feel you need. The moment you begin to tire of the visualization, say, "It is done!"

Take down the flag and hold it close to your body. Close your eyes and, holding the flag to your heart chakra, breathe in deeply and exhale three times, imagining that you are breathing in the self-empowerment you desire. Cross your hands over your chest to hold this energy close to you. Hang the flag in your home in your ritual area. Use it in any future magicks in which you feel self-empowerment is needed. Renew this meditation whenever you feel weak or unhappy, or at least once every three months.

Suggested Variation

Although this meditation was for self-empowerment, you can also make a flag for home protection and harmony. Leave the flag outside to continue capturing and releasing the warding harmonics as needed.

This meditation is good for:

+ When you are worried or afraid
+ Learning how to work with the smooth power of air
+ Releasing negative energy and replacing it with positive feelings

+ Drawing good fortune into your life

+ Stabilizing and empowering the self

Centering Meditation

This meditation is actually a beginning Tai Chi exercise (a form of martial arts that uses breath and energy as the focus—Tai meaning "supreme" and Chi "life force"). Of all the centering meditations I have done over the years, this one has benefited me the most. The more you do it, the better you feel! This exercise also helps to improve your posture. With this meditation remember to stay in the moment and concentrate only on the centering exercise.

Stand with your feet about shoulder width apart, knees slightly bent, head straight. Now just relax in this position. Shake your hands. Shake your right foot. Shake your left foot. Relax back into the original position. Create your MindLight as indicated in chapter 1. Remember to breathe deeply, inhaling from the diaphragm up through the chest and exhaling slowly and evenly. Work with the rubber band technique for a few minutes until you have created a nice MindLight. Position the MindLight just below the navel with your hands. Close your eyes, breathe in, and bring the MindLight up to the heart using your hands. Now lower the MindLight (again using your hands) back to just below your navel. Do this several times, breathing in as you raise your hands and the MindLight, exhaling slowly as you move your hands and the MindLight back down to below your navel. Nice and slow. Relish the feeling! Now move the MindLight with your hands up to the third eye chakra. Bring the light down again to just below the navel area using your hands, making sure to breathe nice and slow. Do this several times. With your left arm hanging comfortably at your side, turn your right palm up and bring it up to the heart chakra as you inhale. Do this as if you had a precious liquid cupped in that hand. When you reach the heart chakra, flip your hand and push down as you move it to just below the navel area. Flip your hand, inhale, and bring the hand up again. Flip your palm, exhale, and push your palm down to its original position. Now try this same procedure with your left hand several times. Finally, create the MindLight again with your hands right below the navel area. Bring the energy up as you inhale to your heart chakra, and then move the energy down as you exhale. Do this at least three times. Relax. Open your eyes. Doesn't that feel great?! Practice centering at least three times a day for an entire month and see just how fast your life improves! I know mine did!

This meditation is good for:

+ Use as a great beginning sequence for any other meditation or working

+ Stress relief

+ Releasing negative feelings or sickness

+ Communing with Earth Mother

+ Learning to manipulate your own energy

+ Experiencing a stable lifestyle

The MindLight Sigil

I developed the MindLight sigil in 2004 while working on quantum physics and personal alchemical change. This cartouche is a stylized drawing using sacred geometry showing how the magickal individual manifests power and change. The oval is representative of the sacred circle—the field in which we create change—a place without negative energy and interruptions.

The central asterisk stands for the primordial void, the spark of thought, the beginning of the manifest. It also equals the eight phases of the moon as well as the quarters and the cross-quarters. The two triangles, locked together create the premise of "As above, so below," invoke our ability to create a cone of power as well as lock together in the sign of infinity—the sigil of mastery.

A trick of the eye creates a stylized figure above and below the apex of the triangles. If you view the figure one way, it is a kneeling individual whose thoughts move to the root chakra and up through the crown; yet, if you look at the figure another way, it is a person poised, looking down, ready to fling an arm up and lift the head at the same time to throw energy

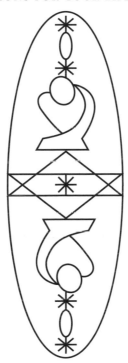

The MindLight sigil. This sigil is a stylized drawing using sacred geometry showing how the meditative seeker manifests power and change. The oval is representative of the sacred circle, the field in which we create change—a place without negative energy and interruptions. Use for all manner of meditations and rituals including healing, prosperity, protection, wisdom, and spirituality. An excellent meditation vehicle, place a copy of the sigil in a conjuring bag or burn in a ritual fire.

out into the universe! The figure above is the figure reflected below, past and present, conscious and unconscious, seen and unseen. In both instances, the person represents the present—the one above looking toward the future, and the one below looking back at the past. The person below gathers the appropriate feeling from the past, pulls it into the present, where the person above holds the energy in the present and projects that energy out into the future to create a positive destiny. The curves of the figure are representative of horns—the power to hook and draw in whatever we need.

The asterisk above the head stands for our creative thoughts and the egg-shape for the potential of Spirit to instill those thoughts with wisdom and healing. The egg can be considered our higher self, our guardian, totem animal, or deceased loved one trying to contact us. The asterisk above the egg is the amazing power that orchestrates the universe, regardless of what name you may call it. There are five asterisks in total—representative of the desire for change.

The cartouche can be used in any and all MindLight operations from manifesting your destiny to working on prosperity or healing enhancement. Following is an example of how to use the MindLight symbol for good fortune!

Crush one unlit cone of incense. Begin the ritual by sprinkling a little of the crushed incense behind you, saying: "For those who came before me, blessing upon you." Sprinkle some of the powder in front of you, saying: "For those who will come after me, blessings upon you."

Hold your hands out, palms up, saying: "Golden Spirit, powers of luminescence, I invoke the and ask for thy blessings upon all who are in this circle."

Draw the MindLight sigil. Light a yellow candle. Holding the lit candle proceed in a clockwise direction to the in a circle until you reach the direction of north. Turn your back to the center of the circle so you are facing the outside of the circle (and north). Say: "I believe that the past, the present, and the future are one in the same. I believe I can unfold my destiny. I remember now that special moment when I was filled with power and joy, and I reclaim that feeling . . . that power right now! I pull this power into the present, and as then, so am I now—filled with mastery and delight!" Turn clockwise to face the center of the circle, and say: "I stand here in the present, filled with positive energy. I am the master (mistress) of my own good fortune! As I step forward, I take this successful, positive abundant energy with me and claim my destiny and enter only the field of happiness and good fortune!" Step forward with emphasis. Then say: "It is done!"

Walk in a straight line to your meditation altar or working space. Set the candle down on the altar. Burn the sigil in a fire safe bowl, saying: "Midnight power—wave of change. Earth and Air, and Fire and Rain; betwixt, between, be now decree! As I will so shall it be! Cauldron glowing—swirling smoke; sparks of light I do invoke! Betwixt, between, be now decree! As I say so will it be! Without the fields of loss or pain, bring to me financial gain! Betwixt, between, be now decree! As I say so it will be!"

Visualize exactly what you want, then snap your fingers to "freeze" the moment. The ritual is concluded when you utter a prayer of thanksgiving, release what you've called, closed the quarters and released the circle. Allow the candle to burn at least two hours. You can relight the candle in sacred space each night and burn for a few moments, or for at least an hour. If you want to continue working on this same spell throughout the month, replace the yellow candle with another or use pumpkin-scented votives.

Alchemy symbol

cMeditation Symbuls

Many seekers work with sigils to help them focus on the movement of energy as attributed (by our choice) to a particular desire that we wish to manifest. This exercise uses the medieval symbol for alchemy (above) not only as the basic icon, but also in relation to instruction on energy movement and sigil empowerment. The first step of this exercise is to look at the above sigil like it is a snapshot *and* like you are looking through the lens of a camera. Study the sigil with this correlation in mind, then continue.

To begin, the largest circle is "the field." Mark it in some way, either by casting a circle magickally, working on a circular surface, on a plate, or within a circle of some image of some kind. The circle helps to define a manifestation point, and it guards against the corruption of thoughts and actions by others. It also helps to keep us from destroying our own work by previous or later worries. You can even spread your hands and visualize a circle on the table, and say aloud: "This is the circle in which I will work." Just be sure to have a strong visualization of this should you choose to use this technique.

Place your "desire" (the visualization thereof) inside the center circle. In this circle all is still. It is a place of no-mind, the cauldron of birth. The circle is the quantum. Your image begins as a small point and then expands to fill the circle. In your mind, make your desire wavy, like a heat mirage. The circle is the mother.

We know that snowflakes and other "explosions" move out in points and then build symmetrically. Move your image of your desire out until it touches the square, one point at a time or altogether as you are capable of. Your mental image should now be housed in the square. The square is the father. Keep the image wavy in your mind, like a mirage or the image of something on a very hot day. However, know in your mind that your image is about to solidify, so it should be a bit stronger in detail than when housed within the smaller circle. The square also represents the four basic elements —the material required to manifest anything on this plane. Allow color to move in from each point, heightening your visualization with a special, glowing vibrancy.

For anything to reach completion on this plane, it must touch Spirit (top), Matter (right point) and Man (left point). Flow your visualization out to the points of the triangle like a mist through a sieve, separating any impurities within the visualization, and solidify the picture clearly in your mind. Hold it as if it is becoming solid right before your eyes, and then freeze it by blowing your breath on it, and at the end of the exhale, affirm strongly that "It is done." And so it shall be.

Magickal Items Often Used in Sigil Work

Incense

Holy water

Magickal oil

Empowered candle

Cauldron or burn pot

String or ribbon

Lock of hair or photo

Magickal powders

Empowered herbs

Favored prayers

Gemstones

Magickal trinkets

Steps for Sigil Work

1) Cast a circle of white MindLight around yourself.

2) Ask for deity assistance.

3) Pass sigil and all supplies over incense.

4) Dot sigil and all supplies with holy water.

5) Write desire on sigil.

6) Light candle.

7) Empower sigil.

8) Attach sigil to hair or photo.

9) Roll sigil. Secure.

10) Dot sigil with magickal oil.

11) Sprinkle sigil with magickal powder.

12) Blow on sigil three times.

13) Burn sigil with herbs, OR

14) Place sigil in conjuring bag with herbs and gemstones or other magickal trinkets. If placed in bag, pass over candle three times.

15) Thank deity.

16) Release the MindLight.

Now let's move on and work with the elements!

CHAPTER FIVE

Enhancing Your Power with the Energy of the Natural World

The meditations in this chapter deal with the world around us and using that energy in a positive, uplifting way. Some of these meditations are a bit longer in duration than those given in the last chapter. With a few of the meditations I've given the formulas for a magickal oil or for an enchanted herbal mixture to assist in the tactile advantages of physical objects that affect your senses mixed with meditation. You don't need to make the oils or employ the herbs for the meditations to work. The formulas, developed here over the last several years, are merely assistance mechanisms, should you choose to use them.

Don't forget:

+ Begin with deep breathing
+ Stay in the moment
+ Click on your MindLight
+ Be patient and touch your still point

Disclaimer: Remember that essential oils should always be used in a carrier oil for your ultimate health safety. A general rule of thumb is for one drop of essential oil, use 10–20 drops of a carrier oil. Before using essential oils, always check with your physician first if you are being treated for a specific medical condition. Pregnant women should not work with essential oils. Body-safe fragrance oils can be substituted in any of these recipes.

Thousand Raindrops Meditation

The Thousand Raindrop sequence was taught to me by a friend who had explored Buddhist teachings and visited India for a time. It is a word-association meditation that I'm sure can be found the world over. This particular meditation requires plenty of time for you to completely explore the current issue without any outside disturbance. You may find gentle, soothing music helpful if the issue you're wrestling with is complicated or upsetting. Place a bowl of clear water somewhere near you. You can also light a white candle and place it beside the bowl if you desire.

Sit comfortably and close your eyes. Begin by inhaling through the nose, and exhaling through the mouth several times. When you are ready, visualize a pool of water. This pool represents the ultimate solution to your problem. Now visualize a drop of water falling into the pool. As the drop enters the pool, say the first word that comes to your mind. Visualize the concentric waves that your drop of water has made. Move on to the next word—the first word that comes to your mind, and "see" the next drop of water slip into the pool. The trick of this meditation is not to direct the words in any way—don't think about them, just let them come—and then release them. One word leads to the next, and then the next, and so on. As you work on the problem in this way the words will turn from dark to light, light to dark, light to gray, etc. Don't worry about it. This is your mind working through your difficulty. When all the words are positive in nature the meditation is complete. This could take you five minutes, or as long as a half an hour or more. The benefit is that when you are finished, you will feel relaxed, in control, and truly wonderful. Don't worry if you don't immediately have the solution you desire. What you need will come to you very shortly.

To Increase the Power of This Meditation . . .

Use a lavender-scented candle or lavender-scented oil if you are dealing with a very stressful problem. Dried lavender, rosemary, and rose petals mixed with two drops of essential lavender oil, or one drop of lavender oil, one drop of rosemary oil, and one drop of rose oil is helpful for navigating your meditation experience toward a more spiritual, higher-mind avenue. This is also a wonderful meditation for a rainy afternoon, where you can hear the raindrops outside as you meditate.

This meditation is good for:

- Problem solving
- Releasing fear

Elemental Flow Meditation

Particularly good if you are feeling stuck, worn, or tired on your pathway through life, the Elemental Flow meditation works on the premise of movement through the elements; however, you may find a mixture of Eastern and Western philosophy in this meditation to assist you in finding greater balance in all things. It is a great meditation for those with limited movement due to an accident, old age, or disability.

Sit quietly and comfortably in a favorite chair. Close your eyes. Take several deep breaths. When you feel you are ready, imagine you are sitting in a shallow pool of water. See the sunlight glint off the reflective surface. Slowly, extend your arms out in front of you and move your arms and hands back and forth (from side to side) as if you are moving your arms through that water and pushing at it gently. Imagine the soft resistance of the water on your arms and hands. Don't strain yourself. Do the movements very slowly and simply relax, enjoying the sensation of peaceful, empowered water. Do this at least eleven times or until you feel fully tranquil. Let your hands fall gently to your lap when you are finished.

With air, you are going to become a bird in flight. Gently raise your arms in front of you and begin waving them slowly up and down, keeping the wrists supple. As you continue the movement, spread your arms like a bird as if you are gently and peacefully flying through the sky. See the blue heavens before you and breathe deeply of the cleansing air. Inhale as your arms move up, exhale as your arms move down. Do this at least eleven times or until you feel fully tranquil. Allow your hands to fall gently to your lap when you are finished.

In fire, imagine that you are the sun. Extend your arms like airplane wings, palms facing up. Slowly raise your arms as if you are the rising sun peeking over the horizon, then bring them over your head and slightly bend them as if you are making a "sun" with your arms. This is the peace of noon. Turn your palms outward and bring your arms gently down, as if the sun is sinking past the horizon. When your arms reach your sides, it is midnight. Turn your palms, and raise the sun again. Continue this sequence at least eleven times, inhaling as you raise your arms, exhaling as you lower your arms. With each sequence, fill your entire body with glowing, white light. Do not finish until you feel completely tranquil. Allow your hands to fall gently to your lap when you feel at peace.

For earth, you will use the image of a seed growing into a tree (your favorite tree). Place your hands in your lap as if you are holding a small ball, fingers not touching. As you breathe in, begin raising your hands and pulling them apart as if you are running your hands along the trunk of a tree. Keep moving your hands upward in this position until your arms are above your head, then open them as if you were a flowering tree. Imagine the boughs flowing and growing from your trunk as you bring your arms out and down, resting once again in your lap. As you "grow your tree," each time envision the colors, the sound of birds, the feeling of the warm sun, and the strength and stability of your tree. When you feel strong and tranquil, allow your hands to rest in your lap.

In Chinese philosophy, metal represents clarity. Sit straight and put your palms together as if in prayer about six inches from your nose, so that your elbows will be parallel to the floor. As you breathe in, keep your hands in the prayer position and breathe in, extending your arms up above your head. See yourself as the sword of clarity. Envision yourself glittering with knowledge. As you breath out, still keeping your prayer hands together, bring them back down until your thumbs are once again in front of your nose. As you move your prayer hands up again, think of yourself reaching out into the universe to capture the information and wisdom that you need in your life. As you bring your arms down, believe that you are bringing this vital information into yourself. Do this sequence at least eleven times. When you feel at peace, let your hands drop to your lap.

Spirit encompasses all things; therefore, the last sequence involves all the previous movements. Don't worry if you mess them up the first few times, but do take note of which element you forgot or didn't quite get. This is the element you may be lacking in your life. Begin by moving your arms from side to side as if you are pushing water, then open your arms and become the bird in flight. Let your arms drop to envision the rising and setting sun. Circle your hands in to form the seed, grow the tree, and allow the boughs to extend down, then move into the prayer, metal-hand position. Raise and lower your arms in that position and as you lower your hands, this time pull them into your heart chakra. Bow your head, then gently open your palms like you are cupping a precious ball of light, then cross your hands gently and pull your hands into your heart chakra. Breathe deeply three times. Open your eyes.

To Increase the Power of This Meditation . . .

Use four candles, one for each element (red for fire, blue for water, green for earth, and white or yellow for air) and dress with your own Elemental Flow Power Oil.

> *Elemental Flow Power Oil:* Blend one drop patchouli essential, two drops essential bergamot oil, one drop gardenia fragrance, and one drop cinnamon essential oil.

For an herbal conjuring bag or herbal offering, mix dried vetiver, lavender, dried apple slices, and ginger. Add three drops of your Elemental Flow Power Oil. This also makes a nice potpourri.

> *To Make an Elemental Flow Powder:* Grind the following into a fine powder: allspice, cedar, chamomile, orris, vetiver, patchouli (not too much, can be overpowering), lemon verbena, and sage (again, not too much, this can "take over" your mixture). Add three drops of your elemental flow power oil. Use herbal powder in gris-gris bags, around candles, or sprinkle outside in ritual circle.

This meditation is good for:

+ When you feel like you're "in a rut"
+ People who have limited physical mobility

Heaven and Earth—
Esbat or Circle Casting Meditation

In many mystical traditions it is believed that the human is the connection between heaven and earth, and through us flows all opportunity of the world combined. How we use that opportunity speaks of our character and integrity. If you have a tough decision to make, try this simple meditation in movement. This meditation can be done sitting down or standing, so it is also a useful one if the individual has limited movement. However, I prefer to do this meditation standing.

Close your eyes and take at least three deep breaths. With your hands extended, visualize that you are holding a very big ball about a foot from your tummy. Now roll the ball until your right hand is on top and your left hand is on the bottom of the imaginary ball. Your elbows are now perpendicular to the floor. In some mystical circles, this position is known as "Embracing the Moon." As you slowly breathe in and out, envision that the ball you are holding is filled with white light and positive power. Slowly begin to separate your hands with the right hand gracefully moving up to the heavens, palm up and your left hand moving gracefully down toward the earth, palm down, and a bit behind you. You'll feel a nice stretch, but don't overextend or strain—that's not the point. Inhale deeply as you do this. Look up at your raised palm, imagining that your left hand has gathered the energy of the earth, and your right hand has gathered the energy of the heavens. Now, as you exhale, bring your hands (and the energy you have gathered) back to their original positions in front of you, as if you are embracing the moon once again. Do this sequence at least five to seven times, then switch hands with your left hand on top of the imaginary ball and your right hand supporting that ball. Move your right hand gently down to the earth, palm down a bit behind you as you raise your left hand to the sky, palm up, with your gaze on your left palm. Gather the energy and pull it back into the ball. Complete this sequence five to seven times. Switch hands once again, keeping your right hand on top. Reach toward the heavens with the right, and toward the ground with the left. This time, look at your left hand—meaning look down instead of up. Gather the energy. Retract to the ball. Do this five to seven times, then switch hands with your left hand on top of the ball and your right hand supporting the ball. Raise your left hand toward the heavens, move your right hand toward the ground, and look at your right hand. Gather the energy. Retract to the ball. Do this five to seven times, then retract to the ball once again. Without dropping the ball, roll your hands so that they are opposite each other, still holding the ball. Now cross your hands and pull them into your heart chakra.

This meditation is an excellent preparation for circle casting. In one fluid movement, pull the ball into your heart chakra, extend your right hand (or your dominant hand) and immediately begin casting your circle using your normal circle casting technique. See the amazing difference?

To Increase the Power of This Meditation . . .

Sacred Space Magickal Oil: One drop basil essential oil, one drop lavender essential oil, one drop clove essential oil, three to five drops honeysuckle fragrance.

Sacred Space Herbal Mixture: Use this mixture outside to prepare sacred space. Add equal parts of hyssop, basil, kava-kava, rosemary, and lavender. Mix. Add three drops of sacred space magickal oil. Blend. Sprinkle around area. Sweep free of the area with empowered broom. Excellent for cleansing, banishing, and bringing positive energies.

This meditation is good for:

+ Circle casting
+ A moving meditation sequence: for a powerful magickal working, do under a full esbat moon for gathering the energy and then putting it into yourself or into any vehicle

Simple Element Meditation

For this meditation you will need four candles, one corresponding to the color of each element. Standard colors are green for earth, white or yellow for air, red or orange for fire, and blue or purple for water. Dress candles with the corresponding element oil (see recipes below). Arrange the candles so that they surround you, one at each compass-matched quarter is good. Sprinkle a bit of the corresponding element magickal powder (recipes given after meditation sequence) around the appropriate candle. Not too much. Take several deep breaths, then envision yourself surrounded with white light. Beginning with the element to which you are most drawn, light the candle of the corresponding color and close your eyes. As you breathe in, imagine yourself breathing in that element. When you feel refreshed, move to the next element that draws you and repeat the procedure. After all the candles are lit, contemplate the order in which you called them into yourself. The one that you chose last is the one you need to work on most. Consider how that element applies to your life right now, and what benefit you may receive by working more with that particular element. When you are finished, take three deep breaths and relax. You can put out the candles and use them for the same type of meditation another time or you can allow them to burn until completion.

> *Earth Element Aromatic Oil:* One drop cypress essential oil, three drops honeysuckle fragrance, six drops patchouli essential oil, one drop vetivert essential, one drop pine essential oil.

> *Earth Element Aromatic Herbal Mixture:* Blend equal parts of vetiver, patchouli, vervain, horehound, and mugwort. Add three drops earth element aromatic oil.

> *Air Element Aromatic Oil:* Six drops bergamot essential oil, two drops clover fragrance, one drop lavender essential oil, one drop tangerine essential oil.

> *Air Element Aromatic Herbal Mixture:* Blend or grind together equal parts of bergamot, eyebright, fenugreek, lemon verbena, and sage. Add three drops of air element aromatic oil. Note: fenugreek and sage can overpower the scent of the mixture, so you may not want to use as much of these herbs.

Water Element Aromatic Oil: One drop apple fragrance, three drops coconut fragrance, one drop camphor, one drop gardenia fragrance, one drop peach fragrance.

Water Element Aromatic Herbal Mixture: Blend or grind together equal parts of eucalyptus, kava-kava, chamomile, myrrh resin, orris, and sandalwood. Add three drops of water element aromatic oil.

Fire Element Aromatic Oil: One drop basil essential oil, four drops ginger essential oil, one drop cinnamon essential oil, five drops dragon's blood fragrance oil that has been steeped with dragon's blood resin. For the brave? Add a minute bit of powdered yohimbe herb.

Fire Element Aromatic Herbal Mixture: Blend or grind together equal parts of allspice, cedar, frankincense, galangal, hyssop, marigold petals, and sarsaparilla. Add three drops of fire element aromatic oil.

This meditation is good for:

- Self-empowerment
- Learning to work with the elements
- Strengthening your abilities with the flow of the elements
- Natal chart work: What elements are missing in your natal chart? Which are weak? You can work on balancing your personality by doing this meditation with particular attention to what you are lacking in your chart.

Thunder Meditation

Learning to gather and move energy with the mind to revitalize the body and soul is something everyone desires and this particular meditation uses the heavenly dance of a thunderstorm to bring balance within the self. For this meditation, some people have wonderful auditory recall and will not need any special aids; however, others may find it easier to purchase a CD or tape that contains the sounds of thunder, lightning, or a pounding waterfall. Drum tapes can also be used to achieve the same effect. Finally, the real thing, an active thunderstorm, can be an exciting and revitalizing experience as long as you are safely positioned, preferably indoors.

Scientifically, a thunderstorm occurs when warm air meets cold air—so in essence, we are dealing with yin (the cold air) and yang (the hot air), or "this" and "that" dancing together, and when they meet they create the glorious manifestation of sound and light. They are the Storm of Becoming. In this meditation, the two forms of air are a part of your being. The receptive side of you (yin) and the aggressive side of you (yang).

Close your eyes and take at least three deep breaths. Position yourself comfortably. As you listen to the sound of the thunder, imagine the receptive part of you accepting the power of the thunder and the glorious manifestation of light. Fill your body with the flash of the lightning. Then, imagine the aggressive side of you using the thunder and the light and the auditory roll of thunder in a positive way. At first, you can bring in the energy as you inhale and push out the energy as you exhale, each time filling yourself with white light. When you feel empowered, you can move on to a specific need. Let's say we would like to do a healing for someone. As the thunder rolls, use your arms to gather in the sound, pulling your arms and hands toward your heart chakra. As the thunder rolls again, use your arms to push that power into a visualization of your friend. Keep working in this way until you feel totally relaxed and energized—that is how you know you are done. This meditation can be very short, or as long as you like. Here you can move from need to need with the inhale and exhale of breath, moving from visualization to visualization. Before you finish, however, we need to close and honor the power, which can be done at the end of a real storm or at the end of your tape or CD. Breathe in deeply, allowing the sound to roll throughout your body, from your head to your toes, one last time. Using the memory of the sound is very good practice. As you exhale, drop your hands to your sides, bowing your head, saying: "I honor the power of the storm. I honor the power of myself. So mote it be."

Suggested Variation

Many people like to use storms, especially thunderstorms, to empower "Thunder Water." For some, Thunder Water is also war water, used when aggressive magick is required. For others, Thunder Water is a water of becoming and healing—used to bring balance to the body, mind, and soul of the practitioner. Thunder Water can be empowered during a storm for this latter purpose and stored in the refrigerator. For seven days, drink some of the water at sunrise (if you wish to bring something toward you) or at sunset (if you wish banishing and cleansing). Nothing else is added to this water and most people use small bottles of spring water as they are easy to empower and contain few additives. If you are looking to bring love into your life, a bottle of wine (if you are over twenty-one in the United States) can be used. To make Thunder Water for healing and good health, hold the bottle with both hands as you practice the visualization given in the original meditation. When the bottle grows warm in your hands, the empowerment is completed.

> *Thunder Aromatic Herbal Mixture:* Pulverize equal parts of the following: cinnamon, dragon's blood, red sandalwood, dried hot peppers, yohimbe, and blood root. This is an expensive mixture but it packs incredible power. Due to the nature of these herbs, do not inhale while preparing and be very careful where you use it. Do not ingest. Empower during a thunderstorm for greatest effect.

This meditation is good for:

+ Pushing out disease and body dysfunction
+ Self-empowerment
+ Sparking the creative self
+ Healing others
+ Banishing negativity from a particular situation

Candle Meditation

This particular meditation is not your normal candle/fire sequence. It was specifically designed to fulfill two purposes. First, there are many individuals who, for whatever reason, are not permitted to burn candles in their environment. Secondly, this is a wonderful meditation to assist you in learning how to visualize a sequence of events. In this sequence we will be envisioning a pot; a thin, straight copper rod; a ladle; and a pillar candle mold. If you have never seen a candle mold, you may want to visit a craft store to observe how they are shaped or go online and simply research "making candles." If you do not have access to the outside world, just imagine that the mold is a metal tube with a bottom. No worries. To help you with this visualization, you may wish to gather these items and look at them or even set them on your altar in front of you (if you so desire). In the real world, a candle mold has to be "wicked" before the candle is poured. For this meditation, we are going to assume that our mold is already set up with the wick in place. All you will have to do for the meditation is pour the wax into the mold without worrying about the technicalities of wick placement. Just believe it is there and it will be.

Breathe deeply in through your nose and out through your mouth at least three times before you close your eyes, then breathe deeply three times again, allowing yourself to completely relax. Visualize a pot sitting before you. The pot is filled with clear, steaming, melted wax. In your mind, choose a color that matches your intent. For example, blue or purple for spiritual wisdom, orange for opportunity, yellow for success, green or purple for healing. Imagine this color as a bright button in your hand. In your mind, drop the color button into the melted wax. Visualize a thin copper rod. Stir the wax in a clockwise direction with the copper rod, repeating your intent in your mind as you stir. As you move the wax with the rod, see the color fill the pot of wax with amazing, colored light. In your mind, put the rod down and pick up a ladle. Fill the ladle with glowing, colored wax. Slowly move the ladle (just as you would in real life) over to the candle mold. Fill the mold with the contents of the ladle. In your mind, do not touch the candle mold with your hands, because in real life the mold would be too hot to touch given the wax is usually at 190 degrees when poured. Now tap the side of the mold three times with the copper rod. This is to set your mental spell and release any residual negativity. In real life, we tap the mold to release trapped air bubbles.

Once you have poured your candle in your mind, begin a deep breathing exercise. Breathe in through the nose, allowing your diaphragm to extend as you inhale, and tighten the diaphragm muscles as you breathe out. Do this at least ten times. Each time you breathe in, think of your intent. Let's use healing for example. Each time you exhale, mentally say: "Manifest." Inhale—healing. Exhale—manifest. Inhale—healing. Exhale—manifest. Keep the candle mold as your visualization as long as you can. Now, in your mind, take hold of the candle by the wick and pull the candle out of the mold. Envision a perfect, brightly colored candle that glows with blessed light. Hold the colored candle to your heart chakra and repeat your intent. Then set the candle down and light the flame, saying: "Fire to light to action to manifestation. I agree that the healing has begun and will not cease until the healing has manifested. So be it!" Take a deep breath and open your eyes, knowing and agreeing that your astral candle will continue to burn until your desire has completely manifested.

This meditation is good for:

+ Strengthening your visualization skills
+ Working on focusing
+ Learning to manifest from the mind

Sunrise and Sunset Meditations

Some of the most calming and fulfilling sets of meditations are done with the sunrise or sunset of each day. With sunrise, it is a time of opening and beginnings. With sunset, a sequence of closure and releasing. Both types of meditations are done with the honor of the universe in the mind and the connection that we have to each other and to the world around us. To find out the exact time of sunrise and sunset in your area, check out your local newspaper under the weather section. If possible, sit where you can see the rising or setting sun. If this isn't a part of your present reality for whatever reason, stick as close as possible to the timing and face the direction of the rising sun (east) or setting sun (west).

Sunrise Meditation

You can perform this meditation with or without tools. I personally like to light a candle in my cauldron and burn incense while I greet the rising of the sun, but these props are not necessary.

Sit in a comfortable position facing the direction of the rising sun (east). Begin deep breathing—in through the nose expanding the diaphragm, out through the mouth contracting the diaphragm muscles. You can keep your eyes open, or close them and enjoy the warmth of the sun on your face as it rises. With your mind, envision a winding creek of sparkling water that leads to the sun. This visualization is to teach you to avoid negativity by learning to mentally move with serpentine ease. Let your mind move toward the sun, extending past your body, past where you are sitting, past the building across the street, or tree, or lake, or whatever is there. Let any sound you hear wash over you and keep moving past those sounds. Slowly raise your hands, palms facing toward the rising sun, then drop your fingers so that they are pointing directly at the sun. As you breathe in, pull the sun's energy into yourself. As you breathe out, connect your mind to the sun, through it, and out into the solar system. Move your fingers gently as if you are tickling the belly of the universe. Don't be surprised if you hear laughter! Now breathe in the sun's energy again, fill yourself with the totality of white light, and breathe out, ending with the tickling motion. Do this as many times as you feel comfortable. When you are relaxed and spiritually energized, slowly lower your hands and say:

"I give honor to the universe this day. I greet the dawn with love and pleasure in my heart. I will create my day with wisdom, clarity, and joy—never forgetting that the Universe and I are one and that I have the ability to move through my day with peace, joy, and harmony. I agree I will exercise this ability to the best of my potential today. So be it."

If you have a job that requires your attendance before the rest of the world awakens or if you must go to school before sunrise (especially in the winter months) don't feel that you can't do this meditation. Simply choose the closest time that you can. The universe is always free with her energies.

Suggested Variations

This particular meditation is wide open for a variety of opportunities involving ritual. It is the time of beginnings and has a pure potential for success. You may also like to add your own composed prayer or song to the meditation sequence. Perhaps you wish to honor something special on a particular day—such as your birthday, the assistance a friend has recently given you while asking for blessings for them, or maybe the passing of a loved one. However, any work you do in the morning should be joyous in nature, celebrating life and the possibility of all things.

> *Sunrise Aromatic Oil:* Two drops cedar essential oil, two drops tangerine essential oil, one drop cinnamon essential oil.

> *Sunrise Loose Magickal Incense or Herbal Mixture:* Finely chipped cedar wood, dried tangerine peels, ground cinnamon, and three drops of sunrise aromatic oil. Or, if you want to have an incense packet for a ritual fire, place cedar wood, cinnamon sticks, and dried tangerine peels in white cotton gris-gris bag. Tie shut. Dab with eight drops of sunrise aromatic oil. Throw in a burning ritual fire.

This meditation is good for:

+ Clearing the aura
+ Beginning a specific project
+ Keeping the self balanced
+ Protecting the self from the challenges of the day
+ Connecting with Spirit

Sunset Meditation

Where the sunrise celebrates beginnings, so the sunset gives us a chance to close our day by releasing negativity or stress, and allows us to honor the good things that have occurred. The problem with a sunset meditation is that, depending upon your job and your family life, you may not be able to achieve the timing as easily as with sunrise. Also, as the days grow shorter in the northern hemisphere in the winter time and life certainly doesn't cease with the setting of the sun, you may find it difficult to fit a long meditation sequence into your responsibilities. If that is the case, you may wish to turn this sunset meditation into a bedtime one where you can spend a bit more time releasing any negativity of the day and allowing your body, mind, and spirit to release any stress you have experienced. If you are having trouble sleeping, you may wish to make a dream pillow of lavender and rosemary to hang on the bedpost, or burn a lavender aromatherapy candle while you do this meditation.

Sit cross-legged on the ground. Close your eyes. Put your hands in a relaxed position, palms up, on the ground on each side of you. Breathe deeply in through the nose extending your diaphragm and out through the mouth, contracting your diaphragm. Breathe this way evenly and deeply several times. As you breathe, imagine the cares of the day rolling off of your body, puddling in the palms of your hands. Turn your hands over and shake them loosely, continuing to allow any negativity in your body to flow out and into the ground. Now, breathe deeply again and wiggle your fingers as if you are tickling the belly of the earth. Again, if you hear laughter, don't be surprised. The earth holds amazing gifts of joy and peace and is delighted when you connect with that energy. Place your hands in a prayer position in front of you, and bow at your waist (as far as your body allows, but don't strain), and say:

"I give thanks to the universe this day. I move into the energy of dusk with love, peace, and joy in my heart. I drink in the softness of the night and the tranquility of the universal sea. May the stars light my path with love and protection and may the moon cast her gentle, loving light into my life as I move into the world of release and restful sleep. Positive closure will be brought to any chaotic energies I have experienced this day and I ask for a blanket of peace to permeate my world. So be it."

At this point you may wish to include prayers for anyone who has helped you this day, or give thanks for something special that has delighted you.

Suggested Variations

If you want to do something at sunset, but just haven't the time for a meditation, you can at least shake off the negativity of the day. Begin with your right arm and shake it about thoroughly, then your left arm. Now your right leg, and then your left leg. Stand up on your toes and drop to your heels, loudly saying "ha!" as you do so. Do this entire sequence three times. Not only will you find it amusing (it usually leaves a smile on one's face), it is also a Tai Chi technique for removing sickness and negativity from the body and therefore serves a good purpose for continued good health.

> *Sunset Aromatic Oil:* One drop rosemary essential oil, one drop lavender essential oil, one drop chamomile essential oil, five drops violet fragrance oil, one drop mint essential oil.

> *Sunset Herbal Mixture:* Mix equal parts of dried rosemary, lavender, mint, and chamomile. Mix with three drops of sunset aromatic oil. Makes a nice potpourri.

This meditation is good for:

- ✦ Closing out a project
- ✦ Honoring work you have done that day
- ✦ Connecting with Spirit
- ✦ Promoting peaceful sleep

Rainstorm Meditation

This is one of my favorites and we can attribute the idea to my youngest son. One day we were talking about how water can be digitized for healing, good fortune, luck, positive intent, etc. My son was unhappy that the skies were dark and a rainstorm had moved in. "It's so gloomy," he said.

"No, it's opportunity," was my reply.

"I don't get it."

"Well, if we can digitize a bowl or glass of water with positive intent and blessings, think what we could do with all those raindrops!" I said, motioning toward the window and laughing.

"That's dumb," he said. "My perception is that it makes me feel depressed."

To me, this was a dare. So, I said, "Really? Watch this!" We could see two people walking down the street in the rain. I closed my eyes and I envisioned that every drop that touched them was empowered with happiness, blessings, joy, and laughter. In a few moments they began to dance in the rain!

My son's eyes widened. "I don't believe it! What did you do?"

I told him. He shook his head and wandered toward his bedroom muttering about the utter craziness of this household, leaving me to do whatever it was I was doing at the time. A few minutes later, dressed in a sweatshirt and galoshes, he tromped into the dining room. "Where's the umbrella?"

"I think it's on top of the hutch. Why?"

"Because," he said, standing on a chair and retrieving the umbrella, "I can bless more people if I stand on the street corner."

Suggested Variation

This meditation can also be used during a snowstorm. As every snowflake is crystallized water, and each snowflake is symmetrical and unique, there are a compendium of prayers you could utilize simply while watching the snow blanket the earth. As snow "covers" the earth and "glitters" in the sunlight when the storm is over—snow blessings for protection of any kind are excellent.

> *Rainstorm Aromatic Oil:* Three drops sandalwood essential oil, two drops clover fragrance, one drop allspice essential oil, two drops musk.

This meditation is good for:

- Empowering the self through water
- Healing the self through water
- Turning negativity into a positive flow of energy
- Learning to work with the weather

Pushing Away a Storm—
The Swimming Dragon

There are times when we need to push negativity out of our lives and "swim" into positive energy. I discovered the power of this meditation quite by accident while studying ancient Chinese energy techniques. It is a simple Qigong movement. Qigong is the birth mother of Tai Chi and there are hundreds of forms of this "movement in energy" system all over the world, especially at the point of its origin—China. While practicing the Swimming Dragon technique one Saturday afternoon, a major storm was brewing. I really didn't think much about it because I like storms, but then I remembered that my youngest son was out with his girlfriend and I didn't really want them to be caught in a downpour. While practicing the form I loosely thought (and I mean loosely) that I just wanted to push that storm away. It never rained. Not here. Not where they were. Not anywhere in the local area. Although I'm not encouraging you to mess with the weather, this experience did bring the point home that if you can push away a physical storm, you can certainly push away a mental storm created by negative energy!

Begin by standing with feet apart, both hands resting on your stomach, one on top of the other. Whichever hand is on top, move that hand out and as far to your side as you can. For example, if my right hand was on top, I would move my right hand out to the right side, as if I was grazing the surface of chest-high water with my hand. Turn gracefully to the right as you move your hand gently as far to the right as you can. As you turn back, your left hand will naturally want to move out to the left, grazing that chest-high water, while your right hand naturally wants to retract to right above your stomach. Allow your entire upper body to flow in the direction of your outstretched hand as you move from side to side, one arm extended, the other arm contracted. After about the tenth time of this, you will suddenly feel like a *big* dragon . . . swimming! Keep this up as long as you like; however, never overexert or overextend your arms to the point where the position is uncomfortable. Do what you can do—no more. The trick is to inhale until your arm is extended, then exhale as that arm comes back to center, inhaling as you switch and extend the other arm, exhale as that arm comes back to center.

The visualization here for this exercise is to inhale positive energy and exhale the negative situation you've found yourself in, believing that you are swimming through a sea of potential and navigating away from any negativity or recent unhappy experience. This exercise is much like the old windmill warm-up that a teacher might have taught you in gym class, the difference here is that the form is done slowly, in a very relaxed and graceful manner, rather than tossing your arms from side to side like a rag doll. If you would like more information on Qigong, try the DVD "Qigong—Beginning Practice" with Francesco & Daisy Lee-Garripoli, produced by Gaiam (www.gaiam.com). This DVD set shows all the exercises along with an interesting documentary on the history and current use of the system.

> *Blessing Aromatic Oil:* One drop myrrh essential oil, one drop jasmine fragrance oil, two drops lemon essential oil, one drop patchouli essential oil, one drop sandalwood essential oil.

> *Blessing Powder for Conjuring Bags:* Crushed and pulverized egg shell, white sea salt, and powdered sandalwood. Grind thoroughly with mortar and pestle. Add one to three drops blessing aromatic oil. Mix well.

This meditation is good for:

- Releasing disease from the body
- Pushing away negative thoughts
- Healing work for others

- Learning how to flow
- Using as an excellent relaxation technique

Meditation of the Void

For this meditation you will need a black cloth (13 x 13 inches), a black candle, and silver glitter. I've also found soft music to be extremely helpful—something that allows your mind to travel "into space." Before you begin, have your specific desire set firmly in your mind. Make it as clear and succinct as possible. We are using black to represent that which was the beginning, without form, without substance. The void is not an evil or negative place. It just "is." It is the still point where everything and every being meet as one.

Place the black cloth flat on a hard surface. Place the unlighted candle to the left of the cloth. The lighting in the room should be low, but not so low that you can't see what you are doing. Sit quietly and stare at the black cloth as you breathe in through the nose (extending your diaphragm) and out through the mouth, contracting the muscles in the diaphragm. Do this at least three to seven times. When you are ready, pick up the black candle. Hold it between both hands. Slowly breathe your intention into your candle with three deep, slow breaths and say:

"In the beginning, there was the void. It is the still point where everything and every being meet as one. A realm of potential, it is a state where every desire can manifest. With the light I form a pattern of becoming!"

Light the candle. Pass the candle flame over the black cloth, then place the candle in the upper left corner of your workspace in a safe candle holder.

Pick up the glitter, and say: "With the light the pattern of becoming is formed. The pattern of this manifestation is . . ." (state your desire).

With the glitter, begin drawing any pattern on the black cloth. Let your hand flow freely. It doesn't have to look like anything in particular. You are allowing your thought to manifest through free-form art. When you are finished, sit back and look at the pattern. Think of what it is that you would like to manifest. See that object or condition rise from the glittering pattern, and like a bird, take flight into the universe. Say: "I agree that it is done!" Allow the candle to burn as long as you safely can. When you must put the candle out, don't blow on it, use a candle snuffer or "clap" it out with the swift movement of your hands over the candle without touching the flame. Gently pick up your glitter drawing and carry it outside. Release the glitter into the air and snap the cloth three times to seal your working. You can relight the candle each night until it has burned to the quick, or you can wrap the candle in the black cloth and put it in a safe place until your desire is met.

Suggested Variations

Before the drawing is made, you can add a specially ground magickal powder that matches your intention to the glitter to enhance the power of the working. If you dislike using glitter, you can also use a pouch of small, rolled gems or crystal points, scattering them in one gentle movement across the black cloth. Other natural objects, such as cowry shells, pumpkin seeds, or small sticks can be employed. For a very dynamic manifestation, empower water with blessings and your desire and freeze in an ice cube tray with very small compartments. Place your black cloth on a cookie sheet. Scatter the ice cubes across the black cloth. As they melt, they will release your desire. When the ice has completely melted, hang the black cloth out-side to dry, asking for blessing of air to carry your desire into the universe. Pour the water on the ground as an offering to Spirit.

> ***Spirit Offering Aromatic Oil:*** One drop essential lavender oil, two drops rose fragrance, two drops lemon essential oil, one drop rosemary, one drop spearmint essential oil.

> ***Spirit Offering Herbal Mixture:*** Blend equal parts lavender, rose petals, lemon verbena, angel wings, rosemary, and spearmint.

This meditation is good for:

- ✦ Learning how to connect with the still point
- ✦ Understanding darkness in a positive way
- ✦ Taking part in a birthing process
- ✦ Dispelling fear of the dark

Water, Fire, Wood, Metal Meditation

In Chinese philosophy water stands for "the void," the beginning of all things, the flow of energy, and the birth of the Spirit. Fire is the light, move-ment, action, and energizer. Wood denotes vision and control. Interesting-ly enough, anger is a negative aspect of wood. Wood is the pattern of the magick. Metal stands for clarity, ritual, wisdom, division, and release—it is the realm of the white tiger.

The first meditation of this sequence is simply to visualize each element and what it stands for, breathing in through the mouth while extending the abdomen and exhaling through the nose, contracting the abdomen. At the conclusion, you should feel some sort of "release." Go through the sequence again, equating water to your ancestral "chi" (your heritage of energy) and to the energy of early spring. Move to fire, and the equation of summer. To wood, the richness of autumn, and finally, to metal, the completion and "rest" of the year. Again, you should feel a type of release at the end of the sequence.

Finally, choose something you wish to obtain within your own character. How about wisdom? Patience? Continuing to breathe deeply and regularly, let your mind move into water, seeing the word "patience" or "wisdom" rise from the water. For fire, allow the words to be spelled out in flames in your mind. For wood, see the words on a block of wood or wooden words. Shining metal words would be next. Reach out in your mind and pull the words into yourself. Take a deep breath and open your eyes.

Suggested Variations

You can choose a candle color for each element and light that candle as you move through the sequence the first time. Allow the candles to burn completely after the meditation, or use them again with the same meditation for seven nights in a row. For a more hands-on effect, hold representations of the four elements as you meditate on them or collect these elements from nature and place them on your altar while meditating with a single white candle.

> *White Tiger Chi Element Oil:* One drop patchouli essential oil, one drop lemon essential oil, one drop frankincense fragrance steeped with frankincense resin, one drop sandalwood.

> *White Tiger Chi Element Herbal Mixture:* Equal parts of patchouli, mugwort, lavender, lemon verbena, chamomile, frankincense, sandalwood, eucalyptus, and myrrh. Mix. Add three drops of white tiger chi element oil. Use in gris-gris bags, around candles, or as potpourri for the flow and movement of the elements blended with your spiritual energy.

This meditation is good for:

+ Learning energy flow within a different cultural mindset

- Strengthening the steps of the power of manifestation.

- Understanding the self

Sunlight Meditation

How many times have you been stuck somewhere with nothing to stare at but the four walls and a patch of sunlight? Turn this alpha moment into a profound bit of magick!

Imagine the patch of sunlight as the field of opportunity. Everything in that patch is filled with possibilities! See the shadow around it as the void of becoming. See the light as the action that can formulate your desire. See the pattern of the sunlight on the floor (or wherever) as the pattern linked to what you wish to manifest. Pull the sunlight into yourself! Agree that your desire is met!

This meditation is good for:

- Learning to concentrate on a specific field with the assistance of light

- Learning how to use light in a positive way

- Using the mind constructively

Snowflake Meditation for Crisis (or just to feel good)

How many times has someone hit you with upsetting information? And all you can think about for hours is what you are going to do about it? Your whole body is tense, especially around the chest, neck, and shoulder area. You might feel sick to your stomach. Your brain is running around like a frenzied rabbit—looking here and there for a solution, a way to cope, some sense of stability. And did you ever notice that you never get hit with this stuff during the week or during the day when you can do something (anything) about it? The worst is at night, or on the weekend, and you are stuck because our regular forms of handling crises are cut off. We are left to deal—alone—in our own brains. Here is a great meditation to start coping calmly and efficiently. This meditation can be done on your feet, sitting, or lying down. No matter where you are or what you are doing (other than driving), you can implement its benefits.

Every snowflake is symmetrically individual—no two snowflakes, so they say, are ever alike. Snowflakes are water molecules that hook up in a hexagonal lattice pattern creating prisms, and all six budding arms naturally grow at about the same rate. A snowflake begins with a core: a particle of dust. In this meditation, the core we will be using consists of our Mind-Light. If we make the connection, a snowflake is really the alchemical hexagram, where each point has esoteric meaning. Snowflake crystals are fairly clear, but when light travels from the air to the ice, the light is reflected and tossed, bouncing around and eventually scattering back out of the crystal. As all rays of the prism are equal, the snow appears white.

Sit or stand comfortably. If standing, keep your spine straight and your head lifted—you are proud of yourself and your accomplishments, even if the crisis is trying to nail your self-esteem with a heck of a shot. You can overcome! Create your MindLight right below your navel. Place your hands over this area and breathe in and out, nice and deep. Allow the muscles in your body to relax—tension and tightness in the muscles cuts off your abilities and depletes your own energy flow, which leaves you open for attack. Move your feet shoulder-length apart.

If you can, close your eyes. Spread your arms like you are an eagle, keeping the light focused right below your navel. Allow that white light to grow simultaneously (like a snowflake) in the following pattern:

- ♦ Up and down (from center to heaven, from center to earth)
- ♦ Right and left (out from your arms)
- ♦ Diagonal (the pathway shown by the position of your feet)

Let the light continue to grow out through the head, down into the ground, from the left hand continuing into the universe, from the right hand continuing into the universe, from the left foot up through the right shoulder and out into the universe, from the right foot up through the left shoulder and out into the universe. See yourself glow like a giant snowflake, remembering the analogy of light bouncing around inside the snowflake. Take several deep breaths in this position.

Reverse the energy. Simultaneously, bring light in from overhead, from the ground, from the left side, from the right side, from the left foot into the body from the right foot into the body, from the right shoulder and from the left shoulder. Take several deep breaths, filling yourself with this white-light power. Stay in the moment. Concentrate only on the light, not on the problem.

When you feel balanced and comfortable, open your eyes.

Wait ten to fifteen minutes. Do the entire snowflake sequence again. Wait one half hour. Repeat the sequence. Each time you do the sequence your mind will become clearer and the crisis will carry less emotional impact, leaving you with a calm, clear head.

This meditation is good for:

+ Learning the beauty, power, and purpose of nature

+ Obtaining mental control in a crisis

+ Strengthening your focus

+ Healing for self and others

+ Learning the steps of manifestation

Remember, the inner and outer worlds are not as separate as they seem—it is all how you approach it in your mind. Let's move on to meditations designed specifically for dealing with life's little irritations!

CHAPTER SIX

Life in the Fast Lane

As we journey on the exciting pathway of life we chance upon a variety of potholes, broken bridges, unexpected barriers, seas of unrest, and ditches of failed expectations. These challenges can provide a wealth of opportunity if we only rise to meet them! The meditations in this chapter are designed to help you over life's little irritations.

Remember to:

+ Employ deep breathing

+ Stay in the moment

+ Use your MindLight

+ Be patient and embrace the still point

Tightrope Meditation

A friend of mine lost his partner a few years ago and found himself in an emotional spiral. One afternoon a buddy took him to the circus, and as my friend watched the amazing feats of the athletes skipping across that narrow, wobbling wire he thought to himself, "That's me! That's me up there! That's how I feel! If I could only get through this terrible time in my life with the grace and power that fellow up there has—I know I could make it!"

That evening, as always, the death of his loved one haunted him. Except this time, my friend decided to create a meditation to help himself. He sat back and imagined that the tightrope was his shaky life and that the platform on the other end was a place of calm and serenity. Very slowly he began, in his mind, to walk across the wire. In telling me this story, he laughed, "Just don't forget to visualize a safety net!" Over the years this simple yet profound meditation has assisted him through many tough emotional spots.

Suggested Variation

If you want to make this an active meditation, hold a broomstick for balance, close your eyes, and walk very slowly across the room, envisioning yourself on that tightrope. Make the wall, a chair, or some other object the "serenity" item. Once you touch it, feel white light and peace enter your body.

This meditation is good for:

- Working through an emotional crisis
- Gaining balance in your life
- Goal programming
- Strengthening your determination

Pentagram Hallway Meditation

This one is excellent for banishing negativity and requires only the space to walk—a hallway is very good. Begin with the right foot, take a step and draw a banishing pentagram (below) in the air with your right hand.

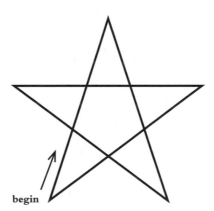

begin

Take a step with your left foot and draw a banishing pentagram in the air with your left hand. It takes a bit of practice, but soon you'll be off and banishing! As you draw the pentagram, say: "Be gone!" or "I banish thee!"

or whatever seems appropriate. This short, but powerful meditation can also be used in a crowd that you need to get through. Take a step, envision the pentagram as a blazing white light in front of you. Take a step with your left foot, envision the blazing pentagram again in front of you. Step, pentagram, step, pentagram, step, pentagram—and soon you will have made it safely where you wish to go!

Suggested Variation

If you are working on bringing balance into your life, draw the yin-yang symbol in the air instead of the pentagram.

This meditation is good for:

+ Banishing negativity in a particular area
+ Banishing illness where you see the disease as an opponent
+ Learning how to physically move while concentrating on a visualization

Stairway Active Meditation

This is a very good active meditation for meeting a situation head-on and overcoming it, while at the same time pushing away negativity to clear your pathway to success. It is also great exercise!

Start at the bottom of the stairs, feet together. Take three deep, even breaths in through the mouth, out through the nose. Look at the top of the stairs. In your mind, see a gateway and glowing, white light. This is the gateway of success. As you breathe in, take a step up (with whichever foot you desire) and as you exhale bring your other foot in line with the first. Inhale, bringing your hands up to your shoulders and push away as you exhale. Do this very, very slowly so you don't lose your balance! Now another step, repeating the same procedure. Continue to go up the stairs, pushing away negativity until you reach the top. Step through your imaginary gateway and pull your hands toward your heart chakra, celebrating your success! You'll be through your difficulty in no time at all!

Suggested Variation

If you don't mind getting your stairs wet, take a small pitcher of empowered water in one hand and a white candle in the other. Take a step and pour a bit of water on the stairs, make a banishing pentagram in the air with the candle. Take another step, repeat the process. Not only does this aurically cleanse your stairway, it feels really empowering! Can't do stairs? No problem! Walk up a ramp instead. No ramp? Walk from one end of your backyard to the other. Or down the block. Or through a field! Just remember to walk slowly and feel the energy against your hands as you softly push, as if you are pushing your hands through water.

This meditation is good for:

- Learning how to physically move while concentration on a visualization
- House banishing
- Banishing an illness where you see the disease as an opponent
- Banishing an astral nasty

Double Spiral Active Meditation

Not only is this a quick calming meditation, it also helps you to release pent-up energy. You can also use it to empower a specific thought.

Begin with your hands in the prayer position about six inches from your heart chakra. Close your eyes and take three, deep even breaths (more if you are upset). Keeping your hands together, begin making a spiral in the air with your hands from the center out in a clockwise direction as you breathe in, then, when you are ready to exhale move your hands up in front of your third eye (palms still together) and draw the other half of the spiral from the outside in. Then reverse. With your hands still at your third eye, make the clockwise spiral from the inside out, then move your hands (still together) down to in front of your heart chakra, and as you exhale, make the second spiral from the outside in. Do this three to five times for best results.

This meditation is good for:

+ Learn how to manipulate energy with positive flow
+ Stress or anxiety relief
+ After a physical workout for continued health
+ After a sudden shock

The Right Thing

In this crazy world we live in, it isn't always easy to do the right thing. Sometimes the right thing entails that we will accept a loss of some kind. We know what we should do, but facing up to it isn't always so simple and the fear that gathers around us fogs that "right thing," occasionally paralyzing us from moving forward in the way that we know is proper and moral. Indeed, we intimidate ourselves. I've discovered that in these situations, there are often several players on the field, each following their own agenda, which is adverse (or at least not particularly helpful) to your overall wants or needs. Doing the right thing takes an immeasurable amount of courage. If you find yourself in this type of situation, then try this meditation.

Sit comfortably in a quiet place at a quiet time. I would like you to think of someone you know who has performed heroically in the past—whether dead or alive, this is not important. What is vital is that you admire this individual for the courage they have shown in the face of unbeatable odds. Mythical characters and creatures are acceptable as long as you believe they have power and courage.

In your mind, I want you to visualize that the individual is reaching out to you with a smile on their face. Visualize yourself touching that person's hands, and when you do, warm, powerful, joyful energy begins to pulse through your body. See that energy as pure, white, incredible light. When you feel very good inside, break the connection and physically cover your heart chakra with your hands. Give thanks, and then allow the vision to fade. Take three deep, even breaths and open your eyes.

And move forward with grace and vision.

This meditation is good for:

- Finding courage within the self
- Self-empowerment when facing a negative group mind or individual
- Choosing wisely what is best for universal flow

Calling All Angels

Over the years I've heard many astounding stories about how the beloved dead have reached out from beyond the grave and assisted us when we are truly in need. Sometimes we have asked for help, and other times help has been there when circumstances were incredibly dire. I've written about several experiences in some of my books (my own and stories from individuals I met while on tour), yet I never cease to be awed and amazed at the incredible mystery we call our universe. If I had any doubts that the dead had power beyond the grave, they were completely squashed while I was writing this book. Once upon a time there were two very unlikely friends—an eighty-year-old nun and a forty-two-year-old male Witch. This nun was an interesting and larger-than-life character who always carried a big, funky pocketbook. On a cold and snowy morning, the nun was murdered as she made her way to a volunteer establishment. When they found her, she had two things clutched tightly in her hands—her rosary and her purse. Her friend was devastated.

The months passed, bloomed into summer, then turned to autumn gold. On one particularly vibrant fall day, the male Witch stepped out of that same volunteer establishment (he donated time there) with a co-worker. In the blink of an eye, the nun was there before him and with one swooping, mighty blow, she smacked him as hard as she could with her pocketbook, sending him reeling. The Witch, shocked and stunned, hit the pavement. The co-worker immediately stooped to the rescue and drew his hand away, covered in blood.

"Have you been shot?" asked the Witch.

"No, you have," came the reply.

"My stars," said the Witch in utter awe. "She pushed me out of the way."

"Who pushed you?"

"The nun!" (Actually, he said her name, but I'm not listing it here.)

The co-worker shook his head. "No, man. Wasn't nobody else on this stoop, least of all a nun. Just you and me. I didn't push you out of the way. But I clearly saw the guy who shot you. I did see you stumble before the shot hit. If you hadn't lost your footing . . . you'd be a dead man."

The world we live in is a fascinating one. If we agree to allow ourselves to think outside the box, to reach beyond common, ordinary assumptions, to touch and accept the things we cannot see—miracles can occur.

The next time you feel that you are in a lot of trouble, or feel inundated with daily, petty problems (or even big ones), go visit your ancestors—particularly people who loved you. Meditate at their resting place. Talk to them aloud. They will hear you. Help is on the way!

You simply have to agree to believe.

Breathing Meditation for Patience

When we are impatient we have a tendency to hyperventilate, or breathe quickly and shallowly, which directly reflects on our thinking process in a negative way. Learning to breathe deeply and enjoyably not only clears the mind, it immediately puts us into a pleasant altered state. Think of deep breathing exercises as a banquet table for the mind and body, filled with the most delectable delights!

For this meditation please choose:

- ✦ 2 pleasurable aromas
- ✦ 2 pleasurable sounds

- ✦ 2 pleasurable sights

- ✦ 2 pleasurable tactile objects

Write them down on a piece of paper.

Close your eyes and breathe deeply in through the nose and out through the mouth. Take your time. No hurry. No rush. When you feel ready, think of the first tantalizing aroma. Let's say it's Thanksgiving turkey. Open your nostrils and really allow that full breath to enter the body. Enjoy the breath. Savor it. Now, let it easily flow out of the body with a pleasured state that visualization can bring. You can even say "Ummmmmm," as you let go of the breath.

How about newly mown grass on a summer day? Breathe in the memory of the aroma, and let it go after you have truly savored it. Perhaps this scent will also bring visions of sunlight, bright green, or vibrant blue skies. That's okay.

Now the next breath. This one is sound. I chose the windchimes I have hanging on my back porch. Breathe in the sound of those chimes—how pleasurable they make you feel. Exhale slowly, with that same wonderful feeling. You can even say "Ahhhhhhh," as you let go of the breath.

Go onto the next sound. Breathe in the sound, and let it go. If positive associations come to the mind, don't dwell on them, just let them go with pleasure.

On to the two pleasurable sights. I chose the horizon at dusk and the sun on the New Mexico mountains at midday. Be careful here. You may have seen something beautiful in the past that you will always remember, but at the same time, sometimes delightful sights are linked to unpleasant memories. Choose a visualization that does not have negative strings. You can even say "Ouuuuuuuuu," as you breathe out.

Finally, choose two tactile objects. Something that you like to touch. Often it is an object that brings memories of security for you. I chose petting my dog—his soft, warm fur on my fingertips—and the memory of running my hands across a still pool of water. As you breathe out, you can say "Ohhhhhhhhhhh."

Take three deep, even breaths, in through the nose and out through the mouth and open your eyes. Don't you feel so much better!

Suggested Variation

If you are running a group meditation, have objects representing the four senses represented above for everyone to experience while they are meditating. When you are finished, the room will be filled with delightful energy!

This meditation is good for:

- ◆ Learning to control panic attacks
- ◆ Incorporating the senses to bring balance
- ◆ Teaching yourself to slow down and enjoy life

Meditations for Restful Sleep

All of us experience periods where our minds are so full of chatter that we have difficulty sleeping or falling asleep. Over the years my family and I have found various visualization techniques to assist us in achieving peaceful, restful sleep. As we all have different personalities, it is interesting to learn what works for different people—all of the ideas that help us involve a visualization where you put yourself in the picture. All of the techniques, whether the people realized it or not, are an act of "letting go." Here are visualization ideas:

1) In your mind, sit beside a stream and visualize yourself picking pebbles out of the water and tossing them into the center of the stream. Set the scene at dusk and mentally hear the running water. To help with this meditation one family member put a fountain beside her bed.

2) Visualize the "dream boat." In your mind, stand on the shore of a lake at dusk and imagine a beautiful, small boat with bobbing lights coming toward you. When it docks you see that it is your dream boat filled with lots of soft pillows, sumptuous covers and sweet smelling flowers. The lights are decorative lanterns. There is a "protector" on the boat to ensure your safe passage into the dream world. The "protector" is never seen fully, but they

have an aura of safety and warmth. Step into the boat either on your own or assisted by the protector. I use a lavender-scented dream pillow to help with this meditation that leads into peaceful sleep.

3) Another family member rides a white dream horse to a place of the ancient ones. Sometimes, he says, he falls asleep before he gets there. At other times he reaches a beautiful mountain top with colorful pennants waving in the breeze. A wise person touches his hand, and says, "Sleep now, for your dreams will bring you . . ." and the blank is filled in with whatever concerns him at the time. Sometimes it is wisdom, sometimes healing, sometimes answers to specific questions.

4) Finally, one person simply counts. He begins at 100 if he is not really tired, or 25 if he's tired and just wants to relax, and counts down, seeing the number in his head as he does so. On occasion he uses a step visualization where each step has a number on it and the step lights up as his imaginary foot touches it and he moves down the staircase.

All of these sleep visualizations have the following in common:

1) The individual stays in the moment of the visualization by focusing only on the imaginary scene—and not on anything else, such as life troubles, worries, or fears. Stay in the moment.

2) All of them let go, allowing their bodies to relax as they move into the visualization.

3) All found that the more they practiced the visualization the faster they went to sleep. Once you have set a familiar pattern that you know works for you, then relaxation takes over and you drift into a peaceful sleep.

Turning Daily Tasks Into Meditative Vehicles

One way I found to keep myself from slipping into a funk when problems threaten to overwhelm me is to turn the daily tasks I find myself stuck with doing into positive meditative vehicles. When we do repetitive processes, like sweep the floor, cook dinner, or even physical exercise at the gym with all the fancy equipment, we are not working our minds. When that happens our wonderful, imaginative mental faculties haul out the mind-trash and start rummaging through it, just to keep itself occupied. Because we are usually in a light alpha state while working at a repetitive process, these worries, fears, or oppressive thoughts become magnified and cause more damage than we realize. It is best to stay in the moment and create an affirmation that negates the worry. For example, when you peel potatoes you peel away from yourself. Your mind wanders all over the place because peeling a potato is less than absorbing. If you aren't bothered by anything in particular, a general banishing statement will do. With every whisk of the peeler, you might say, "I banish all negativity from my home," or "Only harmony and healing remains in my heart." With that outward movement of the hands and arms, you could even say, "I open the pathway to enlightenment," with every stroke.

If you work on a packing line, for example, packing books, or toys, or whatever, you could say, "With every book I place in this box I send love and blessings." Your good energy—your chi—will bring a wonderful gift to a stranger. Believe it— and it will be. How about customer service? What could you do there? Let's say you work at an airport dealing with passengers. Why not make a MindLight of joy and happiness and place it over the customer's head before they step up to your window? The trick is always to "stay in the moment" and to "agree" to allow the positive energy to exist.

This meditation is good for:

- Turning boring routines into positive energy
- Understanding that repetition in affirmations create a powerful energy boost
- Training the mind to focus easily on the positive

Getting Things Done

Ever have one of those weeks where innumerable things seem to crop up on you and suddenly, you're sitting there and saying to yourself, "Oh blast! I forgot to . . ." and then you think of another thing you let go, and another thing that slipped your mind, and you are sitting there with all this stuff you need to do. Hate those moments, don't you? Your mind goes tearing off in several directions and you feel burdened, grumpy, and irritated and you have no idea how to prioritize anything because they all need to get done.

Stop!

Stay in the moment. And pick one thing, do it, and go on to the next. Just remember to stay in the moment with each thing. Or, you can have a little fun and do it this way:

Go find a bunch of quarters and a piece of paper. On the paper, write the different tasks in a haphazard order. You can write them upside down, in circles, or whatever. Make it fun. These are tasks you put off because you didn't want to do them, remember? When you are finished, you have tasks scattered all over the paper—a perfect representation of how your brain feels at this moment, right? Shake the quarters in your hands and drop the quarters on the paper.

Look for the highest concentration of quarters. What task do they cover or are in close proximity to? That's the one you do first. When you are finished, go to the next highest concentration of quarters. Quarters all over the place? Not to worry. Start with "heads up" tasks. When they are finished, go to the "tails." Sound stupid? Not really. You see, your mind likes to confuse itself when it is bored or dislikes a task. By writing down the tasks and tossing the quarters, you have eliminated some of the boredom and have told your mind that you are preparing to do the tasks. Sort of like revving up the player before the big game. Not only that, you've begun to create order out of chaos—which is how we accomplish things anyway!

Or, write down your to-do list and beside each item write down a reward you'll give yourself when it is completed. Make the rewards reasonable (not "I get to watch three football games in a row" after the first task because then you won't achieve the other ones. Or not "I get a big, fat ice cream cone" if you are on a diet). You can even make the rewards dovetail into the next task. Sometimes we really don't mind some of those items on the to-do list; it is just a matter of getting started because of the time you know that duty might take. If you "stay in the moment," the work goes faster.

It's all a matter of perception.

Plus, you get to keep the quarters.

This meditation is good for:

- ✦ Release negative thought patterns that have attached themselves to specific tasks

- ✦ Find courage and determination within the self

- ✦ Learning to move the mind in a positive way

Staying Centered

In the Basic Meditations Chapter we worked on a centering exercise. This meditation takes a step forward based on the same premise. One of the most difficult aspects of moving through this life is learning to stay centered. By keeping our inner balance, we naturally begin to exude balance in our lives and in the world around us. Your energy center lies about one inch below your navel. This particular exercise can be done once a day, several times a day. If you are very brave and truly want a change in your life, do it all day long (which is more difficult).

While you are standing comfortably, move your feet shoulder-width apart. Close your eyes. Breathe deeply several times until you feel comfortable. Imagine a golden ball centered just below your navel. When you have a strong image, open your eyes. You are going to walk with your "center." Rather than leading with your head, you are going to lead with your original power point—that area just below your navel. This may take a bit of practice, but soon it will feel very natural. Walk forward a few steps. Lead with your center, not your head. Turn. Walk several more steps, concentrating on walking with your center point as the lead guide. See how different and comfortable that feels? Practice this for at least a few minutes, remembering to breathe deeply and stay in the moment.

Whenever you walk anywhere, try to remember to walk with your center as the lead. After a bit of time, it will be a totally natural movement for you.

Should you try this technique all day you'll find your life extremely interesting. You will remain much calmer; but, on the first day, my students tell me, all sorts of things tend to erupt around you for the first few hours. This is natural. Your energy field is changing to calm and stable; therefore, negativity will arise to challenge that state. Every time this occurs, take several deep, even breaths and stay in the moment, continuing to move as best you can from the center point. By the end of the day you will realize what an amazing time you have experienced. Enjoy it!

This meditation is good for:

- Learning to overcome feelings of impatience
- Training your mind to maintain balance
- Banish negative circumstances around you
- Very good to incorporate in healing work

Moving Through the Blocks

I am sitting in a high school auditorium with my daughter and her best friend. We are there to see my oldest son in the talent show. My son walks onto the stage. There are a few catcalls and nasty comments. I am extremely proud of him. He looks neither right nor left. It takes courage to stand under those lights and face the world with your talent in your hip pocket.

Behind us, several young women begin to titter. We are the "Witch family" and therefore the object of much (negative) attention. The three of us sitting together look at each other. We don't want to make a scene, yet we'd love to turn around and say something—the Virgo, the Aquarian, and the Scorpio. We don't, because this is my son's time in the spotlight. We demur.

My son takes his position and the auditorium dips to a hush. Before him are stacked cinderblocks. The lights dim. He prepares himself. The girls behind us dummy up. You can feel the anticipation electrify the air. My heart is beating wildly. I know how important this moment is to him.

There is a tremendous "crack!" and shards of cinderblock fly across the stage as the crowd jumps to its feet and roars. He has done it: he has seen through the blocks, and he has destroyed them. I realize I've dug my fingernails into the armrests of my chair. The smiling kid who walked off that stage wasn't just the winner, he was the owner of his personal success.

All of us run into cinderblocks in life. These problems seem so solid when we first observe them that it is difficult to think of anything else. What we must do is remember to stay in the moment and see through the blocks. Believe the problem is porous, stay in the moment, and move through the block as if through air. If we become angry, we lose our power. Instead, relax into the flow—regroup by collecting your power through meditation and the four agreements I talked about at the beginning of this book. Walk forward from your center, vaporizing the problem. Remember, the purpose of meditation is not necessarily to solve a problem, but to find peace so that the problem will be solved as a direct result of finding your center.

This meditation is good for:

- When a negative person or situation keeps you from moving
- When a negative person or situation keeps you from thinking
- Removing blocks you have created yourself

Overcoming Delays

There is nothing more irritating than the red tape of our society, waiting for a check or money that is rightfully yours, or a delivery that should have been made weeks ago. What I have found most interesting is that if you sit down and consider where you are stalling in your own life and then move forward to deal with that issue, the delays will also disappear and what is due to you will mysteriously appear. When you tackle and complete a project that you have put off, the universe opens a gate to bring in balance for your actions.

The meditation part of this particular section entails the contemplation of issues (not in a negative way) where you have "dropped the ball." Rather than being upset about it, just write them down and consider which situations have the highest priority. Take care of them. In my experience, in about twenty-four to seventy-two hours you will be rewarded in some way. Continue to work through that list until all the duties are completed, using other meditations in this book to clear out any frustration or angst. In short order you may be delightfully surprised at the equal benefits you receive, and at the same time you can take pride in the fact that you have finally completed something you've put off for eons!

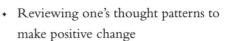

This meditation is good for:

- ◆ Learning to prioritize

- ◆ Reviewing one's thought patterns to make positive change

- ◆ Owning up to responsibility and moving forward, regardless of obstacles

The next chapter focuses on the energy of the heavens and how we can use that power within our own lives. Even if astrology isn't of interest to you, you may find the meditations themselves incredibly helpful in your daily life. There's a lot of information there—let's dig in!

CHAPTER SEVEN

New Moon Meditations

"If you can change a thought, you can change the universe."
—John Wolf

The absolute bonus of this chapter is that you don't have to use astrology at all to implement the suggested meditations in your life. You can page through and choose a meditation that fits your current circumstances and be done with it. Or you can be so excited that I have a new way of working with the planets in meditation to show you that you'll just gobble up all the information and start meditating with planetary power! Either way, all the meditations are designed for your life enhancement in the way you choose.

Just remember:

+ Use your MindLight

+ Stay in the moment

+ Employ deep, cleansing breaths

+ Find the still point and embrace it!

+ Don't forget your agreements

Astrology is often claimed to be the oldest science, as astronomy and astrology were once wed as a single entity. This science (the two aspects together as well as separate) have had an incredible impact on humankind. The study of natal astrology is the contemplation of patterns of energy brought into this dimension by your birth. It can teach you how to manipulate energy as well as indicate why you behave in the manner in which you do. When we view astrology in this manner, we realize that nothing is fixed or fated, save what we bring to ourselves through our own choices. There are various types of astrological studies today, of which reviewing one's natal chart and how it currently interacts with what is happening presently in the heavens is only one venue. In this book we are going to learn to work with the planets on a personal basis in meditation sequences. These meditations are good for students who are learning astrology, those who wish to work with astrological/heavenly energies in magick, and those who wish to learn to pull in the various positive advantages that the planetary energies can bring. In the Pagan world the dialogue between planets (where they are in the heavens in relationship to each other) dictates our eight major holidays.

If you have access to your own astrological program, such as WinStar or SolarFire, you may wish to cast a chart for each holiday (or any day) when planning your ritual or meditation, and use that information to tailor a completely unique activity. This can also be done for just about any situation in your life. WinStar, in particular, has an inexpensive computer program that will serve you well in your magickal work. They also have a full-scale program that is excellent for any type of astrological work you can think of. If you do not have chart capabilities readily available, but are on the Internet, there are many sites that provide free chart casting services. Almanacs are also a treasure trove of information. My personal favorite is *Llewellyn's Daily Planetary Guide*; however, there are many fine and suitable publications on the market. I'm sure one will appeal to your personal taste.

The body (but not all) of modern astrological study focuses on eight of the known heavenly bodies—the planets—Mercury, Venus, Mars, Saturn, Jupiter, Uranus, Neptune, and Pluto; our moon (which is a satellite); and our sun (which is the only star in our solar system). Although astrologers speak of the ten planets (as listed above, including the sun and the moon) astronomers obviously do not make this categorization. The sun and moon are sometimes called the Greater and Lesser Lights (the sun being the greater and the moon being the lesser). Many times students back away from using more detailed astrology in their work because the body of information on the subject is so vast that it can confound the mind. I've heard the comment, "I just want to cast a quick spell. I don't have time to study all that." However, once that same student has a dire and personal need, he or she is forced to realize the gold mine of information that abounds on issues of timing as well as reasoning and development of a particular situation. When that hits home, serious study often begins. As a magickal teacher, I've found it important to at least ensure that the student has a firm and working idea of the nature of the energy of the planets. With this information their spells, meditations, and rituals can blossom at their own pace to meet the needs in that particular student's life. Because astrology is active (the dialogue between the planets and the placement of the planets in the heavens is constantly dynamic) the student begins to learn that there is always information available to assist in a particular situation. You just have to look at it. With all this teacher-type prose, all I'm trying to say is: Take what is given here and make it as simple, or as complicated as you like. Here are the building blocks—run with it. Be creative!

To begin, I've listed the planets with several of their traditional correspondences, including my own oil, powder, ink, and loose incense recipes. These formulas are meant merely to enhance the meditations and are not necessary to prepare; however, they are extremely helpful should you wish to turn the meditations into simple spells or full rituals. Before practicing each meditation I recommend that you take the time to read over the preliminary information that describes each planetary energy. Take your time and relax with the information. The only test you will encounter is that of your own life. If you like to study with vim and vigor—fine. If you prefer a more relaxed, use-it-as-you-need-it scenario—that's fine, too.

If you find these meditations interesting and wish to know more about astrology, you will find a recommended reading list at the back of this book to help you in your further study. You will also find a basic astrological glossary at the end of this book. One of the best ways to work with astrological meditations is to make them somewhat active, using body movement, dance, drumming, or the lighting of candles. Gems are also particularly helpful in concentrating on particular energies. Please note that any candle colors recommended are of my own choice, usually based on standard accepted correspondences. Do feel free to use your own color, hue, and tint selections when working in this realm.

Remember this—meditation is the moment you take a thought and make it into magick.

The Moon

Speed and Orbit: The moon circles the earth in 27 days and 7 hours and spends 2.3 to 2.5 days in each astrological sign. This means that you can work with the moon in every sign in a one-month period.

Retrograde: The moon never retrogrades (appears to go backward) but it does go "void-of-course" often. When the moon is void-of-course she simply isn't speaking to the other planets and is not paying any attention to her answering machine. Things often begun in a void do not come to conclusion (keep that in mind for your workings and meditations). Moon voids are good rest times, and excellent periods for introspection.

The Moon Moves: Approximately 0.5 degrees per hour, or 12 degrees per day.

The Moon Rules: The astrological sign of Cancer, a cardinal sign (starter). The moon is strongest when she is in her ruling sign.

Moon's Element: Water

The Moon's Day: Monday

Basic Energy: Emotion and reflection

Colors: White, blue, silver, ivory, clear

Keywords for the Moon: Creativity, domestic, feeling, roots, flexible, family, growth, imagination, impressionable, intuition, kindness, magnetism, masculine, maternal, matter, mother, peace, void, plasticity, womb, protection, psychism, receptive, sensitive, sympathy, visionary.

Gems: Moonstone, crystal, blue agate, bloodstone, opal, pearls, fancy jasper, mother-of-pearl, moss agate, pietersite, rainbow fluorite, any creek or river stone.

Aromatic Herbal Packet: Sandalwood, eucalyptus, bladderwrack and willow. Also an excellent Ostara herb recipe for conjuring bags.

Aromatic Oil Blend for Moon Energies: One drop camphor, three drops sandalwood, two drops gardenia, and one drop cucumber.

Moon Loose Meditation Incense: Mix equal parts of lemon balm, myrrh, and eucalyptus. Add one drop sandalwood essential oil. Mix with ground wood base for outdoor rituals. Throw on ritual fire or burn on incense charcoal tab. Colored powders can be added for visual effect.

Moon Ink: Add one drop of moon oil to one four-dram bottle of silver ink. Swirl. Add one link of a silver chain. Swirl. Grind sandalwood to a fine powder and add a minute amount. Swirl. Empower under the full or new moon as suits your purpose.

The moon, in astrological terms, is considered a planet (although we know it really isn't). In the world of the occult you will find a compendium of information about moon workings with many books singularly devoted to this topic. Many occultists and astrologers believe that the moon's greatest power lies in the astrological sign it is visiting, with its phases (full, new, waxing, waning, etc.) considered secondary. However, there are others who feel the phase is more important than the sign. Only you can determine for yourself which you feel is most powerful through your own experimentation and magickal work.

The moon's power, fueled by the light of the sun, changes as it moves from sign to sign, like your own feelings that change when you hear different types of music. From foot-stomping country and western to an incredible piece rendered by an Italian violinist that leaves you breathless and awed, to a memorable jingle from a television commercial, the moon can provide a vast array of power to any meditation or magickal working. You simply have to pull this power in—which is what the Wiccan theme of Drawing Down the Moon is all about.

Succinctly, the moon stands for our emotions, our needs, and, in magick, any powerful female figure as well as the needs of children (such as the protection a mother affords to her offspring) and pets. Naturally, the moon rules the fourth house, which includes the family environment, our heritage, our roots, and "endings." Although not often mentioned, the moon rules money in general (although Venus is often equated to money as in value, and Jupiter as in expansion and good fortune). The base of financial energy, however, lies in the moon.

Personal Moon Meditation Formula

Many people know their astrological sign, but when you inquire as to their moon, they sort of look at you funny. Your personality, say the astrological experts, is made up of three dynamic energies: your sun sign, your moon sign, and your rising sign. For this formula you will need to know what sign the moon was visiting at the exact time of your birth as well as the address at the time. Now, if you are one of those people who doesn't have an exact time of birth, don't fret—you can still use the formula.

Each month the moon spends approximately two days (give or take) in each astrological sign, which provides us with a vast network of energy to work with in meditation and life enhancement techniques. Your BEST time for performing extremely incisive work is when the current moon conjuncts your natal moon. This will occur for you once every month at different times of the month depending on the cycle of movement of the heavens, and you will have the opportunity of growing energy (first and second quarter), harvest energy (full moon), and banishing energy (third and fourth quarter moons) throughout the year. To best explain the formula, here's an example:

Rochelle was born with a Scorpio moon. The "address" of her natal moon is 10 degrees 4 minutes Scorpio. Rochelle can use a computer program like WinStar to keep track of when this golden time pops up for her, or she can use a daily planner with an ephemeris. Each month, Rochelle will have a "hot" time—that moment when the transiting moon conjuncts her natal moon. This month when the moon moves into Scorpio, she is in her building phase (first quarter), so Rochelle will want to concentrate her energies on positive growth.

Now, before you throw up your hands and say: "I'm at work a lot. I don't have time to set up an altar or pull out a mojo bag . . . and I certainly can't light a candle! My boss would think I'm nuts!"

Stop!

This formula is just too easy.

You don't need all that stuff.

Let's also say that Rochelle is working on a website design. This particular task is very important to her career. We know that Scorpio energy is intense, so we already have an idea about how Rochelle feels about this work. Rochelle checked her dates (in fact, she took a calendar and marked out a year in advance all the times that the moon will conjunct her natal moon, just so she wouldn't forget), so she knows that today at 4:15 p.m. this important conjunction occurs. She's at work at that time. Not to worry. The ladies' bathroom is a very magickal place. If she finds that she has to be in a meeting, she can work in the hour before (but never after—after is when you've lost the wave). There are two ways Rochelle can proceed—she can add hand movements to the formula or if she can't get away anywhere to do this, she can simply stare at a point on the wall.

The formula is already familiar to you. First, we are going to make a MindLight just like you've been doing every morning since you first picked up this book (Right? You've been doing that?). If not, go back to the book's beginning and review how to make your MindLight.

For Rochelle, this MindLight is all about creating a dynamic and successful website design. Doesn't matter where she actually is on the project. This energy is to carry it through to successful completion, which means where end-users find the work productive and create a high number of hits for the owner.

At 4:00 p.m. (which is when Rochelle can get away for a break), she slips into the ladies' bathroom and into a stall. There, she forms the Mind-Light between her hands. She holds the MindLight at the root chakra, and she says: "I physically agree that this website design I am working on right now will be incredibly successful for myself, the company, and the owner and that it will bring great joy into my life as well as into the lives of the users." As she breathes in she imagines drawing energy up from the ground and into the MindLight. As she breathes out, she imagines the MindLight expanding in pretty colors, as if it is becoming a living thing.

She now moves the MindLight up to her heart chakra, and repeats the statement.

Then up to the third eye chakra, repeating the statement.

And finally up to the crown chakra, saying the statement one more time.

She brings the MindLight back to her heart chakra and pulls the energy in, saying to herself "I agree!" Then, quickly, with a rush of energy, she flings her hands outward, palms up (as if offering this gift to the universe) and says: "Sa!" with an outward rush of breath.

If you don't know the exact time of the conjunction energy, then pick a time when the moon first enters the sign to create your success. The most important point of this formula is NOT to rush the thoughts. Your breathing and the statement you have chosen should be done in a relaxed, easy, gentle flow—as if you are relishing every bit of word-energy in an enjoyable way.

Can you use this formula anytime? Absolutely! Let's say you are having a really crappy day. The kid just wrecked your car. Your mother-in-law is whining about your responsibilities to her. You received an unexpected bill in the mail and you simply don't have the money to pay it—you know, Friday night fight stuff.

Try this formula.

You'll feel like a winner!

New Moon Meditations for You

With a new moon meditation the moon and the sun hold the same zodiac "address," and therefore the planets empower each other. Because the Moon is the faster moving heavenly body, the sun (the slower object) modifies the moon's energy. To hone in on the energies, we need to take a quick look at how the sun in each of the twelve zodiac signs affects the moon, which will affect the theme of your meditation. Since the moon is all about addressing our needs, I've chosen one specific need that you may have and tailored the meditation to that theme. Feel free to create your own meditations based on the keywords given, or use your own intuition. Please feel free to improve upon the meditations given to suit your own desires and lifestyle.

New Moon in Aries

Color: Red

Element: Fire

Available Energies: Power, energy, force, expression, self-reliance, assertive, spontaneous, fearless, enthusiasm, pioneering.

Aromatic Herbal Mixture Suggestions: Basil, black snakeroot, bloodroot, cactus, carrot, damiana (note: damiana is considered poisonous), deerstongue, dragon's blood, galangal, garlic, ginger, hawthorne, holly, pennyroyal, pepper, peppermint, thistle, toadflax, tobacco, woodruff, wormwood (note: wormwood is considered poisonous).

Application: Rituals and meditations for gaining confidence, learning new things, sports, controlling your fear or anger, winning, starting a project, being a pioneer, make announcements, boosting your reading level, taking calculated risks.

Avoid: Skipping over ritual or meditation steps, or hurrying through the working process.

Be Careful: Of your own temper

Note: Remember that Aries energy is not long-haul. Follow up with another spell later on to keep this energy rolling. It is a possibility you will be interrupted, so keep this meditation or ritual quick and to the point.

Aries Moon Aromatic Oil: Five drops dragon's blood scent (with one pinch of dragon's blood resin), one drop essential ginger, two drops essential peppermint, one drop cinnamon.

Aries Moon Meditation
how to create your own
amazing meditation magnum

Three years ago I created a very unique meditation focus using copper, herbs, resins, gem chips, and aromatic oils for the purpose of boosting my focus in meditation and enhancing my mental work. You can hold it, wear it, or put it on your keychain, purse, or magick bag. You can even use it in a gris-gris bag, and the wonderful thing about this type of charm is you can cleanse and use the magnum repeatedly. Inexpensive to construct, once you make one, you'll want to design several for your friends!

You will need:

- 1 foot of ¼-inch copper pipe (you will find this in the hardware store in the plumbing section. Many of the larger stores like Lowe's and Home Depot offer precut lengths starting at one foot). You can make your magnum as large or small as you desire. My first magnums were 2 inches and later I reduced them to the more comfortable size of 1½ inches.

- 2 copper end caps that fit the ¼-inch pipe (you will find these in the hardware store in the plumbing section, usually right by the copper piping. Be sure the ends fit before you leave the store as every once in a while they aren't made properly or are bent).

- Hand-held pipe cutting tool—you can find this also in the hardware section at a reasonable price. It is a small tool and doesn't require electricity.

- Industrial glue—I used Liquid Goop

- Black marker

- ¼ teaspoon powdered dragon's blood resin

- ¼ teaspoon powdered ginger

- ¼ teaspoon powdered frankincense

- ¼ teaspoon of quartz crystal chips or one very small crystal point

+ 1 piece of chipped moonstone

+ One power sigil of your choice drawn on very small piece of parchment paper with Mars ink (see page 211).

+ One red candle

+ Aries moon aromatic oil

+ 12 inches of deadsoft sterling wire (optional)

Instructions

Whenever making enchanted items such as tools, charms, amulets, etc., you will find that how you make them is just as important as the finished product. An Aries spell magnum should be constructed when the moon is in Aries, preferably the new moon. If this isn't possible, you could also make the magnum on an Aries day (Tuesday) or in an Aries planetary hour (see appendix 2 for instructions on calculating planetary hours).

Light a red candle dotted with Aries moon aromatic oil. Bless all tools with a simple prayer of your own making. Measure and mark the copper pipe. Cut the pipe with the easy-to-use hand tool. Glue one copper end cap over one opening of your 1½-inch pipe piece. Allow to dry.

Mix together the dragon's blood, ginger, frankincense, crystal chips (or point), and moonstone. Add one to three drops of Aries moon aromatic oil. Empower using the Mars invocation beginning on page 210. Draw your sigil onto the parchment paper and allow to dry. Again, empower using the Mars invocation. Roll parchment and insert in copper magnum. Add the herb/gem mixture. You might need a toothpick to firmly pack the magnum. Glue the remaining end onto the magnum. Allow to dry.

Using wire art techniques, wrap the copper magnum with the sterling silver wire. You can even create a decent bail for hanging the magnum on a chain, a cord, or a ribbon using the silver wire. Sterling silver (a combination of pure silver and copper) assists in the magickal flow of the piece.

Empower the entire piece with the same Mars invocation. Attach to a red cord or sterling silver chain.

How to Activate Your Magnum in Meditation

Light a red candle and sit in a quiet place at a quiet time holding the magnum in both hands. Breathe deeply, in through the nose and out through the mouth until you feel that you are relaxed and comfortable. Allow the sterling silver chain or red cord to drape easily over both hands.

In your mind create an outdoor temple as ornate or as simple as you desire. Take your time. In the center of the temple is a stunning, shining copper and silver cauldron filled with dancing, mesmerizing flames. In the background you hear someone say: "Behold the infinite power of Mars!" The fire bursts to the ceiling, sending a kaleidoscope of sparks showering around the gleaming cauldron.

A woman or a man (only you will know) dressed in red and gold steps up to the cauldron and says in a booming voice, "Who will accept the divine power of focus and manifestation?" then whirls and points at you. "Do you agree?" this person shouts.

It is now your turn to answer in the affirmative. "I agree!" The moment you agree, the magnum in your hands begins to glow with incredible power. Slowly, bring the magnum to your heart chakra with both hands. Breathe in the power, feel your incredible mind honing to razor-edge focus. Continue filling yourself with power until you feel strong and motivated, then lower your hands and breathe deeply several times. Open your eyes. The meditation is finished.

New Moon in Taurus

Color: Red-orange

Element: Earth

Available Energies: Stability, peace, affection, responsiveness, saving, artistic, devotion, harmony, value.

Aromatic Herbal Mixture Suggestions: Alfalfa, allspice, corn, grains of paradise, henna, lovage, magnolia, motherwort, mugwort, red clover, red sandalwood, saw palmetto, yohimbe.

Application: Meditations, rituals and workings for prosperity, saving money, holding onto something you already have (like a grade point average), building and keeping harmony in the home, investing time and money in a project, long-term goal planning, prayers for people you love, workings for long-term healing, meditations for peace and tranquility.

Avoid: Missing a good opportunity

Be Careful: Of your own stubbornness

Note: Taurus energy has a slow, plodding effect. Be prepared to be late getting your meditation or ritual going, or if you are working with a group— some of the participants showing up late.

Taurus Moon Aromatic Oil: One drop allspice, three drops clover fragrance, one drop sandalwood.

Taurus Treasure Candle Meditation

Mix ¼ cup gemstone chips with ¼ cup coins. Put a candle (your color choice) into a personal cauldron. Surround the very bottom of this candle with your treasure mix. If your cauldron is too small, place the mix outside of the cauldron. Dot candle with Taurus moon aromatic oil. Light candle.

Close your eyes and imagine yourself walking along a lovely beach. The sky is azure blue, the seas calm and serene. Suddenly, a golden ship appears on the horizon. As you breathe, deeply inhaling and exhaling, let the ship come toward you. See it gently rocking on the waves. Feel yourself filled with delight and excitement. When the ship is very close, physically smile, and in your mind, as you look down you will see that your arms are filled with golden treasure. As you look up and around you see yourself surrounded by all the things you need—new clothes, plenty of food, money to pay your bills and live happily without pain or need. In your mind, take this positive energy of abundance into yourself. Take three deep breaths and open your eyes. Slowly move forward and hold your hands over your treasure mix. Say: "Gems of earth and coins of metal, candle flame and abundant kettle! Fill my life with treasure fine, I declare good fortune mine! I agree!"

You can allow the candle to burn or you can do this same meditation (if money is particularly tight right now) every night for seven nights, lighting the candle for seven minutes each night. On the eighth night, the eve of mastery, allow the candle to burn completely. Carry a bit of your empowered treasure mix with you whereever you go during that week. To make your conjuring bag more powerful, add a lock of your own hair and dot the bag with Taurus moon aromatic oil.

New Moon in Gemini

Color: Orange

Element: Air

Available Energies: Intellect, awareness, agility, adaptability, multi-tasking.

Aromatic Herbal Mixture Suggestions: Aspen, bean, bergamot, clover, fenugreek, fennel, maple, mint, parsley, pecan, rue.

Application: Meditations, rituals and workings for any type of learning, or research. Focused thoughts to finish the old and move on to the new, or to help you juggle the many projects you are working on at once without failing, finding a new car, or new job. Meditations for any of the mental arts, including meditation itself, learning a divination tool, pathworking, and telepathy. Meditaitons for learning to understand and deal with siblings.

Avoid: Trying to pack too many magickal operations into one ritual

Be Careful: Of self-denial

Gemini Moon Aromatic Oil: Two drops essential bergamot, one drop essential spearmint, three drops maple fragrance, one drop essential cinnamon.

Gemini Meditation to Increase Your Mental Awareness

This meditation should be performed for at least seven days.

Light a mint-scented candle or a candle dressed with Gemini moon aromatic oil. Sit in a comfortable position in a safe and familiar indoor place at a quiet time. Breathe deeply in through the nose and out through the mouth until you are feeling relaxed and comfortable. With your mind, begin reconstructing the room you are currently sitting in. Investigate the pictures on the walls, walk around the room in your mind, pick up items such as books, papers, little statues, etc. Take your time and create the entire room as you left it when you closed your eyes. Take another three deep breaths and relax, just letting yourself feel comfortable and safe. Open your eyes. What items did you miss in your mental exploration?

Although this meditation seems pointless on the surface, it is really an aid in increasing your mental visualization capabilities. Always start with something familiar, and then very soon you will be amazed at your power of concentration and increased perception in daily life. For those who are truly hard-working souls, practice this visualization exercise for a full thirty days.

New Moon in Cancer

Color: Amber

Element: Water

Available Energies: Emotions, maturity, psychism, peace, protection, being magnetic, sympathy, maternal.

Aromatic Herbal Mixture Suggestions: Aloe, calamus, camphor, coconut, gardenia, gourd, Irish moss, jasmine, hyssop, lemon, lemon balm, lily, lotus, mallow, mesquite, moonwort, moonflower, myrrh, oak moss, poppy, purslane, yellow sandalwood, willow.

Application: Meditations, rituals and workings for women, for maturing without losing your mind in the process, for peace in the home, for protection of yourself or loved ones, for your mother, for psychism, transforming negative emotions into positive ones, dream spells, divination and telepathy. Thoughts and affirmations to draw positive things toward you or protect a friend or family member through pregnancy.

Avoid: Thinking that Spirit owes you

Be Careful: Of being too emotional

Cancer Moon Aromatic Oil: One drop camphor, two drops gardenia fragrance, one drop lemon, one drop sandalwood, one drop coconut fragrance, two drops lily fragrance.

Cancer Scrying Meditation

Dot a white candle with Cancer moon aromatic oil and light it. Place a fresh glass of drinking water beside the candle.

Sit in a quiet place at a quiet time. Take three deep breaths and relax, allowing yourself to feel safe and comfortable. Imagine that you are walking in a beautiful forest, down a path lined by beautiful, colorful, exotic flowers. Count from ten down to one as you walk. If you are having trouble relaxing, count from twenty-five down to one. When you reach the number one you will find yourself in a dreamy, mystical clearing filled with singing birds, the chatter of small animals, and the most beautiful butterflies you have ever seen. In the center of the clearing is a crystal clear pool, reflecting the soft, vibrant blue of a summer sky. Sit by the pool and relax, allowing your being to drink in the captivating scenery of total harmony. Take another deep breath, and relax. Say to yourself: "I agree that which I need to know will reveal itself in the reflective surface of this magick pool." Then lean over in your mind and gaze into the watery mystery. Do not concentrate on remembering the images. Allow them to flow easily and serenely across the face of the pool. Now say, "I agree that I will remember the most important images necessary for my personal growth when I drink three sips of water." Take several deep breaths and relax. Open your eyes. When you are oriented, take three sips of the water beside your burning candle. The images that were most important for you to remember will come back to mind. Those that were not necessary for your inner growth will not resurface.

New Moon in Leo

Color: Yellow

Element: Fire

Available Energies: Strength, being positive, leadership, confidence, generosity, kindness, success, personal validation, charisma.

Aromatic Herbal Mixture Suggestions: Angelica, ash, bay, carnation, celandine, cinnamon, chamomile, copal, frankincense, ginseng, goldenseal, gum arabic, marigold, oak, olive, orange, rosemary, safflower, sunflower, tangerine, tea, witch hazel.

Application: Meditations, rituals and activities for courage, strength, thinking in a positive way, winning, success, learning to be a good leader, to be kind, loyal, and generous. Affirmations for stage drama and acting, fun at the beach or on vacation, wealth in the home, making your talents shine. Workings to find the perfect pet for you, or to help you realize your talents.

Avoid: Overspending on ritual and spell supplies

Be Careful: Don't brag about your magick. Remember the Witches' Pyramid—to know, to dare, to will, and to be silent.

Note: There probably will be some sort of drama going on in your life this day. If you are having a group meditation, be prepared for people to bring their dramas into sacred space. Everyone will want to shine, lead, and be noticed.

Leo Moon Aromatic Oil: One drop chamomile, two drops tangerine, one drop rosemary, three drops frankincense fragrance (with a bit of ground frankincense).

Leo Self-Esteem Power Booster Meditation

You will need a golden cord fifty-four inches long. Anoint the cord with just a bit of Leo moon aromatic oil. You may also wish to burn a gold candle while practicing this meditation.

Take three deep breaths in a quiet place at a quiet time. If you are unusually stressed, continue deep breathing until you feel calm and relaxed. Pick up the cord. Tie a knot at the top of the cord, and say: "I am absorbing!" Create a MindLight ball of energy and let it sink into the knot. Remember to stay in the moment!

Continue tying the knots as you repeat the following statements:

"I am adorable!"

"I am alluring!"

"I am amazing!"

"I am amusing!"

"I am astonishing!"

"I am astounding!"

"I am attractive!"

"I am awesome!"

"I am bewitching!"

"I am breathtaking!"

"I am captivating!"

"I am colorful!"

"I am compelling!"

"I am dynamic!"

"I am electrifying!"

"I am enchanting!"

"I am enthralling!"

"I am exciting!"

"I am fantastic!"

"I am fascinating!"

"I am imaginative!"

"I am incredible!"

"I am intriguing!"

"I am lively!"

"I am magick!"

"I am mesmerizing!"

"I am phenomenal!"

"I am powerful!"

"I am sizzling!"

"I am smart!"

"I am spectacular!"

"I am spellbinding!"

"I am terrific!"

"I am me!"

Take three deep breaths, and say: "I agree!"

Carry the cord with you throughout the month. Practice this meditation every night, touching each one of the knots in succession for seven days—thirty if you feel you really need a boost!

At the end of thirty days, put the cord in a safe place to use again when you feel you need a boost, or bury on your property to hold these marvelous qualities close to you.

New Moon in Virgo

Color: Yellow-green

Element: Earth

Available Energies: Examination, analytical, brilliance, making choices with head, not heart; precision, finding solutions

Aromatic Herbal Mixture Suggestions: Bayberry, cinquefoil, civit, clary sage, ceremonial sage, crabgrass, dill, elecampane, grains and grasses of all kinds, mandrake, nuts, St. John's wort, seedless plants, storax, trees of the forest, valerian, vervain, vetiver, wintergreen.

Application: Rituals and workings for solutions to problems, for finding information, things, or people. Situations where you must make a difficult choice, accuracy in research, getting good grades on tests, eliminating mistakes, analyzing yourself so that you can be a better person, or to uncover any elusive medical problem that has the doctors stumped. Methods for improving your ritual or meditation techniques. Understanding the meaning of service to others or find a person who can help you with a particular task.

Avoid: Getting lost in ritual detail

Be Careful: Of being overly critical

Virgo Moon Aromatic Oil: Three drops bayberry fragrance, one drop essential sage, one drop vetiver. You can add wintergreen, but be careful, as this essential is thought to be harmful, especially to pregnant women.

Virgo Solution Meditation

Empower a bag of unpopped popcorn with the Mercury empowerment invocation on page 201.

Close your eyes and take three deep breaths. Continue to breathe easily and fully until you are totally relaxed. See before you a beautiful harvest field filled with golden wheat, bursting ears of corn, bright orange pumpkins, and shining red apples. An attractive person (only you know the gender) stands in the center of the field holding an armful of fresh-picked corn.

Walk toward this person, enjoying the full-bodied aroma of the rich harvest field. When you reach the person, they smile and hand you several ears of corn. "Do you agree to accept this gift? For within these precious ears of corn lies the positive solution you seek," they say pleasantly. And you respond, "I agree!" and draw the corn to yourself. When you hear this corn popping the solution you seek will gather in your mind. When you taste the popped corn, the answer you require will solidify.

Thank this person and take three deep, even breaths, allowing the field to softly vaporize around you. Open your eyes and orient yourself. If your conversation was longer than this (it can be), write down anything you remember. Pop the popcorn and eat some of it, allowing your mind to draw forth a successful plan of future action. If nothing comes to you right away, don't worry. Sometimes the wisest solutions need time to manifest. Be patient and confident that your needs will be met.

To enhance this meditation you may wish to set an entire harvest altar, singing or chanting softly while you do so, and then move into the meditation.

New Moon in Libra

Color: Emerald

Element: Air

Available Energies: Beauty, love, sociability, cooperation, originality, courtesy, responsiveness, self-education, neighbors.

Aromatic Herbal Mixture Suggestions: Aloe, apple, all fruits and berries, bachelor's buttons, balm of gilead, birch, burdock, catnip, coltsfoot, elder, feverfew, heather, hibiscus, hyacinth, larkspur, lilac, marjoram, orchid, passion flower, primrose, rose, sage, tansy, thyme, tonka beans, trillium, violet, wisteria, willow.

Application: Meditations, rituals, and workings for sharing the arts (music, painting, dance, writing) where you seek the approval of others. Positive thoughts for love, friendship, and romance, and for mediation in conflict. Meditations to ensure you are treated fairly, to enjoy beauty, and to learn to cooperate with others. Workings to better communication between yourself and a teacher or parent. Partnerships of any kind.

Avoid: Making open enemies

Be Careful: Of indecisiveness

Libra Moon Aromatic Oil: One drop essential catnip, three drops lilac fragrance, one drop orchid fragrance, one drop rose fragrance, and one drop majoram essential.

Simple Libra Anti-Stress Active Meditation

This is a movement in meditation sequence. Above all, don't overextend your body. Just move as much as you can, and repeat as often as you like. The trick is to do the movements very slowly as you breathe in and out with each, separate movement.

Take three deep breaths in a quiet place at a quiet time. Stand with your feet slightly apart. Remember to stay in the moment.

Reach your arms up over your head, palms toward the heavens, and say: "I am filled with the energy of bliss."

Touch your toes and say: "I am filled with calm."

Rise to a standing position, with your arms at your sides and palms facing forward and say: "I am filled with harmony."

Reach both arms out on either side and say: "I accept peace."

Pull your arms in and cross your chest with your hands, saying: "Serenity fills me."

Raise your right arm over your head, palm toward the heavens, and drop your left arm down and slightly behind you, palm toward the ground. Look up and say: "I draw power from the heavens."

Switch arms with your left up over your head, palm toward the sky, and right arm down, palm toward the ground. Look down and say: "I draw power from the earth."

Place both hands in a prayer position at your heart chakra, and say: "I walk in balance. So be it."

Close your eyes and take three deep, even breaths. Open your eyes and square your shoulders. Breathe again deeply and slowly three times. This active meditation is finished.

New Moon in Scorpio

Color: Green-blue

Element: Water/Fire

Available Energies: Intensity, rebirth, transformation, illumination, wisdom, karma, instinct, investigative.

Aromatic Herbal Mixture Suggestions: All plants in the sea or under fresh water. Asafoetida, bladderwrack, cypress, eucalyptus, lobelia, plantain—and as Mars co-rules this sign, any fire herbs as well.

Application: Rituals and meditations for a situation that needs ultimate power, must transform, or is karmically related. Workings to hone your instincts, or to get to the bottom of a messy situation. Meditations for wisdom, renew an old project, to stop aggressive action (cold), to bring down a criminal, stop gossip or other unhealthy emotional situations. Workings to sign documents where you will get the best deal. Meditations to end things (though a waning Scorpio moon is best for this). Understanding the cycle of birth, life, death, and rebirth. Reincarnation and past-life regression.

Avoid: Creating a secret agenda

Be Careful: Of your resentment

Scorpio Moon Aromatic Oil: One drop essential cypress, one drop essential eucalyptus, one drop cinnamon, and four drops musk.

Scorpio Meditation to Heighten Your Instinctive Abilities

A few years ago I attended a very interesting totem workshop conducted by one of my students. In this seminar he indicated that the animal you dislike the most is actually indicative of the power you hold within yourself—a power that you fear because it speaks of the untapped depths of your inner being. Now *that* made me think! Scorpio energy is all about the power down below, the volcano beneath the sea of yourself. Many of us don't want to tap that energy because we are fearful that if it is not contained, we will lose sight of our spirituality. Yet it is this same power, operating below the surface of each of us, that provides the reservoir of energy when we need it most. It's like having an uncle who is a hit-man. You never talk to anyone about it, but when you've been threatened—guess who you call?

This meditation requires a bit of research, but it is definitely worth it. What animal, reptile, or insect comes to mind that you absolutely, positively hate with a passion? First, consider on the surface why you dislike this creature so much. Why do you, on a gut level, feel it is so disgusting? Next, actually take an evening and research this beastie. If you love the Internet, use search engines and metacrawlers. If you have no desire to touch the World Wide Web, then off to the library you go! Or to your favorite large bookstore that provides a reading area. Spend at least one hour learning all you can about this particular beastie. Take notes if you like. What does it eat? Where does it live? How does it normally behave and why?

And no, I'm not going to force you to meet this creature in the dark alley of your meditation. A one-on-one is not what I had in mind.

When you are ready, and it may actually take a few days for you to feel you are up to it, sit down in a quiet place at a quiet time and light a single, white candle. Or sit in the sunlight. Take several deep, even breaths until you feel relaxed and calm. If you prefer, you can keep your eyes open and contemplate, rather than close your eyes (in case this being is super scary to you—and that's okay). Think about the positive aspects of this creature which may be difficult at first, but you can do it. Every being on this planet has at least one positive attribute. If you can admit one, then you are on a roll! Then, think about the qualities that you don't like. Why? What, within yourself, is like those yucky points? Here, you must be absolutely and totally honest with yourself. You can do this because no one is ever going to know—except you.

For example, one of my students hates sharks. Every since the movie *Jaws,* he has despised and feared these creatures. In his meditation sequence, he realized that when push comes to shove, even though he tries to be spiritual in every action he does, there can come a time when his anger reaches such a point that he will go into a feeding frenzy on the offending party. This only happens when a friend or one of his children is threatened, but he still fears the power of his own mindless anger.

I have a female student, a Sagittarius with a Sagittarian Super Chart (astrological chart wherein most planets are either in Sagittarius or are in the house that is naturally ruled by Sagittarius), who hates spiders—just abhors them. Spiders are all about "allure" and "capture." A Sagittarian deplores being tied down, yet they love to be the center of attention. She realized that she loves to spin a web of acquaintances, but doesn't want to be "captured" herself. A spider is a loner, independent, and a builder. She now looks at spiders with a whole new way of respect.

What did you learn from your research and your contemplation?

New Moon in Sagittarius

Color: Blue

Element: Fire

Available Energies: Expansion, generosity, faith, optimism, understanding, mercy, charity, hope.

Aromatic Herbal Mixture Suggestions: Agrimony, betony, cedar, clove, honeysuckle, hyssop, juniper, linden, nutmeg, sarsaparilla, sassafras, star anise.

Application: Meditations, rituals and workings to expand any project or talent, to find understanding in a difficult situation. Thoughts and actions to give yourself or friends hope. Affirmations to strengthen your personal faith, to expand your awareness, and to learn generosity when dealing with yourself and others. Workings to borrow money, make travel plans, or visit a foreign country. Learning and studying world religions.

Avoid: Sloppy ritual

Be Careful: Of running from commitment

Sagittarius Moon Aromatic Oil: One drop essential cedar, one drop essential clove, two drops honeysuckle fragrance, and one drop essential juniper.

Sagittarius Meditation for Positive Growth

You should never look at a picture just one time, because if you do, you will miss the mystery of the nuances and your conclusions will be based on only surface impressions. It is the same with a meditation. Visiting the sequence repeatedly assists in settling the changes desired in the mind. There are two parts to this activity. First, take your camera and explore a favorite area outside of your home or apartment looking for scenes that speak to you of positive growth while the new moon is in Sagittarius. Take a hike in the woods, a stroll downtown, a trip to the beach, a favorite garden spot, etc.

Take as many pictures as you like. Have all the pictures developed, or with today's digital capabilities, put them in a computer file. Go through the pictures and choose one that you feel exhibits the way in which you wish to grow. Print this picture. On the back of the picture, write the specific type of growth you desire and hang it in a prominent place where you will see it often. Meditate on the picture a few minutes each day, welcoming positive growth into your life. From time to time, check the other pictures that you took on that day. Did you miss something? Does a different one now appeal to you? When you tire of the picture, or have grown to the point of your desire, take the picture down and replace with a new one from your next Sagittarius moon outing.

New Moon in Capricorn

Color: Indigo

Element: Earth

Available Energies: Structure, patience, thrift, diplomacy, sincerity, restraint, endurance, justice/law, order, self-discipline.

Aromatic Herbal Mixture Suggestions: Beech, bindweed, boneset, buckthorn, comfrey, elm, hemlock, horsetail, horehound, ivy, kava-kava, morning glory, patchouli, pansy, parsley, potato, skullcap, slippery elm, Solomon's seal, spikenard, spruce, yew.

Application: Meditations and rituals and workings to learn to work with authority figures, rules, business or school organizational structure. Activities to help you build your savings account, or to call for divine justice, or to work for a promotion on your job. Meditations to create order out of a chaotic situation, to learn self-discipline, and create the underlying structure of anything (even the video game you are creating). Perfect moon phase for political science majors.

Avoid: Depressing rituals

Be Careful: Of your own ruthless ambition

Capricorn Moon Aromatic Oil: Two drops essential patchouli, one drop essential pine, one drop myrrh, and one drop essential geranium.

Capricorn Meditation for Financial Success

Take several deep, even breaths in through the nose and out through the mouth until you feel calm and relaxed. In your mind, create a round, golden light. See before you a beautiful, fertile field. Watch the light drift down into the ground, and as this occurs, the ground itself turns warm and golden. From this area, a beautiful tree will begin to grow. It may be golden, or green, or multicolored—the choice of color is entirely up to you. See the tree mature in golden light from above. See it flower with strength and beauty. Soon, the tree will begin to grow golden coins and paper denominations of money. In your mind, step forward and stand under the tree. A lovely, warm breeze wafts through the field, rustling the leaves on the tree. Money begins to freely float down from the tree and into your hands. The breeze sings: "The world is an abundant field. All your needs and more are met." You can repeat this mantra, if you like, in the first person: "My life is an abundant field, and all my needs and more are met." Now, in your mind, imagine that there is a natural hollow spot in the tree in front of you. Within the hollow area is a lucky, money-drawing charm. Reach in and withdraw the charm. What do you see? Step back from the tree and say "Thank you," to the universe. Breathe deeply and allow the scene to fade. Open your eyes.

What was the lucky charm?

Now go find a physical item that resembles that charm. Use that item on your prosperity altar and in your future money workings.

New Moon in Aquarius

Color: Violet

Element: Air

Available Energies: Independence, originality, progressive ideas, reformation, universal love, inventive, heightened perception, resourceful, individualism.

Aromatic Herbal Mixture Suggestions: Almond, benzoin, bodhi, broom, citron, dandelion, eyebright, hops, lavender, life everlasting, mastic, mistletoe, palm, pine, rice.

Application: Meditations, rituals, and workings for independence, finding new ways to look at the world, changing structures that you think are wrong (school dress code), finding universal love. Meditations to boost new ideas, or finding yourself and defining yourself as an individual. Rituals and affirmations to help you learn mathematics, science, or astrology. Meditations on strengthening your inner self in new and exciting ways.

Avoid: Ritual interruptions

Be Careful: Feeling too detached

Aquarius Moon Aromatic Oil: One drop almond, one drop lavender, one drop pine, one drop cinnamon, and four drops vanilla fragrance (steeped with a real vanilla bean).

Aquarius Bling-Bling Meditation for Focus

For this meditation you will need a set of bells or a singing bowl and a shiny object that fits in your hand, preferably new without any mental attachments. Some individuals enjoy using Ben Wa balls—which range from ¾ to 1½ inches. Cleanse bells and object in spring water, bless them, and allow them to dry. Before we begin the actual meditation, pick one goal and write it down. Place that goal under a purple candle dotted with a bit of Aquarius moon aromatic oil. Light the candle.

Sit where you will be totally relaxed, holding the bell. The object can rest on a table in front of you or in your lap. Close your eyes. Take several deep, even breaths in through the nose and out through the mouth until you feel relaxed, calm, and comfortable. If an errant thought comes to mind, just say to yourself, "Stay in the moment," and ring one of the bells gently. When your mind is clear and calm, you are ready to begin. Open your eyes. Ring the bell. Allow the sound to travel throughout your body from the tip of your toes to the bottom of your feet. Ring the bell again. Allow the sound to settle into and expand your heart chakra. Ring the bell. Allow the sound to settle into your throat chakra and expand the energy there. Ring the bell and allow the sound to travel into and expand your third eye chakra. Ring the bell and let the sound fill and expand the crown chakra. Ring the bell and feel your feet pull energy up from the heartbeat of the earth. Ring the bell and allow yourself to draw down positive energy from the heavens. Pick up the shiny object with your dominant hand. If you are using a singing bowl, you will have to make the sound and then pick up the object during that sound. If you are using bells, the other hand can ring the bell. As the sound reverberates, move the object in the palm of your hand from left to right tracking the object with your eyes. Ring the bell again and track the object from right to left. Now, make a MindLight focused on your goal—for example, "Harmony in my life in a positive way." Ring the bell again and place the MindLight in the shiny object. Ring the bell and track the object again from right to left with your focus on the MindLight that now covers the object. Ring the bell and track the object from left to right, again envisioning the MindLight covering and in the object. Take a deep breath, ring the bell, and blow softly on the object. This is to seal your goal with sacred breath. Ring the bell. Hold the shiny object with both hands and bring to your heart chakra. Close your eyes. Breathe deeply several times until you reach a total calm place. Open your eyes.

Carry the object with you until the desire is met. Repeat the meditation as many times as you like. Allow the candle to burn completely, or put the candle out and burn every night for seven nights completing the same meditation.

Suggested Variation

Make a tape of ringing bells at sixteen- to twenty-second intervals. Use the tape during this meditation. If you feel you are hurried with the sounds you've made on the tape, use a stopwatch to remake the tape at a speed that is comfortable for you. The interval between the sounds should be one deep, complete, relaxing breath that is right for you.

New Moon in Pisces

Color: Crimson

Element: Water

Available Energies: Visionary, inspiration, psychism, compassion, creativity, devotion, universal peace.

Aromatic Herbal Mixture Suggestions: Acacia, bistort, celery, flax, gotu kola, orris, rowan, uva ursa, yarrow, yerba santa.

Application: Meditations, rituals and workings for improving your imagination, visualization techniques, dreaming, astral projection, telepathy, and divination. Prayers and rituals for the dead. Meditations for finding compassion within yourself or seeking compassion in others. Positive affirmations for creativity, using more music and art in your daily life, and celebrating the creativity of others. Workings and prayers for universal peace, or peace among friends and yourself. To see the big picture rather than getting lost in the details.

Avoid: Self-doubt when focusing

Be Careful: Of illogical reasoning

Pisces Moon Aromatic Oil: One drop essential or fragrance of yarrow (hard to get, but it can be found), two drops jasmine, one drop musk, one drop essential orange.

Pisces Inkblot Meditation for Creativity

For this meditation you will need a bottle of blue ink, an eye dropper, and vellum paper cut into three-inch squares. Choose as many squares as you like. You may also wish to do this sequence by candlelight and with soft, inspiring music of your choice.

On the back of each paper, with pencil, write down one aspect of creativity that applies to the type of inspiration you desire. For example, if you wished to compose a fictional story, you might write the names of the main characters on several pieces, the words "exciting subplots" on another, "incisive dialogue" on a different piece, etc. If you wished to design a piece of jewelry you might write "eye-catching design" on one piece of paper, "dynamic color flow," on another, even a theme—funky, chic, classic, water, fire—any words that speak of the type of creativity you wish to work with. Before you begin the next step, take several deep breaths and allow yourself to touch the still point of calm. You are ready to begin.

Mix up the papers with blank side up. Begin with the first paper. In your mind, create a golden (or colored) ball of MindLight as mentioned in the first chapter. Let this MindLight sink directly into the paper. Now, pick up the ink dropper and place several drops in the center of the first paper, close the paper and crease it firmly (without reading what you have written on that paper). Open the paper and set aside, allowing it to dry. Go to the next paper and follow the same sequence. Continue marking the papers, creasing them, and setting them aside until you are finished. Sit back, close your eyes, and take three deep, even breaths until you feel relaxed and comfortable. You can continue on with this meditation, or you can stop here, and use the dried inkblots as triggers when specifically working on your creative venture. When you have completed the project to your satisfaction, burn the ink blots in a ceremony of personal accomplishment and thanksgiving.

If you continue with the meditation, place the papers, ink blot side up, in a circle on a flat surface. Place a candle in the center of the papers. Light the candle. Sit back and take several, deep, even breaths. Close your eyes and create a golden MindLight. See it bob in the air before you. Open your eyes and recreate the MindLight. Let it sink into the first ink blot. Imagine that the ink blot now glows. See the MindLight rise from the first ink blot and move to the second, into the second ink blot, making it glow. Have it rise from the second and move to the third. Continue this sequence until you have worked with all of the papers and the golden MindLight. Finally, after the last paper, bring the golden MindLight back to you, hold open your hands, and imagine the MindLight, now filled with amazing creativity, is nestled softly in your hands. Bring your hands to your heart chakra and allow the MindLight to enter your body. Take three deep, even breaths, and open your eyes. This meditation is concluded.

CHAPTER EIGHT

Full Moon Meditations

Five-Minute Full Moon Meditations for You

The full moon represents an astrological opposition between the sun and the moon, with the earth in the middle. full moon meditations are exciting because you are taking two energies and melding them into one. You will find as you first read through and then work with the energies on a monthly basis that the opposite signs aren't so opposite at all, and truly complement one another, giving you a marvelous vast array of energies to work with! Remember, the slower moving heavenly body, in this case the sun, will modify the energy of the moon, which is why an Aries full moon (moon in Aries opposite sun in Libra) is not the same as a Libra new moon (which would be moon in Libra and sun in Aries). The best way to learn this for yourself is to keep a diary for three months, making entries only on the full moons. At the top of the page, copy the information I've given you under each entry (the signs and the elements involved), and then write down what your day was like. How you felt. What you encountered. Could you see the energy of the signs in the events around you? What do you think about that? Remember, this is all about you! How you process the information and how you, yourself, can best work with what you feel.

The following twelve meditations take five minutes or less (or more, if you like) and are formulated on your willingness to "stop and enjoy the energy of being." Designed to be done on the full moon indicated you can add as many props (candles, herbs, aromatic oils) as you desire or use none at all. Perhaps when reading through the meditations one specifically speaks to you at this time in your life, but today isn't a full moon, or isn't a full moon in the sign indicated. Do that meditation anyway. If it speaks to you, welcome the message!

Aries Full Moon Meditation

When the full moon is in the starter sign of Aries, the sun is in the starter sign of Libra. Here, we are mixing the moon's placement element, fire, with the sun's placement element, air. Suggested meditation themes might be: advancing your social situation, finding new friends, adding a bit of sparkle and passion to your romance, working on or with music, and rising to any challenge you currently face in an honorable way. The only problem with the full moon in Aries, and you've heard me say it as well as many people who work with astrological energies, is that Aries energy is short-lived. A greater starter vehicle, this energy has a habit of running out of steam very quickly. To get around this, don't bite off huge chunks—keep it short, fast, and sweet—or else you might choke later. Aries full moon activities should have a follow-up meditation, working, or ritual planned at a later date to keep your desire moving full speed ahead. If you are having difficulty visualizing this combined energy, think of a jungle explorer who decides to make the tent a truly aesthetic place out there in the middle of lions, tigers, elephants, snakes, and truly colorful bugs.

For five minutes, slow down every action you take, as if you are in a slow-motion movie. Make every movement (Aries) as graceful as possible (Libra) whether you are cooking a meal, cleaning the dining room, or tending your garden. Granted, this is a moving meditation that should be done when you aren't being observed, as people will think you are nuts! (And we don't need those pesky observers in this sequence.) The beauty of this meditation is to show you the grace of every muscle in your body—to make you aware of how you move. In martial arts disciplines, the student is often taught the sequence of forms in slow motion because there you can find precision in what you do by drinking in the moment of the action. When, in the future, it is necessary to move quickly, you will always hit your mark.

Think about it.

During the month, when you are very stressed, just do a five-minute, slow-motion meditation. Stay in the moment. Examine every movement. You'll be glad you did.

Taurus Full Moon Meditation

When the full moon is in Taurus, a fixed and plodding sign, the sun is in Scorpio, a very fixed and intense energy. Here we are mixing the moon's placement of the earth element with the sun's placement of water (mixed with fire if you so desire). Meditations here would focus on long-term success for any type of investment (time, money, energy, the home, business, etc.) for things that you value. Finding security, investigating one's own financial standing, and seeking stable ways to save money. Scorpio's intense power makes this combination a dynamite meditative opportunity for long-term success, especially in the financial arena. If you are having trouble visualizing this combined energy, think of a man sitting down to a seven-course meal to be entertained by twenty costumed harem dancers and the chef cooking directly over the fire in front of him.

If you don't have balance on your own two feet, how can you have balance within yourself? Begin this meditation on the Taurus full moon and keep it up for five minutes a day for at least three weeks. You won't regret it. And it is very, very simple.

Stand on one foot for as long as you can. Now, put both feet flat on the ground and take a nice, deep, even breath, exhaling fully. Stand on the other foot as long as you can. Again, put both feet flat on the ground, inhale and exhale calmly. Now lift the other foot, and again, balance as long as you can. Keep switching feet, breathing deeply, for five minutes. That's all there is to it. Balance on your feet brings stability in your life.

Gemini Full Moon Meditation

When the full moon is in flowing and mutable Gemini, the sun is in equally flowing and mutable Sagittarius. Here, we have the moon's placement of the air element coupled with the sun's placement of fire! With this blend, Sagittarius modifies the energy of Gemini. Sagittarius is "work horse" energy: it just goes and goes and goes. Now is a good time to put your Gemini ideas into solid, physical action. This is an excellent moon to move any energy quickly and with targeted speed—from thoughts to things. With this full moon you may wish to work on your magickal studies, short written pieces that need power and punch (like advertising copy), issues involving your child's education in the lower grades, work on remote viewing with a friend, or meditate in a different place that is not far from home, such as the woods, a sanctuary, etc. This is a time to work on creativity in writing such as stories, poems, spells, rituals, and meditations. A time to learn about other cultures, religions, and pantheons in short sound bites that you feel comfortable employing in your own work. The full moon in Gemini is the writers' dream! If you are having trouble visualizing this melding of energy, think of a race car driver who spent six years developing a new engine, and now is going to put it on the track for a super win!

Since both Gemini and Sagittarius are naturally scattered, we're going to take advantage of that natural force. All you will need is a clay pot and plenty of open space. No observers, please. Wear protective eye covering, such as safety glasses.

Take three, deep, even breaths in through the nose and out through the mouth. Fill the pot with MindLight. Raise the pot over your head. As you exhale swiftly—smash the pot, allowing the pieces to scatter.

What is the point?

If you are trying to banish something, for example negative thoughts, put those in the pot before you smash it. As the pieces scatter, envision all the negativity within yourself flying away from you. Saying a loud noise as you smash the pot not only makes you feel better, but helps to expel the negativity.

On the other hand, let's say you were trying to get information out there as quickly as possible. Fill your pot with MindLight focused on the thoughts you wish to disseminate. Again, raise the pot, uttering a loud sound as you exhale and smash the pot. As the pieces shoot from the center point, envision your words being carried far and wide.

Note: Do not smash the pot on your toes or right under your nose. Do not smash the pot near other people or pets. If you would like to make this meditation more intense, write what you want to remove from your life, or what you wish carried to others on the pot with indelible ink. Remember to use the MindLight and to stay in the moment.

Cancer Full Moon Meditation

When the full moon is in the starter sign of Cancer, the sun is in the starter sign of Capricorn. With this combination we have sacred water and Mother Earth—an amazing combination for continued good health meditations and workings! Meditations for stability in the home, honoring your personal roots, and even ending matters in a positive way through limits, rules, structure and rewards are good applications of this energy. Protection meditations, too, for family, property, and pets would be good, as well as working on anything that you choose to bring into the home within the next cycle of the moon. If you are having trouble visualizing this energy, think of a matriarch who only carries a clutch bag building the family empire.

For this meditation you will need any of the following: anything small and stackable such as building blocks (the type children play with), a small puzzle, or a picture cut into six or seven pieces.

Place the objects on a white surface. Take several deep breaths in through the nose and out through the mouth. When you are perfectly calm and no thoughts interfere, gaze at the objects before you. For this example we are going to use building strength and security within the home. Create your MindLight and fill it with love and blessings, then slowly put that Mind-Light into the blocks. Stay in the moment. Think of nothing but the blocks. Very slowly, stack the blocks in a pleasing shape or put together the puzzle. When you have created your pattern, sit with your hands in your lap, palms on your thighs. Raise your hands limply (like a puppy begging), until they are at eye level. Straighten your fingers so they point toward the blocks. Flip your hands up (slowly) so that your palms are facing the blocks, and then bring your hands down slowly back to their original position on your thighs. Now, let's do that again with a nice, deep breath as you raise your hands, and exhale as you lower your hands. Keep going. Every time your hands go up, think of the energies around you building in a positive way. As your hands go down, think of that stable energy enfolding you like a warm blanket. When you feel relaxed and refreshed, the meditation is over.

If it has been particularly stressful in the home, do this meditation every evening until the chaos abates. What if someone knocks over your blocks?

That's the person causing the most wild energy, even if it doesn't appear to be so on the surface. If an animal knocks over the blocks, determine who else is in the room at the time, that is your key. If it is just you and the cat, for example, who were you thinking about right before the blocks tumbled? Did you receive a phone call, etc.? If the blocks tumble down, don't fret. Simply do the meditation again.

Leo Full Moon Meditation

When the full moon is in fixed and stubborn Leo, the sun is in equally fixed, but totally individualistic Aquarius. Where the Leo moon brings fire to the mix, the Aquarian sun brings air. Here, we are looking at personal goal fulfillment in unusual, individualistic ways. Incorporate meditations to strengthen your children's self-esteem, your own talents, and your own activities within a group or organization. If you are having trouble visualizing this energy, think of a casino owner looking for new advertising copy that is totally different from everyone else and will shoot his business to the very top. He can hear the crap tables rolling as I write.

Taking the "wanting to shine" energy of Leo and the individualistic, independent character of Aquarius, let's think about where they might find balance. In helping others. Every Leo and every Aquarius I have ever known finds happiness in extending energy to other people.

For this meditation you buy or create for yourself twenty-one cards (twenty-one is a "master" number) that say: "Have a nice day." Keep your cards absolutely non-religious. Good thoughts only. Do not address them.

When you are ready put all the cards on a flat surface. Breathe deeply several times, allowing yourself to be relaxed and comfortable. Then, create a MindLight that looks like the sun with snazzy little bits of electricity rolling off it. Say: "Blessings!" Put that blessing MindLight in each and every card. When you are finished, close your eyes and take a deep breath. This part of the meditation is over.

Now, go right out there and give those cards away. If you like, play like a Secret Meditation Ninja! Just slip those cards to people when they don't notice OR you can be right up front about it and say: "Here, you need a good day!" When they say "What is this for?" you can respond: "Power is in the moment of joy."

Virgo Full Moon Meditation

When the full moon is in mutable flowing Virgo, the sun is in flowing, outer-space, visionary Pisces. This is the perfect opportunity for down-to-earth Virgo to reach out and touch cutting edge, visionary, look at the big picture energy of Pisces. Here, we are working with the element of earth and the digitized power of water! Finding answers to your problems in a visionary way through meditation, using your analysis coupled with a divinatory tool such as the tarot, lots, or reading astrological charts. Meditation in movement is excellent for this full moon, including Tai Chi and Qigong. If you are having trouble visualizing this energy, think of a brilliant German stage actress who came up with a revolutionary idea in which soldiers could communicate with each other via a coded electronic gadget.

This meditation is based on a Tai Chi technique sometimes referred to as Waving Hands. The purpose of the movement is to keep you focused and concentrated on one thing—the palms of your hands. By learning the comfort in this technique you also learn how to focus with positive intent.

Cross your hands over your chest. Very slowly, move your right hand out and away from you so that you are gazing at your right palm—about a foot from your nose. Never taking your gaze from the palm of your right hand, move the right palm in a gentle arc in front of you until it reaches your right peripheral vision. Your head naturally turns to follow the right palm. The eye movement and the hand movement should be simultaneous. Do not break the gaze. When your right hand and eyes are all the way to your right as far as your peripheral vision will go, slowly bring your left hand out in front of you up over your right palm (so that now you see only the left palm), then track the left palm as you move it out and over to left peripheral vision. Bring your right hand into view over the left hand, and track the right palm as you did before. Your movements should always be very slow and not stressful. Keep tracking your palms for five minutes. When you are finished cross your hands over your chest and breathe deeply three times or more until you feel totally relaxed. This meditation is finished.

Waving Hands is a wonderful technique to use when you are very stressed throughout the day and are having difficulty focusing on the task at hand. When you are comfortable with the Waving Hands technique, place a MindLight filled with positive intent into the center of your palm. This makes the meditation extremely powerful; especially if you work any of the healing arts. Reiki practitioners or healers of all kinds may truly enjoy the benefit of practicing Waving Hands over a thirty-day period.

Libra Full Moon Meditation

When the full moon is in the aesthetic starter sign of Libra, the sun is in the boisterous starter sign of Aries. Now we are taking air energy and modifying it with fire. If you are having trouble visualizing this combined energy, think of a well-dressed Libra woman wearing a fire-engine red suit that makes her feel totally empowered, and the possibility of a snap decision is now within her grasp. The energy here can breathe new life into your aesthetic environment, help you to make a difficult decision, and heat up the wheels of justice.

One particular Zen practice involves arranging flowers around three significant blooms. The tallest stands for the center and the connection between heaven and earth. The middle-sized or medium flower stands for the human essence and the third flower or branch is bent, signifying our connection to the earth. From these three positioned flowers, the remainder of the arrangement is completed.

For this meditation, buy a bouquet of flowers. Place them on a white tablecloth along with a water-filled container that you have chosen for the arrangement. Breathe evenly and deeply at least three times or until you feel calm and comfortable. Create MindLight for blessings and empowerment and settle the MindLight into the vase of water.

Begin with the tallest flower, the center focus, and see the light of heaven and the light of earth connecting to this flower. Place the bloom in the vase. Pick up the second flower, that which stands for the essence of humanity, fill it with peace and love and place it in the vase next. Now, add the "sealing" flower that calls the positive energy into the earth and into humankind, the bent flower or branch. Continue arranging all the other flowers and greens around these three points of focus. When you are finished, step back and observe your work, thanking deity (or whatever you believe runs the universe) for this special, quiet time of beauty. Give the arrangement to a friend or relative, or place in the center of your home to help generate harmony and happiness in your environment.

Scorpio Full Moon Meditation

When the full moon is in fixed, intense, powerful Scorpio the sun is in stable, plodding, dug-in Taurus. With this placement we are modifying water with earth. Scorpio is the energy of mystery, of the occult (seminars of the mysteries conducted on a Scorpio full moon always seem to have the highest attendance), investigation, using other people's money or gaining from other people's money, and rituals for the dead called crossing rituals. It's a time to honor your ancestors. Workings done at this time will be long lasting, so be careful what you work for. If you are having trouble visualizing this melded energy, think of Sherlock Holmes and Dr. Watson. A Scorpio full moon is a perfect time for police officers to really put their nose to the investigative wheel—Taurus fruits will be very satisfactory.

A big part of this meditation is finding an ornate key. In the next month, after you've read this passage, you'll probably come across the key you need. Things happen that way. This key is for unlocking secrets; therefore, if your job entails such things you might find this meditation incredibly helpful. As a suggestion, not a prerequisite, once you have found the key it should be buried in a jar for nine days with dirt from your ancestors, with a mixture of dried patchouli herb, eyebright herb, and mint. You can also add a drop of Scorpio moon aromatic oil and Taurus moon aromatic oil. After the key has "set" for nine days, it is ready for use.

But you don't have to do that if you think it is creepy.

The next prop depends entirely on what you wish to "uncover." Let's say you are looking for a new home, or a way to sell your own home. Use a map of the property or a map of the general area. What if you are working on an investigation of some type? The physical file (or one of them) of the issue would be helpful. What if you know there is office gossip and you are trying to get to the bottom of untrue rumors? Use a physical plant that you can take to the office (as long as you agree to take care of it, of course).

When you are ready to do the meditation, sit quietly in a comfortable place with the key in your hand and your "prop" nearby. Take three deep, even breaths (or more) until you are relaxed and at ease. Remember to stay in the moment with your visualizations—don't let your mind wander. Pull it gently back to the meditation at hand. Imagine now that you are in an ornate hall with many softly gleaming doors. Doors as far as the eye can see. The door you want, however—the one that holds your secret—is at the end of the hall. Begin walking down the hall counting the numbers on the doors from twenty-five down to one. The door you want is numbered: zero. As you walk down the hall you can make the numbers glow to keep you right in tune with your visualization. As you near the door, do not be surprised if the key in your hand begins to feel warm. When you reach the zero door, take a deep breath and say to yourself: "I agree that I will find the answer, and as I open this door, I open the correct pathway to bring me this information without harm to myself or my loved ones. I agree!" Put the key in the lock and open the door. Inside the room glows, and in the center of the room is your prop. In your mind pick up the prop, put the key in your mental pocket, turn, and leave the room locking the door behind you. Outside the room the hallway is filled with brilliant, soothing light. Count from three to one and open your eyes, taking a nice, deep breath as you do so.

Very shortly, the answer you seek will come to you. Carry the key with you, if you like, and put the prop in a strategic place—wherever your gut tells you to put it.

You can use your key as often as you like as many times as you like. If you used the jar, rinse off the key with spring water, bless it, dry it off and place it back in the jar until next time. If you did not use the jar, rinse and bless the key, and wrap it in white or black cloth as your inner self dictates.

Sagittarius Full Moon Meditation

When the moon is in busy, busy, busy mutable Sagittarius, the sun is in chatty, chatty, chatty mutable Gemini. Fire is modified by air! Here is a great chance to expand your knowledge through study. Maybe you built your dream car, but something isn't running right. A back-to-the-drawing-board scenario for contemplation will result in a solution. Or, perhaps you've seen something you like, and begun working on making that object or idea a better one. This full moon is all about improvement through inspiration! Think of an engineer who must build a ship, but in a totally different way to meet new criteria. When it is launched, it will be the eighth wonder of the world.

I call this meditation Touching Sound. Sit in a comfortable place. Close your eyes and take several deep, even breaths until you are relaxed. Just listen.

Let the sounds around you come into your consciousness, but don't iden-
tify them. For example, if you hear a car going by, don't think about what
kind of car it is. Just enjoy the sound. Extend your mind out to each sound
and put a color to it. For example, sitting here, writing at my computer,
I first hear cars going by on the road. I'll make that sound purple. I hear
the fountain in the dining room. Ouuu—blue. The tick of the grandfather's
clock—golden. My son walking down the hall—orange. Cricket song—silver. Except, it would be like this.

Swish: Purple

Burble: Blue

Tick Tick Tick: Golden

Clump Clump: Orange

Crick Crick: Silver

Murmur: Light blue

When you are totally in the moment, relaxed and calm, let go of the
sounds to white light. Just be.

When everything seems busy and hectic, touch the sound.

Capricorn Full Moon Meditation

When the full moon is in starter but firm Saturnine Capricorn, the sun
is in let's-have-a-family-reunion-where-we-can-all-cry-over-good-memo-
ries Cancer. The blend now is water modifying earth. If you have trouble
visualizing this energy, think of Queen Elizabeth being convinced to cough
up the money to build the strongest fleet of ships on the planet (which happened). Here, we would be trying to restructure our home, business, and
magickal life to meet our needs.

This is a very simple meditation, but an extremely powerful one. A friend
of mine actually got a new home when no possibility of obtaining one was
in the picture. First, write your needs, not your wants, on 3x5 cards—one
need per card. Take a break. Go back and look at your needs again. Are there
wants in there? If so, take them out. On the bottom of each 3x5 card you
kept, write the words "or better."

How many cards do you have?

Now you need that many bottles of spring water.

Empower the spring water by pointing the bottle to the west, then to the east, from the north and then to the south—then quickly "punch" the water through the center of the configuration you've just drawn in the air, saying: "Blessings upon you!"

Open the bottle. Roll up the 3x5 card. Insert the card into the water, saying: "Blessings upon my need. This need is met with what is required or better!" Take several deep, cleansing breathes, then create your MindLight. See, in your mind, the MindLight hovering over the top of the bottle, then slipping down into the water. As it touches the water the entire bottle (in your mind) glows with brilliant white light. Aloud, say: "I physically agree that this need is met with what is required or better in a positive way. I mentally agree that this need is met with what is required or better in a positive way. I emotionally agree that this need is met with what is required or better in a positive way. I spiritually agree that this need is met with what is required or better in a positive way. I agree!"

Go through each need in this way. When you are finished, put the bottles in a safe place until your need is met. If this is a big deal and urgent, repeat the affirmations every night holding the bottle. Visualize yourself as happy, safe, and healthy as you say your statements aloud. Finish with three deep, cleansing breaths, allowing yourself to relax into the arms of earth energy.

Aquarius Full Moon Meditation

When the full moon is in fixed talk-to-the-hand Aquarius, the sun is in fixed you'll-do-it-my-way Leo. This blending is the modification of air by fire. If you are having trouble visualizing this energy, then think of a male teen who has just had his eyebrow pierced and his father booming: "You march straight in that bathroom and take those out!" A very positive way to use this energy is to take your unique and exciting ideas and put them "out there" in a very dramatic way with lots of glitz and glitter! Think of how you could use your courage, leadership abilities, and personal independence to enhance your revolutionary ideas.

Everyone has something that they enjoy watching because the visual brings feelings of peace and calm—birds, clouds, a waterfall, butterflies in the sunlight, waving grass on an open field, or the view from the top of a tall building (maybe the lights at night and the full moon overhead?). The best way to use that glitz and glitter of Leo and Aquarius is by allowing that power to build from total serenity, because then it is clean, beautiful, and natural—not tainted with vainglorious ideas. And don't think what you like to watch is off-the-wall. I prefer watching alligators at the zoo. Okay, so I like waterfalls, but if I could pick, it would be alligators. I love to watch them swim. They are so slow and undulating when in a relaxed state; yet you know of the unlimited power they hold within their being.

What do you like to watch that helps you to feel calm, peaceful, and filled with harmony?

Now—for five minutes— visualize it!

Or even better, go find that flower, fountain, fish tank, etc., and spend at least five minutes enjoying the view!

Pisces Full Moon Meditation

When the full moon is in mutable, dreamy, conspiracy-oriented Pisces, think of the sun in mutable, must-provide-order Virgo. Here, earth modifies water. It is a time to take your more visionary ideas and actually set them down on paper with some sort of structure. If you have trouble visualizing this one (and this really happened), think of a Pisces driving up and down the same road looking for a zoo for over two hours and the Virgo finally saying, "Just give me the damned map!"

For this meditation, all you need is a blank wall. Sit quietly, breathing in and out several times until you are relaxed and calm. Stare at the wall. Don't stare hard. Just relax and look at the blank wall. In your mind, allow the wall to dissolve. In it its place, see the amazing realm of outer space filled with the glittering light of the stars. One of those stars carries the information you need to solve a particular problem. Don't worry about what that information might be. Just accept and know that within the light, there is the answer. In your mind, reach out and touch that star. See it flare and fill the entire room with the light. Close your eyes and accept the positive energy.

Take several deep breaths and open your eyes, confident that the answer you seek is already within you and when the time is right for you, it will be revealed in the best way possible for your use.

The Best Balancing Meditation You Will Ever Do

Whether we are discussing martial arts or magick, religion or science, in the end it is all about balance. A productive life is one wherein the major player (which would be you) has attained a sense of inner satisfaction of the self, which extends a type of peace and power outside of you, touching others in a positive way. Struggling to find that grace, for some, will take an entire lifetime.

But not for you, because you have already gotten on the fast track to self-improvement in a variety of ways. Anyone who wants to take the power of quantum science (magick) and mix it with their own life has already shown that he or she has the guts, the power, the determination, and the faith that anything can be accomplished. And that, my friend, is the biggest hurdle!

Now it is a simple matter of putting it into practice!

Ah! Someone is saying, "Hey! I read those words before in here somewhere!" That's right, you did. In the first chapter. And now I'm going to show you the best meditation you will ever do—because, it is all about you.

First, answer this question: What astrological sign are you? Very good.

Second, what sign is opposite your own? Don't know? No problem! Just check the full moon information and you'll find it.

Most people (not all) don't like their opposite sun sign. They don't like the energies because those energies, the deep ones that make the sign individualistic, are those ways of behaving that we might aspire to and secretly wish we could do, but condemn because we think those people go overboard. How rude! You would think that they could temper themselves a little better! Really!

Except they see the same thing in you.

Which is what makes the world such an interesting place.

All you have to do is think about the qualities that you really like in the sign opposite yours. Make a list if you find that helpful. Then collect one item for each quality that you would like to call your own. I would suggest that all the items be small so that they can fit in a conjuring or gris-gris bag. It's that easy. Place all the items on a table, your altar, or outside on the ground. The important point is that no matter where you are sitting (or standing) you can reach all the items easily. Now, close your eyes, take three deep, even breaths, and say: "I take the positive energy of (name the sign) into myself!" With your eyes still closed, reach out and touch one of the items. Hold it in your hands, with eyes still closed. Feel the item to determine what it is. Then say: "I accept this gift!" and pull the item to your heart chakra, thinking of the type of energy you matched to the item you are holding. Once you have visualized the energy as part of your being in a positive way, place the item in your lap or beside you and move to the next. When you have touched and accepted all the items and energies, open your eyes and take a deep breath. You can light a candle to signify sealing your gifts within yourself. Place all the items in a gris-gris or conjuring bag and carry with you throughout the week, if not throughout the following month. Be aware of which type of energy you chose first, and which energy was intuitively last. Actively work on bringing all the energies you requested into your daily life throughout the month. At the end of the month, sit down with all the items in front of you once again, and contemplate your new growth! If you would like to continue to work on integrating particular energies within the self, then repeat the meditation. If not, bury the items somewhere on your property to keep those energies in your root environment.

Advanced Moon Exercise

Match the moon in each sign to a particular type of music, splice the tunes together, and do a meditation, visualizing that the moon is your dancing partner. You will be amazed at the results and I guarantee you, if you use this to teach students the power of the moon in the signs, they will remember!

CHAPTER NINE

Sun and Planetary Meditations

Our reality is a dance of endless energies, from the stars and planets above to the busy human manifestations below. By learning to experience the energies of the heavenly bodies in a meditative way, we can create our ultimate desires through the still point of manifestation.

As above . . . so below.

The Sun

Speed and Orbit: Earth takes approximately 365 days to travel around the sun, and it spends approximately thirty days in each sign. Therefore, you have thirty days to focus your will on a particular astrological sign energy. Remember that the sun is a star and therefore also carries star power.

Retrograde: Never retrogrades

The Sun Moves: Appears to move on an astrological chart approximately one degree per day.

The Sun Rules: The astrological sign of Leo; a fixed sign. The sun has the most power when it is in its own sign.

The Sun's Element: Fire

The Sun's Day: Sunday

Basic Energy: Focus and will

Basic Meditation and Working: Success

Colors: Gold, yellow, bronze

Keywords for the Sun: Aggressive, authority, confidence, courage, determination, dignity, egocentric, faith, fortitude, individualism, leadership, loyalty, optimism, overbearing, poise, power, reliance, success, stubborn, vitality, willful.

Sun Invocation for Empowering Items: O Glorious Sun, who lies at the center of our solar system, father of the skies who travels across the vault of earth's starry heavens bringing golden light and love, infuse this working with star power, success, confidence, generosity and joy! Ruler of Leo, exalted in Aries, element of fire—bring to me my desire! I agree!

Gems: Aragonite, sunstone, citrine, amber, iolite, yellow jaspers, yellow jades, tiger's-eye.

Aromatic Herbal Packet: Rosemary, sunflower, marigold, chamomile, and bay. An excellent Lammas recipe for conjuring bags.

Aromatic Oil Blend for Sun Energies: Three drops frankincense, one drop myrrh, one drop chamomile, and one drop anise.

Sun Loose Meditation Incense: Mix equal parts of cinnamon, rosemary, sandalwood, and frankincense. Add one drop chamomile essential oil. Herbs can be mixed with a ground wood base for outdoor blends. Throw into ritual fire or burn on incense charcoal tab.

Sun Ink: Mix one drop of aromatic sun oil in one four-dram bottle of gold ink. Swirl. Add one link of a gold chain. Swirl. Crush a minute amount of frankincense and add just a bit. Swirl. Empower at high noon.

The sun, a powerful star, gives fuel to the moon and represents our focus, our will, and our ego. In magick, the sun equates to personal power, long-term success, and father figures. Naturally, the sun rules the fifth house of the zodiac lineup, which includes children, risk, brief sexual experiences (fun sex), and, most of all, our talents and how we apply them.

Sun Success Meditation

Everything yellow! Success should be a feast of good fortune! Before you begin this meditation, spend an entire day looking for "things that are yellow or gold." When I took my Spiritism coronation I learned the most valuable lesson in magick—your effort is what counts. Too many times over the years I've met people who have expected the mysteries of the universe to be handed to them on a gold-edged platter. It just doesn't happen that way. In Spiritism I learned that substitutions were not acceptable unless you were in dire circumstances, because part of the magick involves the energy of "seeking to go find" the item needed in the formula.

Here, you are going to "seek to go find" anything yellow or gold. Anything that can fit on a table or altar top and can stay still while you are meditating. A new yellow cat, therefore, would not fit this meditation—although a goldfish would, if you are into it and will take extremely good care of it, since its welfare depends on your good fortune.

Humor aside, the bottom line is—everything in the colors of yellow and gold. Keep the season in mind. If you are doing this ritual in the late summer or early fall, place marigolds on your altar as a centerpiece. If it is in the dead of winter, wrap the outside of a clear bowl with gold foil and fill with water and golden tea lights, etc. Before your meditation begins, set all items on your table or altar, including a gold or yellow candle that is dressed with aromatic sun oil. (If you are allergic to scents, don't panic—you don't have to use them, although they are great triggers for the mind.) On a square piece of parchment write your name in the center with empowered sun ink. Then, on each margin write the word "success" as many times as it will fit. Finally, draw arrows from each word to your name. Fold each of the corners of the paper toward your name. Put this paper under your sun candle.

Over the candle, say: "From the land across the river" (hold your hands out toward the candle).

"To my hands across my chest" (bring your hands toward you and across your chest).

"May the pathway now be open" (open your hands out to the universe).

"And this work become my best" (pull your hands in and cross them over your heart chakra).

Close your eyes and take three deep, even breaths. You want your feet firmly on the floor because you are going to draw prosperous energy up into your body. Breathe in through the nose, out through the mouth. Say to yourself: "I agree to accept golden, harmonious success into my life. I agree that I deserve to be successful." Envision a golden staircase in front of you (with a golden hand railing if that will help). In your mind, mount the staircase, counting as you go up each golden step in your mind. At the top of those stairs is your success, in the form of a shining star. As you climb up each step, you will say to yourself that you are becoming more and more successful. Climb as many steps as you possibly can without losing focus. As you climb you will begin to feel lighter, freeer, and more successful because you are totally focused on that golden energy and nothing else. There isn't room for worry! When you lose count, stop, and make note of the number. Take several deep breaths and relax. Enjoy the feeling of calm and serenity.

Open your eyes. On a piece of paper, write down the number of steps you managed to climb in your mind. Factor that number down to its lowest denomination. For example, I made it to 152 steps, so I will add 1+5+2, which equals 8 (Ah! The number of mastery and the sign of the infinite!). This then, is the number I will work magick with, the number of ingredients I may use in a success working, or perhaps the number of days that I will continue to do a single candle spell. It also lets me know that my success is hinged on 8 as in timing—could be 8 hours, 8 days, 8 weeks, or perhaps 8 months. Allow your sun success candle to burn completely if you can and leave your success altar untouched the same number of days as your "magick success number."

QUICK NUMBER GUIDE FOR THIS MEDITATION

1: Beginnings = New Moon Phase = Candle Magick

2: Partnership = Waxing Crescent Moon = Herbal Magick

3: Learning = First Quarter Moon = Visualization

4: Stabilization = Waxing Gibbous = Drumming or Music Magick

5: Change = Full Moon = Poppet or Image Magick

6: Reflection = Waning Gibbous = Knot Magick

7: Movement = Last Quarter = Spoken Charms

8: Mastery of the Environment = Waning Crescent = Sigil Magick

9: Gateway of Fulfillment = Lunar Eclipse = Tai Chi, Qigong, Martial Arts

10: Completion = Solar Eclipse = Meditation magick, factored to 1

11: Dawn = Mastery of the Self = Good works to others, which is magick in action (and factored to 2)

21: Spiritual Mastery = Dusk = How you do it, not what you do (and factored to 3)

As you can see, the numbers ten, eleven, and twenty-one carry a double message for you.

Can you use this meditation with any planetary energy? Absolutely. Just change the color of the steps to match the planetary energy and change your goal as appropriate.

Mercury

Speed and Orbit: Mercury orbits 88 Earth days and moves around the astrological chart approximately 4 times each year and spends about 7.5 days in each sign (not including retrograde periods).

Retrograde: Mercury retrogrades 3 times per year for 3 weeks per retrograde.

Mercury Moves: Approximately 4 degrees per day

Mercury Rules: The astrological signs of Gemini and Virgo. Both are mutable signs. Mercury is the most powerful when it is in either Gemini or Virgo, as these are the signs this energy rules.

Mercury's Elements: Air (Gemini) and Earth (Virgo)

Mercury's Day: Wednesday

Basic Energy: Speed and flow—is also a "carrier"

Basic Meditation and Working: Communication

Colors: Silver, blue, light blue, white, clear

Keywords for Mercury: Active, adaptable, agility, alert, analytical, articulate, aware, brilliant, changeable, communication, critical, dexterous, diffusive, discriminatory, duality, efficient, expressive, indecisive, intelligent, irresponsible, messages, precise, reason, restless, sensory, skeptical, verbose, versatile, writing.

Mercury Invocation for Empowering Items: Mercury, quicksilver messenger of the gods, he who dances about the earth carrying wisdom and perception, whose versatility brings positive change and creative thinking, I invoke thee and call upon thee in my hour of need. Permeate this working with celestial speed and untold wisdom so that my desire may manifest in the most positive way. Ruler of Virgo and Gemini, exalted in Virgo, elements of Air and Earth! Combine this night in sacred birth! I agree!

Gems: Amazonite, amethyst, aquamarine, chrysoprase, chrysocol-
la, lodestone, lapis lazuli, leopardskin jasper, labradorite, quartz
crystal, sapphire, sodalite, turquoise, howlite, and zoisite.

Mercury Aromatic Herbal Packet: Bergamot, fennel, copal, lavender,
lemon verbena, mandrake (poisonous), and mint.

Aromatic Oil Blend for Mercury Energies: Three drops bergamot, two
drops clover, and one drop mint.

Mercury Loose Meditation Incense: Lavender, marjoram, mint and
clover with one drop lavender essential oil and one drop mint
essential oil. Herbs can be mixed with a ground, wood base for
outdoor incenses. Use on charcoal incense tab.

Mercury Ink: Some recipes used to contain liquid mercury, however, this is highly toxic and not recommended. If you visit an
art store you will find inks in a variety of colors for airbrush-
ing techniques. With a little mixing, you can find the correct
consistency to use with a crow quill or other style of pen nib.
Here, turquoise is a good choice, or you could opt for silver or
the standard blue ink. Add one drop of Mercury oil, swirl, one
link of silver chain, swirl, and powdered mint (just a bit). Lavender, when pulverized, is somewhat fluffy, and may not suit your
needs. Empower Mercury ink at dawn.

Mercury symbolizes the way you think and the process you use to get
what you want, which is then extended through communication and action.
Because magickal people believe that "thoughts are things," Mercury's power can be truly amazing! This quick little fellow of the zodiac naturally rules
the third house and his magick is attributed to communication, siblings, and
lower forms of education. Transportation is also thrown in there for good
measure, which is logical if you think about it—a thought is the transportation of your feelings combined with your needs. He covers the first stages
of writing, that creative process of linking thoughts together for various
forms of expression including writing rituals, stories, spells, poetry, guidelines, journals, etc. It also includes the thought process for building projects,

putting together martial arts forms to create a kata, or dance moves to create the entire ballet or a music video.

Mercury Meditation for Communication from a Higher Source

Field trip! Whoo-hoo! Spirit sends us messages all the time, we just aren't always ready to accept the information! Use this meditation the next time you need wisdom, advice, or the solution to a problem. In a quiet place, in a quiet time, light a blue candle dressed with Mercury oil. Surround the candle with gems and herbs of Mercury correspondence. Close your eyes and take three deep breaths. Allow yourself to relax and settle in comfortably. Say to yourself: "I agree to set the field of wisdom around me." In your mind, create a round, pulsating blue light. Allow that light to grow and diminish and you breath. Breathe in—the light contracts. Breathe out—the light expands. Now, reverse. Breathe in—the light grows larger. Breathe out—the light diminishes. Within this light lies the information you seek. Reverse. As you breathe in, pull the wisdom into yourself. As you breathe out, send your self-doubts away. When you are completely relaxed, breathe deeply three times, and then open your eyes. Put out the candle.

Place some of the gems and a little of the herb in a conjuring bag to carry with you, because now you're going on a road trip. You will need a notebook and pencil if you don't have a great memory, so be sure those are in your purse or back pocket before you leave. As you step out the door, say: "I agree that I will find wisdom today!" Go someplace different (but safe, of course). A walk in the park, a short trip to a museum, community gardens, even an amusement park. On your trip make note of anything that is out of the ordinary; anything odd, unusual, striking, different. Write down keywords of what you see, hear, taste, or touch that is different from everyday occurrence. When you are back home and feel you are ready to digest the information, write your keywords down on a different piece of paper. Dot the paper with Mercury oil. Place the keyword list beside your blue candle. Place your conjuring bag on top. Repeat the exact same meditation that you did before—breathing in the blue light, expelling your doubts. When you are finished with the breathing exercise, don't open your eyes. Instead, catch the first keyword from your list that happens to come to mind. And then the second and third. Open your eyes. Therein lies your solution. Think about it.

Venus

Speed and Orbit: Venus orbits 225 Earth days and spends approximately 18.7 days in each sign (not including retrograde periods).

Retrograde: Venus retrogrades every 18 months for approximately 40 days.

Venus Moves: Approximately 1.6 degrees per day

Venus Rules: The astrological signs of Taurus (fixed) and Libra (cardinal). Venus is the most powerful when she is in her own signs, Taurus and Libra.

Venus' Day: Friday

Venus' Element(s): Earth (Taurus) and Air (Libra)

Basic Energy: Socialization and education

Basic Meditation and Working: Fast cash, love, and friendship

Colors: Light and dark greens, pink, peach

Keywords for Venus: Affectionate, art, attractive, beauty, considerate, constructive, cooperative, courtesy, devotion, evasive, feminine, flirtatious, flowers, gentle, harmony, impressionable, indifferent, indolent, love, obstinate, original, refinement, responsive, sociable, vacillate.

Venus Invocation for Empowering Items: Queen of Dawn's first blush and evening twilight, she who orchestrates both love and war, whose temples graced the ancient world, whose kisses brought agreement and adoration, to you I now implore: synchronize my work so that force and form work in harmony. Ruler of Taurus and Libra, of strength and beauty, exalted in Pisces, creatures of earth and air, daughter of the moon and feminine embraces, fill my work with love and care. I agree!

Gems: Rose quartz, red aventurine, lavender fluorite, garnet, peach moonstone, peridot, rhodochrosite, rhodonite, rhyolite, spinel, and unakite.

Aromatic Herbal Packet: Catnip, rose, vetiver, cherry bark, and orris.

Aromatic Oil Blend for Venus Energies: One drop rose, two drops musk, one drop jasmine, and one drop sandalwood.

Venus Loose Meditation Incense: Rose, vetiver, and jasmine. One drop of lilac oil. Add to wood base for outdoor ritual work. Throw on ritual fire or burn on charcoal tab.

Venus Ink: The color you choose depends on what you are working for. Passion lends itself to the deep reds, where friendship might be pink or even light blue. Again, a trip to the art store for a variety of colors may be helpful. If not—go with standard green. Add one drop of Venus oil to a four-dram bottle of green ink. Swirl. Add one chip of rose quartz. (Note: You can use powdered gems; however, I recommend that if you do this, you wear a face mask as breathing in the dust can be harmful to your lungs and you also need eye protection from flying splinters.) Swirl. Add a minute amount of crushed rose petal. Empower at dusk.

Sigh. Venus. The planet of love and war. The most loving mother, who would cut the throat of someone trying to harm her children without a thought of remorse. The queen of feminine power. Steel under tons of lace. This is Venus. Venus energy has a great deal to do with our socialization skills based on our inner desires, and whether or not we appear adoring to Sam or the worst possible enemy to Lisa. Venus is also how we extend our thoughts out from the physical body and into the realm of the field of interaction with others. Venus naturally rules the second house (things we value, which can include money) and the seventh house—partnerships (people we "own"—my husband, my girlfriend, my boss, etc.).

Venus Meditation for Self-Harmony

There is nothing worse than being at war with yourself. If we can walk in balance inside, then we are far more able to gain winning friends, lovers, and great business partners on the outside. If we hate ourselves, or parts of ourselves, we directly reflect that insecurity (whether we mean to or not) onto our family, friends, and in our work relationships. How you extend yourself to others is a direct indication of how you feel about yourself. Therefore, this meditation is all about you! Unlike the other meditations given so far in this book, this meditation is something that you will do every day—how long depends on what you wish to work on within yourself. The good thing is it requires only moments of your time and the willingness to make changes in yourself as you go along. What changes depends entirely upon you! This Venus Meditation is a behavior modification technique to help you find and keep the balance you seek!

First, you will need a wall mirror that no one else is going to pay attention to. You might want to hang it in a closet (for now). You will also need a big stack of Post-It Notes and a green candle, representing your future growth. Dress that candle with your Venus aromatic oil. Light the candle. Breathe deeply. Relax. Again. Relax. A third time. Good! Time to write! List all the things you simply hate about yourself—one thing per Post-It Note—however, none of the changes are to be physical (like "I hate my hair, ""I hate my body"—that's for later). Stick the Post-It Notes randomly on the mirror, saying: "I agree I will change this habit." Now. Write all the things that are just "blech" about yourself. Things you let slide. Things you think about changing sometimes, but never get around to it. One item per Post-It Note. Stick them up on the mirror (any place is fine), too. Next, write down the qualities you wish you had, for example: More patience. Move gracefully. Listen to others rather than interrupt. One wish per Post-It Note. Stick them on the mirror! Afraid someone will read what you've written? You can always do it in code, or go through magazines and find pictures that represent the changes you wish to make—that will work, too, and no one will know the difference. Finally, write down three physical changes you would like to make in yourself. Line them up neatly on the left side of the mirror, but not on the mirror.

Hold the green candle in front of you and look at yourself in the mirror. What do you see? Just pieces of you. These are the good pieces (as in the pieces that walk in harmony and interact well with others) that people see every day (even though you might not notice them). Do you see a lot of yourself there? I bet you do! Integrating balance isn't going to be hard at all because there's so much good about you already shining through! Okay! That's all for today! Put your candle out.

Tomorrow we begin to work!

First thing in the morning, go to your secret mirror, close your eyes and run your hands over the papers. Pull off one paper. Open your eyes and read what you have written. For this week you will work on this quality. Use the other meditations in this book to pull the energies in, think about the quality, and find pictures and instances to bring this quality into yourself. Say: "I agree to accept this quality within myself" each morning and evening (indicating the specific behavioral pattern).

Pay attention to the opportunities that Spirit brings you that exhibit what you are looking for. Keep a journal if you think it will help. Remember, we are only working on one quality per week at a time. You can enhance your personal work by using the correspondences listed in the Venus section. For example, for the first quality you pulled off the mirror you may like to make a conjuring bag with Venus herbs and gems, and place that quality into the bag with a lodestone or magnet to draw those energies toward you. You may wish to burn white candles dressed with Venus oil every night—placing the candle on the paper you pulled from the mirror. Use your imagination! Be creative!

At the end of the week, burn your Venus candle for five minutes, and contemplate how much you have changed within the week. If you think you haven't quite mastered it yet, then continue to work on that enhancement throughout the next week. If you believe you are well on the way to change, then move on to the next random Post-It Note on your mirror. Continue to go through all the Post-It Notes in this way. Eventually, you will have removed all the Post-It Notes from the mirror—and guess what else? I bet that you will also be removing one if not all of the physical change Post-It Notes beside the mirror. Change on the inside is reflected on the outside, but until you work with energy like this you may not be aware of how true this really is!

Note: Sometimes you will find an opportunity to work on several qualities or modes of behavior at one time. When I worked through this meditation my list included: modifying my behavior in the way I reacted to stressful situations, learning to carry myself with more grace (I was like a wild zebra in Tiffany's), learning to listen more carefully to what Spirit was telling me, and getting my lazy self out of this house and away from the computer that I dance with almost 24/7. I also wanted to make quality time for my adult children—not that hurry-up-don't-interrupt-me-I'm-working-and-don't-have-the-time.

Good results happened like this:

I pulled a Post-It Note: the grace one. Throughout the week I looked for different opportunities and saw that they had released David Carradine's old television show. Beside the new release were a Tai Chi video and DVD for beginners. Carradine always looked pretty graceful, I thought, so I took the tape and the DVD home. I tried to follow the beautiful people on the beginner's tape for the first week. Argh. I kept getting confused. But, I liked what I saw, so I went on the Internet and starting looking for Tai Chi teachers in my area. The closest one to me was at a women's gym. I hate gyms, but my oldest daughter loves them and was very enthusiastic about checking it out. She almost had to drag me kicking and screaming inside, but once in there, I loved it! The first few weeks of class were tough, because it was something all new to me, but by the end of the month I was really starting to enjoy it and was practicing at home almost every day. After two months I pulled out the tapes and DVDs I'd purchased (I was amassing a collection) and started expanding my practices. By the third month I wasn't moving like a gazelle, but I was feeling better physically, had lost a few pounds around the middle, and had discovered a way to work out my daily stresses with physical meditation. Not only that, but Tai Chi night became the sacred time of the week that I spent entirely with my oldest daughter. Even when Tai Chi class was cancelled once or twice we still met for our usual dinner engagement. Not only was I able to make quality time for a loved one, my self-esteem really improved because I was working on something that required a different environment other than sitting behind a desk all the time. For me, it was a win-win situation that all started with a mirror full of Post-It Notes and a Venus candle.

$\mathcal{M}$ars

Speed and Orbit: Mars orbits 687 Earth days—almost two years—and spends approximately 57.3 days in each sign (not including retrograde periods).

Retrograde: Mars retrogrades every 26 months for 10 weeks (70 days).

Mars Moves: Approximately 0.5 degrees per day, which would be a movement of 30 minutes.

Mars Rules: The astrological sign of Aries (cardinal) and Scorpio (fixed) (classical). Mars is at his most powerful when he is in the signs he rules—Aries and Scorpio.

Mars' Element: Fire and "the fire down below," liquid fire (Scorpio).

Mars' Day: Tuesday

Basic Energy: Action

Basic Meditation and Working: Change, force, movement, and war

Colors: Red and orange

Keywords for Mars: Assertive, combative, constructive, courage, defiant, destruction, dynamic, energy, expressive, fearless, force, frank, heroics, impulsive, leadership, passion, power, pioneering, self-reliant, spontaneity, violent

Mars Invocation for Empowering Items: Mighty Mars of iron will, ferocious force of action and leader of passion, he who empowers the earth with vitality and courage, who brings change in movement, seed this working with your forge of unending strength and shield my enchantments from prying eyes. Wolvish howl of transformation, ruler of Aries, exalted in Capricorn, the element of fire, energies this working! I agree!

Gems: Red jasper, carnelian, tiger iron, red coral, red sardonyx, red agate, red aventurine, tigerskin jasper, fire opal.

Aromatic Herbal Packet: Allspice, galangal, ginger, four o'clock seeds or dragon's blood resin.

Aromatic Oil Blend for Mars Energies: One drop ginger, one drop cinnamon, one drop allspice, three drops cedar.

Mars Loose Meditation Incense: Allspice, basil, cinnamon, and ginger. Add one drop cinnamon oil. Use a wood base for outdoor ritual fires or burn on charcoal tab.

Mars Ink: To red ink add one drop of Mars oil. Swirl. Add a minute amount of dragon's blood resin (pulverized). Swirl. Add one link from a copper chain. Swirl. Empower over a ritual fire.

Additional information: Keep in mind that Mars has two moons, Phobos and Deimos (diameter of fourteen miles and seven miles, respectively), which can actually aid in your meditations. Mars, then, becomes a trinity of energy.

Although all the planets carry and dispense (metaphorically speaking) their own forms of energy, Mars is perhaps the most well known for its definitive skill of powerful activation. The culmination of Mars energy is how we mix our feelings (the moon), and our focus (the sun), into thoughts (or Mercury) and into outward behavior (which can be modified by Venus). Mars is the vehicle we drive all those things around in the outside world. In magick, Mars always means "Action!" Naturally, Mars rules the first house (the self) and the eighth house (death, sex, taxes, other people's money, the occult in some forms, mysteries, and investigation). The sign Mars is visiting tells us the "style" in which that energy will manifest.

Mars Meditation for Appropriate Action— "Just Make It Right"

As you well know, it is incredibly difficult to live a spiritual life given the nature of humanity. In fact, it is so tough that a lot of people give up, but not you. Nope. You are one of the determined ones.

"Just Make It Right" was a magickal tune sung by a very old and dear friend of mine not too long ago. Something incredibly unfortunate occurred in this person's family life. I said, "What do you want us to do?" The person paused, contemplated, then said quietly, "Just make it right." "Done!" I said. "That is precisely what we will work for."

Over the course of that month several other issues popped up where more and more of us were saying to each other, "You know? We agree that the best course of action is actually to just make it right."

Many times we might not want to work to "just make it right" because this statement interferes with our plans, especially if we've gotten greedy over something, or we've managed to tie ourselves into a fix where we know "just make it right" is going to spin balance in our own court as well as where we volley. Also, we may be afraid of the power. "Just make it right" could mean a lot of things if we are talking about simple checks and balances. For example, in a situation where the magickal person is acting as a co-dependent, they may not want to see their sister, father, or husband in a drug rehabilitation center if they have to help put them there; or fear that "just make it right" could mean that immediate karma comes knocking. If Johnny's or Susie's or Kim's Karma Bank is in a negative balance, anything can happen.

On the other hand, "just make it right" energy keeps us (the magickal person) from being judge and jury in any matter, making sure that we don't accuse someone who is innocent, or harm people by accident because we weren't thinking clearly—something that happens in the mundane world every day all over the planet. "Just make it right" does not ever result in friendly fire. Still, "just make it right" isn't something you play with to simply have fun—"just make it right" is an active meditation to use when you need a really big gun.

Which is what Mars energy is all about. Targeted action in the appropriate direction.

This meditation is incredibly simple.

It is also carries great power.

Dress in red from head to toe. Dot a red candle with Mars aromatic oil. Hold the candle close to your heart chakra. Repeat: "Just make it right" several times as well as any other information (who the candle is for, etc.). Put the candle in a safe place to burn. Go for a walk, or to your exercise machine, or march up and down the steps (don't overdo it)— the important thing is that with each step, you say, like a mantra: "Just make it right."

When you are finished, come back to your candle. Sit down. Breathe deeply and evenly until you feel totally relaxed. And then, one last time, say: "I agree it just needs to be made right!" (you can always add "in a positive way," which is what I do).

Does "just make it right" work? An attempted murderer is definitely paying for their crime.

Jupiter

Speed and Orbit: Jupiter orbits approximately 11.9 Earth years (usually rounded to 12 years) spending approximately one full year in each sign.

Retrograde: Once per year for 120 days or approximately 4 months

Jupiter Moves: Approximately 30 degrees per year, or 0.08 degrees per day.

Jupiter Rules: The astrological signs of Sagittarius (mutable) and Pisces (mutable, classical). Jupiter is most powerful when in the sign of Sagittarius or Pisces.

Jupiter's Elements: Fire (Sagittarius) and water (Pisces)

Jupiter's Day: Thursday

Basic Energy: Expansion

Basic Meditation and Working: Growth and spirituality

Colors: Lavender, violet, and purple—sometimes orange

Keywords for Jupiter: Aspiration, benevolent, charitable, confident, dignity, expansion, extravagant, faithful, generous, growth, gullible, human, humorous, indulgence, kindness, merciful, optimistic, orthodox, philanthropic, poise, pompous, radiance, religious, reverent, understanding.

Jupiter Invocation for Empowering Items: Massive Jupiter, powerful ruler of gods and men, he who brings loyalty, generosity and faith from the celestial powers, fill this working with your greatness and good fortune and the freedom I need to create the necessary change in a positive way. Hurl your thunderbolts to create an opening so that my magick may pass the earthly world. Ruler of Pisces and Sagittarius, exalted in Cancer, elements of water and fire, flow and force from the ultimate source! I agree!

SUN AND PLANETARY MEDITATIONS

Gems: Howlite, chrysanthemum stone, amethyst, mahogany obsidian, sugalite, sardonyx, serpentine, tiger's-eye, and old crazy lace agate.

Aromatic Herbal Packet: Clove, hyssop, sarsaparilla, sassafras, nutmeg, and sage.

Aromatic Oil Blend for Jupiter Energies: Two drops honeysuckle, one drop maple, one drop sage, one drop clove.

Jupiter Loose Meditation Incense: To cinquefoil, clove, nutmeg, and sage, add one drop sage or clove oil. Mix with a ground wood base for outdoor ritual fires or burn on incense charcoal tab.

Jupiter Ink: To violet ink (you can mix blue and red together to achieve violet), add one drop Jupiter oil, a minute amount of crushed amethyst (remember face mask and eye protection when crushing), and a minute amount of ground sage. Empower over a mirror or body of reflective water.

Additional information: Jupiter has sixteen known satellites that fall into three groups: inner eight, including the four Galilean moons; the middle four, and the outer four. The Galilean moons are the largest: Io, Europa, Ganymede, and Callisto. This is excellent for any meditation with the number four—including the four elements, the four watchtowers, the four archangels, the four directions, etc., and bringing expansion in from those four directions.

Jupiter is the good fortune planet of the zodiac, encouraging expansion and spirituality. This planet's energy is all about what we expect to gain. His major function is growth—taking what we have and making it bigger. The problem with this is that sometimes you can have too much of a good thing. Because it is a planet of spirituality, it can also be a gateway to our ancestors and the world beyond the veil. Jupiter naturally rules the ninth house, the place of distribution of our energies, publishing, religion, long journeys, higher education and the extension of the law into society. He also co-rules the twelfth house, the place of dreams and visions.

Jupiter Meditation for Ritual Assistance

For this meditation you will need a white candle, a purple candle, a bowl of water, Nag Champa incense, a bell, one coin, a new, white cloth, a pencil or pen and a piece of notebook paper.

Many times we know that we want to do something about a situation, but we are unsure of precisely how to go about it. We can look at ritual books and find great information; but there are occasions when we really feel we have to go with our own intuition. This meditation helps you do just that!

To begin, cleanse your coin in fresh, blessed water, then pass it over a candle flame. Run the coin through the incense, then bury it in graveyard dirt from your ancestors for nine days. That done, you are ready to begin this meditation.

Close your eyes and envision yourself surround by white light. Take three, deep, cleansing breaths. Open your eyes. Dot your white and purple candles with Jupiter oil. Light the candles and place them like a "gateway" in front of you. Between the candles place the bowl of water. You can add an empowered crystal to this bowl for more conductivity if you like. Ring the bell nine times. Repeat the opening conjuration:

The stillness touches deep inside
In silent darkness Mother sighs.
I reach within with breath and light
And conjure Spirit warm and bright.
The primal matter, the fire of mind
Vibrational waves to particles kind
I am the flask, the Witch who brings
The change desired, that curious ring
Of power and magick that must agree
From Earth and Heaven it lies in me.
From black to red, then white to gold
As above and so below
One to two, and two to three
The fourth is One
I do agree!

Place your hands over the water and ask that the spirits of truth and light empower your working. Agree that the correct answers will come to you. Sprinkle your coin with this water. Pat dry with white cloth.

State your purpose clearly and succinctly. For example: "I want to do a working for higher spirituality for myself."

Your coin is a simple "yes/no" vehicle. Heads is yes and tails represents no.

Take three deep, even breaths and relax. Keep the lights low. Soft music can be helpful. Allow yourself to float in a dreamy, light state. If you feel tense or disturbed, the information you receive may be garbled. If you are very upset about something, try one of the other meditations in this book first (or a favorite not listed here).

You can flip the coin to determine which path of power to use (candle magick, herbal magick, visualization, drumming, gem magick, knot magick, sigil magick, etc.).

OR you can add today's date to your birthdate and factor down the numbers:

Let's say your birthday is October 31, 1980. October is the tenth month. $1+0+3+1+1+9+8+0 = 2+3=5$

And today's date is June 21, 2010. $6+2+1+2+0+1+0 = 1+2 = 3$

Add 5 and $3 = 8$

According to the chart below, the best type of magick for today is sigil magick.

One = Candle Magick

Two = Herbal Magick

Three = Visualization

Four = Drumming

Five = Knot Magick

Six = Poppet Magick

Seven = Gem Magick

Eight = Sigil Magick

Nine = Petition Magick

Don't let this simple chart stop you from creating your own. Mine is merely a guideline. Once you have chosen your path of power, you can use the coin to determine what ingredients should go into your working. For example, our number here is eight—sigil magick. Begin considering sigils that you find acceptable.

Pentacle? Throw the coin. Was your answer yes? Then the pentacle should be your focus. Did you receive a no answer? Then go on to the next sigil that comes to mind, perhaps the infinity sign, or runes, or Reiki symbols.

You can make this working very elaborate by adding color, scents, and music by asking the yes/no questions, or you can stop right here, and allow your creativity to take over. This particular meditation is a booster for your brain, to help you move past any confusion on what needs to be done. When you are finished with the coin you can sit back, take several deep, even breaths and close your eyes. Relax and let the information you've put together settle into your psyche. You don't need to push anything. When you are done, open your eyes and thank the universe. You've got a lot of work to do!

Saturn

Speed and Orbit: Saturn orbits approximately 29.5 Earth years to complete its cycle around the chart, spending approximately 2.4 years in each sign.

Retrograde: Saturn retrogrades once per year for 148 days or approximately 5 months.

Saturn Moves: Approximately 12.5 degrees per year or 0.03 degrees per day.

Saturn Rules: The astrological sign of Capricorn (cardinal) and Aquarius (classically, fixed). Saturn is most powerful when visiting Capricorn or Aquarius.

Saturn's Day: Saturday

Basic Energy: Contraction, limits

Basic Meditation and Working: Banishment, rewards, rules and guidelines, enforcement of the law (where Jupiter is the law of spirituality), protection, healing—such as banishing infections (use white candles for this) or closing open wounds (use bloodstone in black conjuring bag and white candle). Incorporate the ankh symbol in your prayers and meditations if you are working someone close to death.

Colors: Black, grey, white, or midnight blue

Keywords for Saturn: Caution, defensive, diplomatic, fearful, humility, justice, law, old, patience, pessimism, respect, responsible, restrain, rigid, serious, severe, sincere, stern, thrifty, time.

Saturn Invocation for Empowering Items: Ancient Saturn, gatekeeper, guard of the crossroads, of bones and the honored dead, he who preserves and guards the astral gates of manifestation, who leads the Lords of Karma and crystallizes that which is needed and removes all negative blocks from my path, grant me the authority required over all legions to manifest my will in a positive way. Ruler of Capricorn, exalted in Libra, element of earth, banish all evil energies that stand in the way of my perfection. I agree! (Note: The word "legions" in this refers to Saturn's eighteen moons.)

Gems: Dumortierite, autumn jasper, brecciated jasper, yellow jasper, malachite, onyx, smokey quartz, black river stone, black tourmaline, black jade, black agate, fossil agate, blue aventurine, blackstone (a jasper), obsidian, and snowflake obsidian.

Saturn Aromatic Herbal Packet: Mullein, patchouli, kava-kava, and lobelia (poisonous). Sometimes grave dirt is added.

Aromatic Oil Blend for Saturn Energies: One drop myrrh, one drop cypress, two drops patchouli.

Saturn Loose Meditation Incense: Patchouli, pine, and cedar. As pine and cedar are already wood bases, you don't need to add an addition one. One drop of patchouli oil. Throw in ritual fire or burn on incense charcoal tab.

Saturn Ink: To black ink add one drop of Saturn oil, a minute amount of ground patchouli, and a very tiny amount of graveyard dirt (from a beloved ancestor's grave). Empower at a crossroads.

Additional information: Saturn has eighteen moons, of which the largest is Titan and is the second largest moon in the solar system (smaller only than Ganymede). Other moons of Saturn are Rhea, Tethys, Dione, Lupetus, Enceladus, and Mimas. The number eighteen factors magickally to the number nine, and as Saturn is "the closer" of the original classical lineup of planets, it should be noted that nine is the number of the dead.

When you think of Saturn, think of a security door. He tries to keep our foibles from overwhelming ourselves and the world. Classically, he is the last gateway before one crosses the veil. His energy is often equated with rewards we have earned, and losses we experience. Saturn has two main functions in magick: to banish and to set (as in setting a spell in the material world). Saturn is also equated with older people, such as grandparents or mentors over fifty. Saturn naturally rules the tenth house, which is the domain of one's career or rewards and losses based on our previous actions. Sometimes Saturn stands for the parent (not necessary the father) that imposes the most rules and limits in the family. He also (classically) co-rules the eleventh house—rewards or losses from the outside world that are tied to your salary, organizations you belong to, as well as your public goals.

Black Salt Recipe

Note: This is not to be ingested. Black salt is usually made at the dark of the moon, or during a banishing moon on a Saturday. Its purpose is to eliminate all negativity (thus the main ingredient of salt and the coloring of black— back to the void). The charcoal used in this recipe is extremely fine and will puff. It will go up your nose, all over the counter top and be a real nuisance, so I suggest that you do your mixing and conjuring out of doors. As you work, repeat the following conjuration:

In thy name, Hecate (or the Morrighan, or Papa Legba, etc.)
Mistress (Master) of the Crossroads,
from the sea and from the grave
from the light and to the shade
from the deed to a deed
Release me.
Evil no more, hate no more, pain no more.
Thou art banished in the eyes of the universe!
I agree!
So mote it be!

Begin with one cup of regular salt in your mortar bowl. (Use an old one, black salt stains). Add to this, a bit at a time, activated charcoal powder which can be purchased through many herbal dealers. When the salt is the color and consistency you desire, add to it one tablespoon of graveyard dirt taken from the graves of seven ancestors. Empower at a crossroads. Keep in an airtight container. Warning: Do not inhale or ingest this mixture while making or conjuring the recipe.

Saturn Colds and Flu Herbal Mix for Conjuring Bags

Combine equal parts of lemon verbena, mistletoe, eucalyptus, lavender, and rosemary. Put in white conjuring bag. Dab with eucalyptus essential oil and three drops Saturn oil. Tie with white ribbon. Empower by the light of a white candle. Hang bag over sick bed.

Herbal Packet to Exorcise Evil

Mix equal parts of dried lime peel, coffee, lavender, red pepper, garlic, black peppercorns, cat's claw, carnation petals, and a bit of copal. Add one moth ball. Dab black conjuring bag with black pepper essential oil. Tie with black ribbon and hang over front door. Note: Please be sure that your pets are not exposed to the moth balls; if the animal ingests them, it is extremely harmful.

Crossroads Meditation for Positive Decision-Making

Many of our more difficult decisions in life seem complicated because several avenues of choice may be open to us, but we're not sure which pathway presents the best energies and opportunities for all involved. Some of us miss positive growth experiences because we fear that we may fail or that our choices may affect others in a negative way that we hadn't counted on. This meditation is to help you make a clear, positive choice for everyone involved.

For this meditation, you must choose a real crossroads. Try to pick one that is not extremely busy, but one where you will be completely safe (this is important!). You may also want to take a notebook and pencil as well as an offering to Spirit that will be placed in the middle of the crossroads (or close to the road) in thanksgiving for the information you need. Be sure you know which road is closest to east, west, north, and south. Where you will not be conspicuous, close your eyes and take several deep, even breaths, in through the nose, exhaling softly out through the mouth. Breathe, if you can, with your diaphragm instead of with your chest. This is a more cleansing way of using sacred breath. In your mind, say: "I agree that I will find the most positive solution and discover the best possible pathway for myself. I look for the answer, now!"

Open your eyes. Note the make, model, color, and number of occupants of the first vehicle that enters the crossroads. Look, too, at the direction whence it came, and which direction it is going. Did it go straight? Did it turn? Did it turn toward the future (left—you may have to change course a bit, because you are about to veer off into uncharted waters) toward the past (right— better back up and think through your plans again because what you think is a step forward is really a step back)? Did it come from behind you (past actions—full speed ahead) or in front of you (opportunity is coming toward you)? Before you leave, say aloud: "Spirit, please open the gateways that are the best for me to walk through, and close those gateways that will serve me no good." Leave your offering. For even more information, drive on the same road that your divinatory vehicle did for one mile. Note anything odd or unusual in that mile. Is there construction? Does the area seem prosperous, decadent? Add this information to your notebook as well.

Take your notes home and put them under your pillow. Light a white candle dressed with Saturn oil for seven minutes each night for seven days. Place your conjuring bag beside the candle while the taper or votive burns. Give yourself at least seven days to digest the information you've been given. By then you will most likely find a clear pathway of appropriate action. Remember that Saturn's natural number is seven; therefore, you will most likely receive results in seven days, fourteen days, or twenty-one days.

> *Uncrossing Aromatic Oil Blend:* One drop bay essential oil, one drop lemon essential oil, two drops rose fragrance, one drop camphor essential oil, one drop cinnamon essential oil. This mixture is used if you feel someone is targeting you with evil or negative intent, or if you've simply had a run of bad luck and are looking for a change in fortune.

> *Uncrossing Aromatic Herbal Blend:* Mix equal parts of: bay leaves, dried lemon peel, dried rose petals, and dried rosemary. Add several cinnamon sticks. Mix. Blend in three to six drops uncrossing magickal oil. Use in gris-gris bags, around candles, or as loose potpourri in an afflicted room.

The Three Outer Planets

The following three "outer" planets are not in the original classical lineup; therefore, they are not associated with particular days (though some modern occultists have chosen their own). These planets move very slowly throughout the heavens. When associating with the inner planets (the sun, moon, Mercury, Venus, and Mars) the effect of their energy moves faster due to the quicker speed of the inner planets. When associating with Jupiter or Saturn (sometimes called the social planets), the effects are a little longer in coming. When carrying on a dialogue among themselves (Uranus, Neptune, and Pluto), the effects are sometimes slow to manifest.

The three outer planets, Uranus, Neptune, and Pluto, are not classically popular in their realm of magickal use due to the recent histories of discovery. Uranus was discovered March 13, 1781; Neptune on September 24, 1846; and Pluto on February 18, 1930. The body of data, then, especially for Pluto, is not as expansive as that of the other planets. This does not mean that we haven't measured their energy effect, nor that we can't use them in magick and meditation. We do know enough about how they behave at this point to work them into our magickal applications. The only thing we need to remember is:

a) They are slower-moving heavenly bodies, and therefore applications for which the energies are employed may take longer to manifest. To get around this, you can modify their energy behavior with the energies of the faster moving planets.

b) When change does occur from the use of this energy, the results stand longer—so do be careful.

Uranus

Speed and Orbit: Uranus takes approximately 84 Earth years to complete a cycle. Spends approximately 7 years in each sign.

Retrograde: Retrogrades once per year for 148 days or approximately 5 months.

Uranus Moves: Approximately 4.3 degrees per year or 0.01 degrees per day.

Uranus Rules: The astrological sign of Aquarius (fixed). Co-rules with Saturn. Uranus is most powerful when in Aquarius.

Uranus' Element: Air

Basic Energy: Intensity

Colors: Electric blue, silver, lavender, very light green

Keywords for Uranus: Individual, eccentric, electric, unique, extraordinary, explosion, earth shattering, individual, jolt, independence, light-years, shock, and energetic.

Uranus Invocation for Empowering Items: Uranus! Celestial being of spectacular high-powered performance! Hear me! Hear me! Hear me! Instill this working with positive, awesome, explosive energy! Warp and weave of eleven looms of light and twenty-one blessings of creativity that scatter extraordinary uniqueness across the skies like pearls lifted from the sea. Flagship of individuality, exalted in Scorpio, ruler of Aquarius, element of electric air and digitized water—reveal thy power in this working! I agree!

Gems: Teketites

Uranus Aromatic Herbal Packet: Hyssop, basil, kava-kava, rosemary, and lavender.

Aromatic Oil Blend for Uranus Energies: One drop basil, one drop lavender, one drop clove, two drops tangerine, one drop spearmint, two drops honeysuckle.

Uranus Loose Meditation Incense: Hyssop, basil, rosemary, and lavender with one drop of Uranus oil. Add to ground cherry chip wood base for outdoor ritual fires, or burn on incense tab.

Uranus Ink: To violet or silver ink in a four-dram bottle, add one drop Uranus oil, a quartz crystal chip (or ground crystal—use eye protection and face mask), and a very minute amount of salt peter.

Additional information: Uranus has twenty-one moons—a master number. Some astrologers believe that Uranus is the higher octave of Mercury. Titania is the largest moon, Cordelia and Ophelia are Shepard moons straddling the Epsilon ring. Uranus has eleven rings—another master number. Remember, eight is the mastery of skills, eleven is the mastery of self, and twenty-one is the mastery of your higher being.

Uranus is the planet of "more power, more power, more power." The popular sitcom *Home Improvement*, which featured Tim "the Tool Man" Taylor, is indicative of Uranus action. Sudden, huge, blow-up stuff. Wicked intense. With a breathless "Sweet!" afterward, if you tempted the Fates unscathed. Uranus is techno and up-to-date, individual and eccentric. It is the "I-want-to-stand-out-from-the-crowd" energy. It would be happier if Saturn was not a part of the lineup of planets. Uranus rules the eleventh house—the place of crowds, oddly enough. Some astrologers believe that Uranus is the higher octave of Mercury—and that can be true, if the energy is used wisely.

Uranus Drumming Meditation for Self-Mastery

What better way to use the incredible power of Uranus energy than in working for your own self-mastery? Mastery is what well-placed Uranus energy is all about. Taking your personal power and creating individualistic head-above-the-rest energies to a point of excellence and then giving your skills to the group mind at large in an effort to better the human condition.

You can do it!

One of the most exciting ways to work with Uranus energy is through drumming, and don't think you need to go out and buy an expensive drum. Last year, at one of our healing circles, I'd lent all my drums to the other participants. I was cooking the steaks on the grill, but I wanted to join in, too. I took my wooden cooking instruments, closed the lid of the grill, and joined right in! Talk about sound and fire! Oooh, baby! And whoever heard of someone drumming on a big grill? It certainly was Uranus!

If you own a drum, you've probably already done drum trancing, but if you don't? This is just the coolest magick in the world! You've got to try it! Drum trancing is simply drumming at letting yourself go. At first you will feel stupid, then all of a sudden—man, you are somewhere else! You are at the still point and you have created an amazing field of sound and rhythm. It is then the magick begins!

You can drum anywhere on anything. When my kids were in school and in special activities, I, like a zillion other parents, had to wait, and wait, and wait (because school systems have no concept of time and how valuable yours may be). Many an afternoon and evening, you'd find me sitting in the parking lot, bored stiff. At first, I was really frustrated. What were they doing in there? Finally, one day, I turned on the radio and started drumming on the steering wheel. (No! I am not musically inclined—can't read a note.) As I drummed, I thought of things I wanted to get done, things I wanted to change within myself . . . you name it. I made up little rhymes in my head that suited what I was trying to accomplish. Yeah—I received strange looks, but today, I have nineteen books published.

I so much believe that drumming can literally change your life that I bought several drums of all shapes and sizes as I could afford them and encouraged my students to use them here at our rituals and healing circles.

My husband and I often carried drums with us on tour, encouraging people who had never touched a drum to experience the thrill without condemnation. Students who train with me have to learn to use the drum in magick as a requirement. I still can't read music. I still can't keep a good beat, but I sure do whomp up the magick!

Drum on an empty trash can. Drum on the kitchen counter with your hands. Drum on the washing machine with hangers. (That's interesting.) Drum on a bowl of empowered water with wooden cooking spoons. (That's cool.) Drum on the bottom of a big kitchen pot with dowel rods or even better, 13-inch pieces of broom sticks. In fact, you can drum on the floor with those broomsticks! Can't keep a beat? Neither can I, but it doesn't stop me! When I pour candles, I drum on the candle molds with copper sticks. And all the time I make up crazy rhymes—stuff that is just a hoot that I can't print. Sorry!

It works.

You try.

Dare ya!

Uranus—sound and motion for a truly marvelous meditation that is totally your own!

Neptune

Speed and Orbit: Neptune takes approximately 165 Earth years to complete a cycle and spends approximately 13.8 years in each sign.

Retrograde: Neptune retrogrades once per year for 150 days or approximately 6 months.

Neptune Moves: Approximately 2.1 degrees per year, or 0.005 degrees per day.

Neptune Rules: The astrological sign of Pisces (mutable) co-ruling with Jupiter. Neptune is most powerful when in Pisces.

Neptune's Element: Water

Basic Energy: Illusion

Basic Meditation and Working: Unfettered creativity, protective camouflage, glamouries.

Colors: Sea green, muted greens and blues, turquoise

Keywords for Neptune: Dreamy, creative, conspiracy, misconception, gossip, camouflage, altered perception, chaos, stormy, foggy, concealed, illusion, fantasy, bait and switch

Neptune Invocation for Empowering Items: Neptune! Ruler of the seas of the collective unconscious, bringer of dreams and visions, giver of profound wave upon wave of alluring creativity—Bless me with glittering inspiration of positive poetry in motion! Fill my work with spellbinding enchantment! Instill delightful captivation! Neptune energy ebb and flow, make my work the best of show! Neptune! Exalted in Cancer, ruler of Pisces, element of empowered water let me dance upon the gleaming waves of creativity to bring the mystical magick home! I agree!

Gems: Anything from the sea (shells, coral, pearls), blue agate, bloodstone (thought to provide invisibility to the wearer).

Neptune Aromatic Herbal Packet: Bladderwrack, mugwort, lavender, rose, eyebright, and orris. Specifically for divination: damiana (poisonous), patchouli, orris, myrrh, broom (poisonous), eyebright, and cedar.

Aromatic Oil Blend for Neptune Energies: One drop sandalwood, One drop gardenia, three drops carnation. For divination: three drops patchouli, one drop myrrh, one drop cinnamon, one drop carnation.

Neptune Loose Meditation Incense: To sandalwood, eyebright, orris, and myrrh, add one drop of Neptune or Neptune divination oil. As sandalwood is already a wood base, no others need be added. Burn in ritual fire outdoors or on incense charcoal tab.

Neptune Ink: Some practitioners use invisible ink that they purchase at novelty shops. Others mix half and half green and blue into a four-dram bottle.

Additional information: Neptune has eight moons with Triton as the largest, which is actually bigger than Pluto and moves in a retrograde motion—now that ought to tell ya something!

Neptune is what dreams and visions are made of, and if you are a creative person, on the surface this is a wonderful thing. Glamourie magick is definitely ruled by Neptunian influences, and so is meditation, vision questing, automatic writing, "spirits" of all manner and form, divination, and fears. Neptune is the realm of the dream vacation, the dream career, the dream home, and the dream lover. Neptune does not understand, nor will it ever admit that the word "reality" exists. With Neptune, the world is full of ethereal colors, amazing sights, and delicate to horrific sounds that pop in and out in a rainbow fashion. In its more unfortunate sense, Neptune is the king of drugs, alcohol, and mind-altering herbs. Neptune is the fog that makes life liveable through wise, creative pursuits and a dense, cloying darkness if we cannot keep the field of reality in sight. Neptune naturally rules the twelfth house, a place of dreams and visions, hidden enemies, and modes of oppression (jail, large corporations, institutions, hospitals, critical illness) and in some situation, the field of the "mysteries."

Neptune Meditation for Creativity (No Matter the Subject)

Creativity isn't limited to writing, painting, dance, or poetry—the standard "arts" as we know them. People in all walks of life use their creativity from building the Mars space station to designing a new method of plumbing. Even the most mundane items we handle every day (like toothpaste) had their "time" of creativity and their additional periods of improvement. Although Neptunian energy can often exhibit its more seamy side in our day-to-day lives, we can channel that force into something truly magnificent and beneficial! Remember, it's all how you use it!

Neptune energy is all about looking outside of the box—about allowing ourselves to think beyond normal limitations. First, consider where you need to apply your creativity. For example, let's say you are building a race car engine and you need creative help on your design. If you had to choose who would be the most unlikely person to assist you, who would you come up with? Choose the very first person, animal, or object that comes to mind. The very first. Let's say you thought of a little old lady with a shawl and a pocketbook bigger than her head. Good, you are already thinking outside of the box. First, I want you to take a plain white envelope, put a few Neptune herbs in it and maybe a gem or two. Seal it. Dot it with magickal Neptune oil. On the outside of the envelope, write: "A gift for you." Put the envelope under your pillow.

Now, we're going to go into meditation!

Sit in a quiet place at a quiet time. Take several deep breaths. At this stage, say to yourself: "I agree to invite creativity into my life in a positive way." Count down from ten to one and when you reach number one, think of yourself in the area where you do all your work—the place that relies on your creative thinking or solution. In front of you is a great big set of doors. They sort of magickally appear even though you've never seen them in that area before. Above those doors are the words "Expert Creative Advice." And beside the doors is a big sign that says: "Push Button for Creative Service."

Push the button.

The doors slide open.

And lo and behold, it is our own little old lady with the shawl, orthopedic shoes, and huge purse. Allow her to introduce herself. You can introduce yourself as well. She has come here to help, so don't be combative. Instead, state your problem and why you need assistance. After a bit of conversation (where she may give you sage advice or not.) she will open up her purse and bring out a white envelope. On the envelope it says "A gift for you." Then she says: "This will solve all of your problems!" and smiles.

Tell her thank you and give her blessings.

Take three deep breaths and open your eyes.

Perhaps you already have those creative juices flowing and you want to get right to work. If not, don't worry. Sleep on it. The next morning, just as you are waking up, say to yourself: "I agree to make this an incredibly rewarding and creative day!" Then get up and carefully fold the envelope and take it with you wherever you go. Soon enough, you'll feel a dynamic surge of creativity and off you'll go!

When I first practiced this meditation years ago the person who came to mind was Albert Einstein. And here I am today, talking about quantum physics, magick, and meditation. You just never know! The last time I used this meditation was in the writing of this book. I did the meditation, then began writing furiously. After a bit, I added up my words—3,000! Wow. Gee, I thought, it must be really late. I turned and looked at my grandfather clock. Only one hour had passed. Just one single hour. No more.

℘luto

Speed and Orbit: It takes approximately 248 Earth years for Pluto to complete a cycle. Pluto spends 20.6 years in each sign.

Retrograde: Pluto retrogrades once per year for approximately 6 months. People often leave magickal groups (or join them) right before a retrogradation or as soon as the retrogradation is open—as if there are two windows per year in the choice of spirituality.

Pluto Moves: Approximately 1.4 degrees per year or 0.0003 degrees per day.

Pluto Rules: The astrological sign of Scorpio (fixed), co-ruling with Mars. Pluto is most powerful when in Scorpio.

Pluto's Element: Fire and ice or fire and water (both apply)

Basic Energy: Empowerment

Basic Meditation and Working: Change through empowerment—miracle energy, quantum thought.

Colors: Brown, mahogany, cinnamon, red, white

Keywords for Pluto: Empowerment, miracles, pattern, strategy, increased perception, resourceful, possibility, dynamic.

Pluto Invocation for Empowering Items: Pluto! Centerfield of intricate pattern that brings the world to manifest, lend me your aid! Fill my work with compelling excellence combined with bewitching strategy! Infuse the day with resourceful perception and coalesce with legendary success! Pluto! Lord of Personal Empowerment, exalted in Aries, Ruler of Scorpio, leader of blazing fire and liquid molten, create the amazing pattern I desire and manifest my will! I agree!

Gems: Tiger iron, red jasper, quartz crystal

Pluto Aromatic Herbal Packet: Horehound, spearmint, four o'clock seeds, calamus, ginger, and frankincense.

Aromatic Oil Blend for Pluto Energies: Three drops violet, one drop lilac, two drops honeysuckle, one drop myrrh, one drop cinnamon, one drop ginger.

Pluto Loose Meditation Incense: Ginger, cinnamon, sandalwood, lemon peel, eucalyptus, and ginseng.

Pluto Ink: Four-dram bottle of brown ink with one drop of Pluto oil. Swirl. Steep with one tiger iron bead for seven days. Then add a minute amount of crushed 4 o'clock seeds. Swirl. Empower at 4 a.m., when it is said that all the positive energies of the world come together for appropriate empowerment and change.

Additional information: Pluto has one moon which is actually its partner, Charon (not to be confused with Chiron, the comet). Where Pluto is covered with frozen methane, Charon is covered with frozen water. Therefore, Pluto energy is a pattern maker—a snapshot or a "still," the manifestation of the design at the zero point. Photography is usually exceptional in quality with Plutonian aspects/transits in the heavens.

Pluto naturally rules the eighth house—the house of great depth. I call it "the house of fire down below." To me, Pluto is the volcano under the sea that creates the tsunami. Pluto is all about personal empowerment and how we can investigate ourselves and our own behavior to become better, more balanced, happier individuals by our willingness to dig deep and change ourselves. Other eighth house correspondences include sex, death, taxes, other people's money, investigation on any matter, healing ourselves and others, and certain areas of the occult. Pluto allows us to bring energies into perspective.

Pluto Empowerment Meditation

Pluto is a magnificent energy that allows one to let go of restrictive and worn-out behaviors, making space to build complete and brand-new life patterns. Pluto is the djinn of the zodiac. He has the power to create and the power to destroy. Most of all, he has the ability to "empower." Plutonian energy also seems to adore the power in art, particularly photographic skill.

This active meditation includes the use of fifteen cowry shells, dried beans, or pebbles, as well as two candles in the color that you feel is most empowering to you. One candle stands for the planet Pluto and the other for its moon, Charon. Choose a time and place where you will not be disturbed. Dot the candle (if you like) with Pluto oil. Light both candles.

Hold the shells or pebbles in your hands. Take several deep, even breaths. Close your eyes and allow yourself to become totally relaxed. Once you have reached that still point where no thoughts about the day or your desires interfere, say "This is the pattern of my empowerment," and throw the stones or shells onto a flat surface. Take note of the pattern, but do not try to make any assumptions about the shape or how it applies to your life at this time. Close your eyes and visualize that you are out in space, pulling the empowerment of Pluto and its moon into yourself. Take three deep breaths and open your eyes.

Next, take a good photograph of the pattern you have thrown. If you don't have a good digital camera, you may wish to turn on the lights to ensure a good snapshot. Allow the candles to burn through to completion if you can. Develop the picture on your computer or take it to a film processing store. Tack the picture up in a place where you will look at it often. Think to yourself—this is the symbol of my empowerment! This is my signature symbol for my positive growth! This symbol will help me let go of things that aren't good for me in a positive way, and in that empty spot, new growth and joy will flourish!

The Emerald Tablet Exercise

The Emerald Tablet of Hermes is considered the original impetus of Hermetic philosophy and divine alchemy. According to legend, the text was carved on emerald tablets by someone unknown (attributed to the name Hermes) and placed in the King's Chamber of the Great Pyramid of Cheops. No one is sure of the original language and the Latin translation became known as the Key to the Mysteries by the tenth century. Indeed, it is from Egyptian magicks and Hermetic philosophy that most modern-day Pagan religions find their roots. Although we have masked and massaged our practices to such a point that a strong line to the past is blurred in our daily activities, the ultimate principle works just as it did thousands of years ago.

The Emerald Tablet, simply put, is a key to activating science—the art of quantum physics. This exercise represents a lesson in activating the power within yourself and merging that spark of divine with that which runs the universe to accomplish the purpose you indicate. It is thought that if one works with, and completely understands, the Emerald Tablet that he or she will hold the key to the universe.

There are numerous translations over the centuries by some of the greatest philosophers of history. Here is one translation of the Emerald Tablet. Read through it once to "set" the overall idea, then I suggest reading these same words every single day. Every time I read it, I find new meaning—an incredible occult puzzle of quantum proportions!

Truly, without Deceit, certainly and absolutely—

That which is Below corresponds to that which is Above, and that which is Above corresponds to that which is Below, in the accomplishment of the Miracle of One Thing.

And, just as all things have come from One, through the Mediation of One, so all things follow from this One Thing in the same way.

Its Father is the Sun.

Its Mother is the Moon.

The Wind has carried it in his Belly.

Its Nourishment is the Earth.

It is the Father of every completed Thing in the whole World.

Its strength is intact if it is turned towards the Earth.

Separate the Earth by Fire: the fine from the gross, gently, and with great skill.

It rises from Earth to Heaven, and then it descends again to the Earth, and receives Power from Above and from Below. Thus you will have the Glory of the whole World. All obscurity will be clear to you. This is the strong Power of all Power because it overcomes everything fine and penetrates everything solid.

In this way was the World created. From this there will be amazing Applications, because this is the Pattern. Therefore am I called Thrice Greatest Hermes, having the three parts of the Wisdom of the whole World.

The second time you read the Emerald Tablet, change "That which is below corresponds to that which is above" to "That which is inward corresponds to that which is outward" and think about the two hemispheres of the brain I told you about, and how when the gateway is open and the two hemispheres are communicating simultaneously (the still point) manifestation occurs.

Takes on a whole new meaning, doesn't it?

Let's work through this passage in a new way (and no, I'm not re-translating it, it is so beautiful as it is, we're just changing our perception). Ready?

I agree—

That which is inward corresponds to that which is outward, and that which is outward corresponds to that which is inward and these agreements must work together to create the whole. When the whole is created, perfection is reached. Just as all things come from me, through my inner thoughts and outer actions, so all things in the world are manifested in the same manner. Everyone is capable of this manifestation.

For my desire to occur my will must be in agreement with my emotions, and my thoughts must be in agreement with my physical self. This combined power manifests my chi (the combined mixture of my personal energy) which is thought to be seated in my solar plexus area. By taking deep breaths and breathing properly, I can enhance my personal power, especially if I take the time each day to be still and practice. These agreements create my reality. My thoughts have power only if the agreement remains intact, is sent outward from within myself, and then taken back into myself through the gateway. This gateway must be free of my ego. Once I have internalized the power within, combined with my power of that which is without, then can I manifest anything I desire, by sending the energy back through the gateway one last time. This energy overcomes any difficulty and is manifest on all planes.

In this way was the World created. From this there will be amazing Applications because this is the Pattern. Therefore there are three parts to any manifestation.

Physicist Moray B. King, in his book *Tapping the Zero-Point Energy,* cites several reasons for the inability of conventional technology to detect what he calls "zero-point energy."

+ It is incoherent.

+ The energy is everywhere. Its detection requires measuring an energy difference.

+ Less than one quantum of energy is cohered at any one node.

+ It flows orthogonally to our space (virtual).

+ It rapidly changes frequency. Linear detectors cannot resonate coherently with it to follow signal.

+ The very high frequencies do not readily interact with matter.

Historically, awareness of this energy is anything but new. Pythagoras called it *pneuma*. Later it was called *od* by Von Reichenbach, *animal magnetism* by Mesmer, *vital force* by Hahnemann (the founder of homeopathy), and *ether* by pre-Relativity physicists. Lately, the Russians have been referring to it as *bioplasma*, and even George Lucas in *Star Wars* called it *the Force*. Post-Relativity physicists like David Bohm now postulate its existence and call it *the superquantum field*.

Stop waiting for life to happen. Live in the moment and own your glory! Magick is only science, after all. You can turn it on—or you can turn it off.

The choice alone is up to you.

MindLight . . . defines *your* world.

Silver RavenWolf

Creating Magickal Oils

What Is a Magickal Oil?

A magickal oil is the mixture of plant or resin essential oil created by varying processes (pressing, boiling, simmering, or fermentation), fragrance (which is sometimes synthetic and on other occasions pre-cut essentials)—or both. Fragrances and essentials are housed in what is called a carrier oil. This oil literally carries the scent as pure essentials or fragrances are too powerful in aroma for daily use and can sometimes be considered a health hazard in pure form—such as wintergreen essential. Pregnant women should not work with essential oils.

The quality of the carrier makes or breaks any perfume or magickal oil and is thus considered an extremely important ingredient—just as valuable as the essential or fragrance. Although most people think only of the scent—it is the carrier that actually determines the worth of the oil. There are many carriers on the market today from inexpensive (grape seed oil) to real pocket-book crunchers like jojoba (in 2005, the current market price for a gallon of jojoba is over two hundred dollars). By rule (though products can differ) the more expensive the carrier, the longer the shelf-life and the better grade of the oil. Grape seed may last only three months where jojoba has a 100-year shelf life as long as it is not subjected to intense heat, sunlight, or cold. Jojoba is *Simmondsia chinensis*, a chemically waxy ester that is derived from a desert plant and is a smooth, non-greasy formula. Of all the oils currently available it is the closest to sebum, your own natural skin oil, rich in vitamin E, has the most carrying power for the essential or fragrance, and has an extremely long shelf-life. To our knowledge it is considered the safest carrier on the market, both people and pet friendly. When working with essentials, the rule of thumb is to use ten times the weight of the essential. For example, if you used one drop of patchouli essential you would add ten drops of carrier. To be safe and regulate aroma, up to 25 or more drops of carrier can be used.

Where Do Magickal Oil Recipes Come From?

Magickal oils are extremely popular in ritual and spellcasting as their aroma is thought to trigger personal energy patterns as well as work in sympathy with your purpose. The more you work with a particular magickal scent, the faster the blend will work for you! Energy patterns of essentials and fragrances are chosen with great care to ensure that they match the overall intent of the oil. For example, you wouldn't want to choose an essential that carries active Mars energy for an oil designed for relaxation and stress reduction. Correspondences for the compendium of recipes currently on the market were developed from folk lore, old grimoires, planetary associations, and personal experimentation. Once developed and proven to work well, oil formulas are notoriously guarded by the practitioner—just like the famous perfume blends developed by current designers in that industry. As some essentials and fragrances are stronger than others, you will find that each formula contains one heartbeat essential or fragrance which will overpower other ingredients unless it is used in modification. One drop of cypress, patchouli, vetivert, basil, hyssop, etc., is all that is needed to carry through the entire oil. No more than one drop of cinnamon or wintergreen should ever be used as they can be harmful to the skin in large doses. Always check the tox level of any essential if you are mixing oils on your own, as some essentials can be harmful to pregnant women if not used properly. The more essentials in an oil formula, the more expensive it is likely to be.

Fragrances are extremely popular in magickal oils because body-safe formulas can be easily obtained, and because most essentials do not carry a sweet, aromatic odor. Fragrances are used to enhance the practitioner's mental state, blending a sometimes harsh fragrance into a more pleasing formula.

Care of Your Magickal Oil

Your magickal oil is a tool—like a wand, an herb, or a sigil, the pattern of the oil is developed to meet a specific or general need of the magickal practitioner. Keep oils in a cool (not cold), dark area when storing for best product consistency. Magickal oils are never, ever meant to be ingested. If this somehow occurs, call your Poison Control Center immediately. Always cap oil tightly after use, and be sure to wash hands after every application. If you are prone to allergic reactions, always test an oil before liberal use. Oils should be treated with respect. A magickal oil should be empowered every thirty days for six months to keep the formula at top energy performance.

How to Empower Your Magickal Oil

Simple empowerment involves holding the bottle of oil in your hands and asking your choice of divinity to bestow a blessing. Then, holding the bottle out to the four directions (beginning normally at the north for manifestation, or the east, following the path of the sun), ask that the powers of the directions also bless and consecrate the bottle. If the designer oil is of a specific nature (such as Just Judge, Jinx Removal, etc.), you may wish to be more specific in the blessing you request. Uncap bottle. Hold your hands over bottle and again request blessings from Spirit (or a specific deity) and then say: "I conjure thee, O essence of oil and essential, fragrance and herb, to do my bidding in a positive way. Let thee not be detained by any negativity and fly they energy straight to the need as I so desire!" Stir the oil three times clockwise with dropper, and say: "I know you will do this for me! It is done!" Blessings are often intoned while the oil is being used as well—such as when a gris-gris bag or statue is anointed. Be sure to thank Spirit any and every time you use a magickal oil or any other blessed tool.

Many popular craft books include instructions on cleansing, consecration, and empowerment. If you are unsure of how to use your oil, you may find my book *Solitary Witch* extremely helpful in your work.

Anointing Oil Blend Recipe

Combine one drop essential mint, one drop essential lavender, one drop essential rosemary, and one drop essential lemon with three drops rose fragrance and six drams jojoba carrier oil. Shake well. Add one dried rose petal in the bottle. Cap tightly. Empower under a full moon. Remove rose petal after seven days. Use for general blessings and anointing objects and tools.

How to Use a Magickal Oil in Spellcasting and Ritual

Anoint candles. Rub from the outside in to the center to draw energies toward you—rub from the center out to send unwanted energies away from you. Anoint magickal tools in the same manner. Dot gems and stones and place in the moonlight for greater power. Rub on hands briskly (if you do not have allergies) to encourage energy flow through all the major chakras of your body. Be sure to check the ingredients of the oil to ensure it is body safe. Anoint your altar by dotting with a pentacle design to consecrate the surface or focus on a specific working. Anoint your shrine or holy statues intoning the Eightfold Blessing:

> *Blessed be my feet that walk the path of spiritual service.*
> *Blessed be my knees that kneel at the sacred altar.*
> *Blessed be my womb (phallus) that gives forth life.*
> *Blessed be my heart formed in beauty and strength.*
> *Blessed be my lips that speak only truth and wisdom.*
> *Blessed be my eyes so that I may clearly perceive my destiny.*
> *May I be cleansed, consecrated and regenerated in the service of humankind.*

Draw sigils on doors, windows, and other objects. Place a bit of oil on your fingertip and draw the sigil on the object. It is okay if you run out of oil as the essence continues through the design. Add to your own magickal powders or herb mixes. Add a few drops at a time, mix thoroughly with wooden spoon, allow to dry. If the aroma remains overnight, then the powder or herb is holding the scent and you can store in a glass container—no plastic. Anoint conjuring or gris-gris bags. Three drops is usually enough. Add a few drops to your simmering potpourri pot. Sprinkle on logs before lighting magickal bonfire. Be careful. Oil is flammable. Stand back and toss with any large amount if the fire is already burning. A bonfire oil magick ritual is truly inspiring! Anoint petitons to deity. Add to holy water. If you want a clean blend, use an emulsifier (follow instructions on emulsifier label).

Planetary Hours

The selection of an auspicious time for beginning a magickal working is an important matter. When a thing is begun, its existence takes on the nature of the conditions under which it was begun. Each hour of the day is ruled by a planet and takes on the attributes of that planet. You will notice that planetary hours do not take into account Uranus, Neptune, and Pluto, as they are considered here as higher octaves of Mercury, Venus, and Mars, respectively. For example, if something is ruled by Uranus, you can use the hour of Mercury. The only other factor you need to know to use the planetary hours is the time of your local sunrise and sunset for any given day, available from your local newspaper. Note: Your sunrise and sunset time may vary from the example if you live in a different location. Your latitude/longitude are already figured into your local paper's sunrise and sunset times.

Step One. From your local paper, find the sunrise and sunset times for your location and your chosen day. We will use January 2, 1999, 10 degrees latitude, as an example. Sunrise for January 2, 1999, at 10 degrees latitude is at 6 hours and 16 minutes (or 6:16 a.m.) and sunset is at 17 hours and 49 minutes (or 5:49 p.m.).

Step Two. Subtract sunrise time (6 hours 16 minutes) from sunset time (17 hours 49 minutes) to get the number of astrological daylight hours. It is easier to do this if you convert the hours into minutes. For example, 6 hours and 16 minutes equals 376 minutes. 17 hours and 49 minutes equals 1,069 minutes. Now subtract: 1,069 minutes minus 376 minutes equals 693 minutes.

Step Three. Next you should determine how many minutes are in a day-light planetary hour for that particular day. To do this, divide 693 minutes (the number of daylight minutes) by 12. The answer is 58, rounded off. Therefore, a daylight planetary hour for January 2, 1999, at 10 degrees latitude has 58 minutes.

Step Four. Now you know that each daylight planetary hour is roughly 58 minutes. You also know, from step one, that sunrise is at 6:16 a.m. To determine the starting times of each planetary hour, simply add 58 minutes to the sunrise time for the first planetary hour, 58 minutes to that number for the second planetary hour, etc. Therefore, the first hour in our example is 6:16 a.m.–7:14 a.m. The second hour is 7:14 a.m.–8:12 a.m., and so on. Note that because you rounded up the number of minutes in a sunrise hour, the last hour doesn't end exactly at sunset. This is a good reason to give yourself a little "fudge space" when using planetary hours. (You could also skip the rounding-up step.)

Step Five. Now, to determine which sign rules which daylight planetary hour, consult your calendar to determine which day of the week January 2 falls on. You'll find it's a Saturday in 1999. Next, see page 247 to find the sunrise planetary hour chart. If you follow down the column for Saturday, you will see that the first hour is ruled by Saturn, the second by Jupiter, the third by Mars, and so on.

Step Six. Now you've determined the daytime (sunrise) planetary hours. You can use the same formula to determine the nighttime (sunset) planetary hours, using sunset as your beginning time and sunrise the next day as your end time. When you get to step 5, remember to consult the sunset table on page 248 rather than the sunrise table.

Planetary Hours

Sunrise

HOUR	SUNDAY	MONDAY	TUESDAY	WEDNESDAY	THURSDAY	FRIDAY	SATURDAY
1	Sun	Moon	Mars	Mercury	Jupiter	Venus	Saturn
2	Venus	Saturn	Sun	Moon	Mars	Mercury	Jupiter
3	Mercury	Jupiter	Venus	Saturn	Sun	Moon	Mars
4	Moon	Mars	Mercury	Jupiter	Venus	Saturn	Sun
5	Saturn	Sun	Moon	Mars	Mercury	Jupiter	Venus
6	Jupiter	Venus	Saturn	Sun	Moon	Mars	Mercury
7	Mars	Mercury	Jupiter	Venus	Saturn	Sun	Moon
8	Sun	Moon	Mars	Mercury	Jupiter	Venus	Saturn
9	Venus	Saturn	Sun	Moon	Mars	Mercury	Jupiter
10	Mercury	Jupiter	Venus	Saturn	Sun	Moon	Mars
11	Moon	Mars	Mercury	Jupiter	Venus	Saturn	Sun
12	Saturn	Sun	Moon	Mars	Mercury	Jupiter	Venus

Planetary Hours

Sunset

HOUR	SUNDAY	MONDAY	TUESDAY	WEDNESDAY	THURSDAY	FRIDAY	SATURDAY
1	Jupiter	Venus	Saturn	Sun	Moon	Mars	Mercury
2	Mars	Mercury	Jupiter	Venus	Saturn	Sun	Moon
3	Sun	Moon	Mars	Mercury	Jupiter	Venus	Saturn
4	Venus	Saturn	Sun	Moon	Mars	Mercury	Jupiter
5	Mercury	Jupiter	Venus	Saturn	Sun	Moon	Mars
6	Moon	Mars	Mercury	Jupiter	Venus	Saturn	Sun
7	Saturn	Sun	Moon	Mars	Mercury	Jupiter	Venus
8	Jupiter	Venus	Saturn	Sun	Moon	Mars	Mercury
9	Mars	Mercury	Jupiter	Venus	Saturn	Sun	Moon
10	Sun	Moon	Mars	Mercury	Jupiter	Venus	Saturn
11	Venus	Saturn	Sun	Moon	Mars	Mercury	Jupiter
12	Mercury	Jupiter	Venus	Saturn	Sun	Moon	Mars

Basic Astrological Glossary

Air Signs: Gemini, Libra, and Aquarius are the three signs of the zodiac attributed to the qualities of the element of air. Also known as the air triplicity, Libra is the cardinal (or starter sign), Aquarius is the fixed energy sign, and Gemini is the mutable (flowing) air sign. Each behaves differently in magickal and meditational work. These signs are strongest when visited by the moon (which reflects the energy), the sun (which focuses the energy), or Mars (which uses the energy in an active way). Although the other planets activate the air energy in their own way, these three heavenly bodies are considered to be the most powerful on a magickal basis. Their energy is also short term.

Apply and Application: Words used when describing aspects (the dialogue between planets that is actually a mathematical angle—a measurement of the distance between heavenly bodies that actually makes patterns in the sky if you drew straight lines between them. Such patterns are denoted as squares, triangles, oppositions, sextiles, conjunctions, etc.). What is confusing is that aspects and transits are much the same thing—the word "aspect" is used in a natal chart, and the word "transit" is used for current moving planets (not a snapshot in time like your natal chart). Both are patterns built on the same measurements. An applying aspect is a window of time that begins when a planet reaches a certain distance from another planet, which will eventually (depending upon the speed of the planets) create a geometric pattern, most commonly called an angle. This window lasts until the geometric pattern becomes mathematically "exact"—this is the zero point. You will feel and see events brought on by your past choices coming into focus as one planet nears the other. Often an event precisely linked to the energy of those planets takes place within the twenty-four hours before the zero point occurs. Once the distance between the two planets is exact, the continued movement of the planets away from the geometric pattern (or angle) is called a separating aspect. The zero point is like the eye of a hurricane. If you remember that, you are good to go! Remember, applying means the energy is coming toward you and separating means that the energy is now dissipating. However, in classical astrology it is believed that the fastest moving planet in the aspect can "carry the light" of that aspect to the next planet it visits, coloring the situation in a unique way. In magick, I have definitely seen this to be the case, and it makes sense because our own actions always ripple out from us.

Aspect: When planets are at certain angles from each other, the planetary energies interact (sometimes called a dialogue of energy) depending upon the nature of the planet, the angle, and the speed at which each planet is moving. These critical angles are called aspects. Each aspect has a name and common attributes. Traditional astrology uses the Ptolemaic set of aspects (named after the Egyptian scholar Cladius Ptolemy); however, there can be hundreds of sets of angles, depending on what astrological system you use.

Asteroid: A heavenly body that is smaller than a planet and is encompassed by the sun's orbit. Usually found in bands and often consisting of rocks and frozen ice. The most common asteroids used in magick are Ceres, Juno, Pallas, and Vesta, and each is attributed to a particular goddess energy.

Ceres: Associated with the descent of the goddess and is caring, nurturing, maternal, and protective. Use her for meditations on your children, your pets, nurturing aspects of yourself, and protecting those people and things that you love.

Juno: Roman wife of the god Jupiter, associated with magick done for marriage, commitment, and relationships. Use her for meditations on your partnerships.

Pallas: From Pallas Athena, the goddess of wisdom, war, accomplishment, creativity, using one's talents, and studying. Use her when it is necessary to meet a challenge, or win a fight using your brain as well as your brawn.

Vesta: Roman goddess of hearth and home, and used in magick and meditation in relationship to these subjects. Use Vesta for disciplining yourself to a particular task, building or remodeling your home or environment, gardens, ritual rooms, etc. She can also be appealed to for children and pets, and for general stabilization and prosperity. A goddess of fire, she is good to invoke for making magickal objects and working with magickal oils and candles.

Astrology: "Speech of the stars," derived from the Greek word *astron*, meaning "star," and *logos*, which means "discourse" or "speech." The study of the energy influence of heavenly bodies on any behavior, activity, or condition on people, places, and things.

Burning Way: An old axiom, but incredibly useful in magick. Supposedly, if any planet falls between 15 degrees Libra and 15 degrees Scorpio, it has entered the "Burning Way" and trouble is afoot. However, I've discovered that if the planet in the position is in your favor, either natally or by a horary or electional chart, then you will be the winner against all odds. This is especially true with the planet Mars. The moon travels through the "Burning Way" at least once a month, the sun once a year, etc. The most noticeable, I've found, is when Mars travels through the "Burning Way."

Cardinal Signs: These are the "starter" signs of the zodiac and there is one for each element: Aries (fire), Cancer (water), Libra (air), and Capricorn (earth). These signs usher in the equinoxes and solstices and therefore are seen as times to create beginnings.

Conjunction: The conjunction is when two planets are in the same longitudinal measurement position and within orb (space between them). In laymen's terms it looks like one planet is on top of the other—they are dancing together in the same "space." Therefore their energies are thought to "meld" for a short time. If more than two planets look like they have the same address on the astrological chart, this is called a "stellium" and the power of these planets acting together is very forceful. Conjunctions are great in meditation for energetic focus. A conjunction is a very active and dynamic aspect. A new moon is a conjunction of the moon (reflective) and the sun (focus) energies. The sign in which this conjunction occurs denotes the flavor elementally, and the type of force: starting (cardinal), fixed, mutable (flowing). For example, let's say you check your daily planetary guide and you see that the sun and Venus are in conjunction today—this is a good aspect! Meditate for beauty, acquiring objects or positive energies, love, and happiness! The "stars" smile upon it! Let's say Mars is conjuncting Saturn today. Working on designing good rules and guidelines for your magickal group would work well, meditating on what is right for yourself and your people. This is a positive way to use this energy. Conjunction energy is all about focus.

Degree: A degree is 1/360 of a circle. Each degree is divided into 60 minutes, and each minute is divided into 60 seconds. The time it takes for a planet to move from degree to degree around the circle is the main timing mechanism used in astrology and the magicks associated with it. Degrees are also used as "addresses" (like the address on your house or apartment) when locating where a planet is at any given time.

Earth Signs: Taurus, Virgo, and Capricorn are the signs associated with the element of earth, and are thought to have the qualities of that element. Also called the earth triplicity. Capricorn is the cardinal (starter) sign, Taurus is the fixed energy sign, and Virgo is the mutable (flowing sign). These signs are strongest when the moon (reflection), the sun (focus), and Mars (action) are visiting them, although the other planets do bring the flavor of the sign into their energies as well. Prime earth meditation times would be when one of these three planets is in an earth sign.

Eclipse: The blocking of light from one heavenly body by another heavenly body. Eclipses of the sun and moon figure prominently in magickal and meditation applications. A lunar eclipse is said to affect situations for approximately six weeks, where an eclipse of the sun is said to last for six months.

Electional Astrology: Studying various charts to determine the best day and time possible to enact an event, such as a wedding, beginning a new job, putting in a proposal, or obtaining a loan.

Fire Signs: Aries, Leo, and Sagittarius are the zodiac signs associated with the element of fire, and are thought to have the qualities of that element. Also called the fire triplicity. Aries is the cardinal (starter) sign, Leo is the fixed energy sign, and Sagittarius is the mutable (or flowing energy). Fire meditations work extremely well when the moon (reflective), the sun (focus), or Mars (action) are visiting fire signs.

Fixed Signs: These are the stubborn ones; Taurus, Leo, Scorpio and Aquarius. Magick or meditation done in a fixed sign, or using a planet that is currently in that sign, will "set" the work and give long-term results. Therefore, be very careful what you wish for when working with these energies. Meditations for stabilization, solidity, firmness, and support work very well when the moon or sun is in these signs.

Horary Astrology: The study of an astrological chart based on the time of a question. Horary has its own rules and relies on classical astrology (which does not use Neptune, Uranus, or Pluto), although modern interpretations are sometimes used.

House System: I don't mention it in this book, but it bears noting. A house system primarily dithers over where the cusp lines fall (divisions between the segments of the 360 total). Some systems are equal house where all the slices of the astrological pie are the same and others are unequal. Which house system an astrologer uses to cast their charts is a personal choice.

Mundane Astrology: A branch of astrological study that interprets the charts of nations, eclipses, and solstices to monitor and analyze political events.

Mutable Signs: Gemini, Virgo, Sagittarius, and Pisces. These signs can move with the flow and interact with just about anyone on anything. Meditations for flow, movement, rising above conflict, spirituality, communication, and higher wisdom work well under these signs.

Opposition: Is a powerful aspect and is when planets are in a 180-degree longitudinal angle from each other. The most well-known opposition in magickal work is the full moon, where the Moon is on one side of the earth and the sun is on the other. Oppositions are dynamic and exciting to handle as they require that you pull in the appropriate energy for the situation from each planet and merge them into something bright and positive, a step forward on the path of life. Oppositions can manifest the best of two worlds or the worst of two worlds, depending on how you use them. An excellent herb for working with an opposition is basil because it traditionally puts energies in sympathy with each other. The opposition energy is all about being aware of the world and how you can use the energies outside of yourself to improve yourself and your life standing. Signs of the same type of activity (cardinal, fixed, mutable) are linked by squares and oppositions. As we discuss the Grand Cross in the Squares paragraph, let's now discuss the T-Square pattern, formed by an opposition and a square. The T-Square is a "developmental" harmonic pattern. You are taking two different energies and you are rising to the challenge of meeting that square with a blending of all three sign and planetary energies. Rather than looking at this in a negative way, the T-Square will give you access to inner resources you never knew you had. As Basil Fearrington says in his book *The New Way to Learn Astrology*, define the opposition first, then consider the square energy. He goes on to say: "Venus opposing Mars suggests an awareness of passion within individual expression. Saturn squaring this axis will introduce dimensions of control or discomfort upon that passion. It is almost as if Venus and Mars, an intimate couple, enter into someone's home who is decidedly Saturnian. Instead of being able to express themselves, they will be uncomfortable with the limitations they experience" (page 96).

One of the best ways to work with these aspects is to make them three-dimensional on your altar using candles in corresponding colors, gemstones, or other items with visual appeal. A very empowering meditation is to turn those candles into "actors" in your mind. First, read what is going on in the heavens. Check out the planet's basic energy and current placement and then add the dialogue that might match. This type of meditation can help you overcome any fears or doubts about the energies around you and opens the way for positive solution gathering, working with current patterns rather than against them.

Orb/Orb of Influence: The range of degrees within which an aspect is considered to have an effect. Orbs differ by aspect and by the choice of the astrologer. A rule of thumb is that if planets are within ten degrees of forming the pattern (square, conjunction, opposition, sextile) and closing to make that pattern exact (mathematically), something is likely to happen. When the pattern in the sky is exact, this is the "zero point of manifestation."

Many astrologers and magickal folks time their work immediately before this zero point to "catch the wave."

Retrograde: A planet that appears to move backward in the heavens for a period of time is called a retrograde planet. You'll find retrograde planets uniquely useful, particularly for meditation. Retrogrades can help you catch a big wave of long-term energy and ride it through to completion. The retrograde motion (going backward) is an illusion created by the orbit of our own earth. See pages 202 through 206 in my book *Solitary Witch* for complete magickal information on how to use planetary retrogrades for your positive life enhancements.

Sextile: The sextile is when planets are in a 60-degree longitudinal relationship to each other. Sextiles are seen as windows of opportunity; however, if no action is taken, the energy will dissipate. In magick and meditation, sextiles are great for "bringing things to you" if you act on the first magickally and then in physical form. Using lodestones and magnets can enhance your working in a positive way. Sextile energy is all about opportunity and where support can be found if you choose to use it.

Square: The square is when the angle between the planets is 90 degrees and is thought to bring tension to any situation. Squares often represent challenges that we must rise above, or better yet, an energy that requires us to put our "best foot forward." Squares encourage us to gather our forces and exert them in a positive, intelligent way. Sometimes this requires great courage. Squares are thought to show where a person regularly experiences inner turmoil and anxiety and can denote stress and worry. However, squares, say the astrologers, show where the most development in a situation will occur. It is where a situation can turn from better to worse, or worse to better; and therefore is an excellent vehicle for change! Active meditations with body movement are wonderful activities during any squared influence. Visualize yourself rising above the storm, gathering your power and applying that power in a positive way. Where the square has a lot of "inner" activity, the opposition speaks of outer activity (like disagreements between two people or modes of behavior). Squares are all about inner tension and the development of the self and life path. Signs of the same type of activity (cardinal, fixed, mutable) are linked by squares and oppositions. A Grand Cross, four squares which also form two oppositions, affects one's identity from the bottom up. It is a pattern of two oppositions that meet in the middle. The directions are all separate, but somehow become complementary, feeding off of each other. People often have trouble making decisions when a Grand Cross is in effect, not knowing which way to turn, or where to place their constructive energies. The trick is to go to the center in your meditation, to pull in the positive energies from each direction, and then to focus that combined force outward in a positive, goal-oriented way. Naturally, when you have issues flying in all different directions toward you—your very identity is at the core of your choices.

Transits: The changing positions of the planets as they move through the signs of the zodiac. Transits influence planets and points in any type of chart and can trigger events. Although a single transit alone rarely triggers a situation, single transits work well for planning magickal and meditational applications as you focus on that type of specific energy. A "transit," according to Basil Fearrington in his book *The New Way to Learn Astrology*, is like a sentence. The energy of the outer, slower moving planet in any combination acts like a modifier to the energy of the inner planet activity.

Trine: The trine is when planets are 120 degrees apart longitudinally. Above all, the trine denotes ease of expression, yet, it can also be a period of laziness if we are not too careful, and then the opportunities it presents are lost. A Sun/Jupiter trine is a wonderful business, career, and spiritual advancement period if you can apply yourself to those energies. Trines, in their own way, can hold on to a negative situation, so be careful. Even though a trine is thought to be a good aspect, it can hold you back— keep you from doing what you should be doing because change requires effort. Trine energy is all about flow and movement and your choice to find the easiest path. Note that astrological signs of the same element are linked by trines. When three signs of an element are involved in a trine through the placement and orbs of the planets (three addresses), you then have a situation called a Grand Trine. There are four types of Grand Trines—one for each element. Grand Water Trine, Grand Fire Trine, Grand Earth Trine and Grand Air Trine. Here, there is an amazing flow of that elemental energy to be tapped.

BIBLIOGRAPHY

Barbour, Julian. *The End of Time: The Next Revolution in Physics.* New York. Oxford University Press, 1999.

Bruce, Colin. *Schrodinger's Rabbits: The Many Worlds of Quantum.* Washington, D.C. Joseph Henry Press, 2001.

Cole, K. C. *The Hole in the Universe: How Scientists Peered Over the Edge of Emptiness and Found Everything.* Orlando, Florida. Harcourt, Inc., 2001.

Davies, P. C. W. and Brown, J. R. *The Ghost in the Atom.* Cambridge, UK. Cambridge University Press, 1999.

Davies, Paul. *The Mind of God: The Scientific Basis for a Rational World.* New York. Simon & Schuster, 1992.

Feynman, Richard P. *QED: The Strange Theory of Light and Matter.* Princeton, New Jersey. Princeton University Press, 1985.

Fortune, Dion. *The Cosmic Doctrine.* York Beach, Maine. Samuel Weiser, Inc., 2000.

Gell-Mann, Murray. *The Quark and the Jaguar: Adventures in the Simple and the Complex.* New York. Henry Holt and Company, 1994.

Greene, Brian. *The Elegant Universe: Superstrings, Hidden Dimensions, and the Quest for the Ultimate Theory.* New York. Random House, 2000.

Gribben, John. *Schrodinger's Kittens and the Search for Reality: Solving the Quantum Mysteries.* New York. Little, Brown and Company, 1995.

Hawking, Stephen. *The Universe in a Nutshell.* New York. Bantam Books, 2001.

Laughlin, Robert B. *A Different Universe: Reinventing Physics from the Bottom Down*. New York. Basic Books, 2005.

Randall, Lisa. *Warped Passages: Unraveling the Mysteries of the Universe's Hidden Dimensions*. New York. Harper Collins, 2005.

Smolin, Lee. *Three Roads to Quantum Gravity*. New York. Basic Books, 2001.

Walker, Evan Harris. *The Physics of Consciousness: The Quantum Mind and the Meaning of Life*. New York. Perseus Publishing, 2000.

Wolfram, Stephen. *A New Kind of Science*. Champaign, Illinois. Wolfram Media, Inc., 2002.

 Read unique articles by Llewellyn authors, recommendations by experts, and information on new releases. To receive a free copy of Llewellyn's consumer magazine, *New Worlds of Mind & Spirit*, simply call 1-877-NEW-WRLD or visit our website at www.llewellyn.com and click on *New Worlds.*

LLEWELLYN ORDERING INFORMATION

Order Online:
Visit our website at www.llewellyn.com, select your books, and order them on our secure server.

Order by Phone:
- Call toll-free within the U.S. at 1-877-NEW-WRLD (1-877-639-9753)
  Call toll-free within Canada at 1-866-NEW-WRLD (1-866-639-9753)
- We accept VISA, MasterCard, and American Express

Order by Mail:
Send the full price of your order (MN residents add 7% sales tax) in U.S. funds, plus postage & handling to:

> **Llewellyn Worldwide**
> **2143 Wooddale Drive, Dept. 0-7387-0985–9**
> **Woodbury, MN 55125-2989, U.S.A.**

Postage & Handling:
Standard (U.S., Mexico, & Canada). If your order is:
> Up to $25.00, add $3.50
> $25.01–$48.99, add $4.00
> $49.00 and over, FREE STANDARD SHIPPING

(Continental U.S. orders ship UPS. AK, HI, PR, & P.O. Boxes ship USPS 1st class. Mex. & Can. ship PMB.)

International Orders:
Surface Mail: For orders of $20.00 or less, add $5 plus $1 per item ordered. For orders of $20.01 and over, add $6 plus $1 per item ordered.

Air Mail:
Books: Postage & Handling is equal to the total retail price of all books in the order.
Non-book items: Add $5 for each item.

Orders are processed within 2 business days. Please allow for normal shipping time.
Postage and handling rates subject to change.

Solitary Witch
The Ultimate Book of Shadows for the New Generation

Silver RavenWolf

This book has everything a teen Witch could want and need between two covers: a magickal cookbook, encyclopedia, dictionary, and grimoire. It relates specifically to today's young adults and their concerns, yet is grounded in the magickal work of centuries past.

Information is arranged alphabetically and divided into five distinct categories: (1) Shadows of Religion and Mystery, (2) Shadows of Objects, (3) Shadows of Expertise and Proficiency, (4) Shadows of Magick and Enchantment, and (5) Shadows of Daily Life. It is organized so readers can skip over the parts they already know, or read each section in alphabetical order.

Selling Features

- By the author of the best-selling *Teen Witch* and mother of four teen Witches
- A jam-packed learning and resource guide for serious young Witches
- All categories are discussed in modern terms and their associated historical roots
- A training companion to *Teen Witch* and *To Ride a Silver Broomstick*

0-7387-0319-2
8 x 10, 608 pp., 53 illus. $19.95
appendices, index

To order, call 1-877-NEW-WRLD

A Witch's Notebook

Lessons in Witchcraft

Silver RavenWolf

What if you could peek inside the journal of a skilled and powerful Wiccan and read all about her exciting forays into the Craft? What if that Witch was the ever-popular Silver RavenWolf?

Silver's own pearls of wisdom gained along the bumpy road to spiritual enlightenment can be found in *A Witch's Notebook*. This hands-on guide is designed to work from moon to moon—leading students through five months of spiritual advancement. In discussing cleansing, sacred symbols, renewed spirituality, and magickal ingredients, Silver urges Wiccans to step outside the usual confines of Witchcraft and explore other belief systems. This book also includes exercises, spells, and herbal information to assist in forging one's own unique spiritual path.

0-7387-0662-0
264 pp., 6 x 9 $12.95

To order, call 1-877-NEW-WRLD
Prices subject to change without notice

To Ride a Silver Broomstick

New Generation Witchcraft

Silver RavenWolf

Throughout the world there is a new generation of Witches—people practicing or wishing to practice the craft on their own, without an in-the-flesh magickal support group. *To Ride a Silver Broomstick* speaks to those people, presenting them with both the science and religion of Witchcraft, allowing them to become active participants while growing at their own pace. It is ideal for anyone: male or female, young or old, those familiar with Witchcraft, and those totally new to the subject and unsure of how to get started.

Full of the author's warmth, humor, and personal anecdotes, *To Ride a Silver Broomstick* leads you step-by-step through the various lessons with exercises and journal writing assignments. This is the complete Witchcraft 101, teaching you to celebrate the Sabbats, deal with coming out of the broom closet, choose a magickal name, visualize the Goddess and God, meditate, design a sacred space, acquire magickal tools, design and perform rituals, network, spellcast, perform color and candle magick, divination, healing, telepathy, psychometry, astral projection, and much, much more.

0-87542-791-X
360 pp., 7 1/2 x 9 1/8, illus. $14.95

To order, call 1-877-NEW-WRLD
Prices subject to change without notice

Transformative Meditation

Personal & Group Practice to Access Realms of Consciousness

Gayle Clayton

Never underestimate the power of a small group of conscious, committed individuals to change the world. As humanity grows ever more complex, we need to balance technological advances with an evolution of higher consciousness. One way to do that is through group or collective meditation.

This system of meditation creates a single identity that transforms the individuals, the group, and later, the world. Select groups and teachers have already incorporated collective meditation into successful practice. Now, *Transformative Meditation* introduces this system to everyone. It presents an overview of meditation systems, explores the various levels of transformative meditation, and teaches you how to move the group to upper astral planes, how to chant to create a higher identity, and how to increase moments of mystical awareness.

0 7387-0502-0
240 pp., 6 x 9 $12.95

A Time for Magick
Planetary Hours for Rituals & Spells

Maria Kay Simms

This is a practical guide to applying aspects of astrology known as electional and planetary hours to ritual magick and spellcraft. In short, it allows you to take charge of your destiny by directing planetary energies to your best advantage! It is designed for the magickal practitioner who has little or no astrological expertise.

A master astrologer and Wiccan High Priestess demonstrates easy tips for astrological timing in this modern rebirth of the long-out-of-print planetary hours material of Llewellyn George. Here you'll learn about the planets and their correspondences, including a special interpretation based on your planetary hour of birth. You'll find chapters on timing by the Moon and on how you can make quick, practical use of an astrological calendar to pick best times for mundane and magickal action. A special meditation plus a complete and detailed ritual for the Sun, the Moon, and each of the eight planets guide you to bring their energies within and truly understand their themes magically and spiritually.

1-56718-622-X
312 pp., 6 x 9 $12.95

To order, call 1-877-NEW-WRLD
Prices subject to change without notice

Meditation for Beginners

Techniques for Awareness, Mindfulness & Relaxation

Stephanie Clement, Ph.D.

Perhaps the greatest boundary we set for ourselves is the one between the conscious and less conscious parts of our own minds. We all need a way to gain deeper understanding of what goes on inside our minds when we are awake, asleep, or just not paying attention. Meditation is one way to pay attention long enough to find out.

Meditation for Beginners explores many different ways to meditate—including kundalini yoga, walking meditation, dream meditation, tarot meditations, and healing meditation—and offers a step-by-step approach to meditation, with exercises that introduce you to the rich possibilities of this age-old spiritual practice. Improve concentration, relax your body quickly and easily, work with your natural healing ability, and enhance performance in sports and other activities. Just a few minutes each day is all that's needed.

0-7387-0203-X
264 pp., 5 3/16 x 8, illus. $12.95

To order, call 1-877-NEW-WRLD
Prices subject to change without notice

Instant Magick
Ancient Wisdom, Modern Spellcraft

Christopher Penczak

What if you could practice magick anytime, without the use of ceremonial spells, altars, or magickal tools? Items such as candles, special ingredients, and exotic symbols are necessary to perform many types of magick, but these items aren't always feasible, attainable, or even available. The purest form of magick—tapping into your own energetic awareness to create change—is accessible simply through the power of your will.

Popular author Christopher Penczak explains how to weave natural energies into every facet of life by inspiring readers to explore their own individual willpower. This book features personalized techniques used to weed out any unwanted, unhealthy, or unnecessary desires to find a true, balanced magickal being. Penczak's innovative, modern spellcasting techniques utilize meditation, visualization, words, and intent in any situation, at any time. The results can seem instantaneous and the potential limitless.

0-7387-0859-3
216 pp., 6 x 9 $12.95

To order, call 1-877-NEW-WRLD
Prices subject to change without notice

To Write to the Author

If you wish to contact the author or would like more information about this book, please write to the author in care of Llewellyn Worldwide and we will forward your request. Both the author and publisher appreciate hearing from you and learning of your enjoyment of this book and how it has helped you. Llewellyn Worldwide cannot guarantee that every letter written to the author can be answered, but all will be forwarded. Please write to:

Silver RavenWolf
Llewellyn Worldwide
2143 Wooddale Drive, Dept. 0-7387-0985-9
Woodbury, MN 55125-2989, U.S.A.

Please enclose a self-addressed stamped envelope for reply,
or $1.00 to cover costs. If outside U.S.A., enclose
international postal reply coupon.

Many of Llewellyn's authors have websites with additional information and resources. For more information, please visit our website:

www.llewellyn.com